ZEN ECOLOGY

ZEN ECOLOGY

GREEN AND ENGAGED LIVING
IN RESPONSE TO
THE CLIMATE CRISIS

Christopher Ives

Wisdom Publications
132 Perry Street
New York, NY USA
wisdom.org

Library of Congress Cataloging-in-Publication Data
Names: Ives, Christopher, 1954– author.
Title: Zen ecology: green and engaged living in response to the
    climate crisis / Christopher Ives.
Description: New York, NY: Wisdom Publications, [2024] |
    Includes bibliographical references and index.
Identifiers: LCCN 2024033906 (print) | LCCN 2024033907 (ebook) |
    ISBN 9781614299547 (paperback) | ISBN 9781614299783 (ebook)
Subjects: LCSH: Consumption (Economics)—Religious aspects—
    Buddhism. | Human ecology—Religious aspects—Buddhism.
Classification: LCC BQ4570.E23 I94 2024 (print) |
    LCC BQ4570.E23 (ebook) | DDC 294.3/373—dc23/eng/20240814
LC record available at https://lccn.loc.gov/2024033906
LC ebook record available at https://lccn.loc.gov/2024033907

ISBN 978-1-61429-954-7   ebook ISBN 978-1-61429-978-3

28 27 26 25
5 4 3 2 1

Cover design by Marc Whitaker. Interior design by Gopa & Ted2, Inc.
Set in Palatino Nova Pro 10.25/14.8.

Wisdom Publications' books are printed on acid-free paper and meet
the guidelines for permanence and durability of the Production Guidelines
for Book Longevity of the Council on Library Resources.

Printed in Canada.

Contents

Publisher's Acknowledgment   vii

Acknowledgments   ix

Introduction   1

PART I. IDENTIFYING THE CORE PROBLEMS

1. Entanglement in Materialism   9

2. Freneticism, Distraction, and Ignorance   27

PART II. SLOWING DOWN AND PAYING ATTENTION

3. Mental Spaciousness and Presencing   45

4. Verbal and Physical Spaciousness   67

PART III. GREENING OUR INDIVIDUAL LIVES

5. Green Mental States and Green Living   87

6. The Home as a Place of the Way   111

PART IV. CONNECTING TO OUR PLACE

7. Realizing Our Embeddedness in Nature *as* Nature   129

8. Reinhabitation   143

PART V. TAKING ACTION IN COMMUNITY WITH OTHERS

9. Community   157

10. Buddhism and Activism   179

11. Taking Action   197

Notes   217
Bibliography   237
Index   247
About the Author   255

Publisher's Acknowledgment

The publisher gratefully acknowledges the generous help of the Hershey Family Foundation in sponsoring the production of this book.

Acknowledgments

While I am the author of this book, from a Buddhist perspective it has arisen because of myriad other inputs: facets of Buddhism I've encountered, publications I've read, people who've supported me. I feel gratitude for all of them, but especially the following people.

First and foremost is my wife Mishy, who over the decade I was creating this book brainstormed with me about my ideas, the title and subtitle, and spots in the book where I refer to Indigenous people and their lifeways.

I thank Stonehill College students who in recent years have taken my upper-level course "Buddhism, Nature, and Environmental Ethics," in which we wrestle with many of the topics in this book. Interacting with them has helped me dive deeper into the issues and organize my thoughts.

I give thanks to participants in programs I've offered at the Barre Center for Buddhist Studies over the past fifteen years, especially my 2023 program "Buddhist Resources for Engaging the Climate Crisis." Time and time again they helped me look at things differently and directed me to writers who have influenced what I've crafted here.

I also feel grateful that this monograph is being published by Wisdom Publications. Laura Cunningham and Chris Hiebert did a masterful job of editing the manuscript. They not only refined my prose but provided insightful suggestions about how to develop my ideas. I thank Patty McKenna and the rest of the marketing team for their work creating the gorgeous cover and whose savvy

has made this book available to a broad audience, and Ben Glea-
son, who, with his distinctive skills, handled the production process, as well as Tucker Foley, who created an excellent index. And
I bow to Wisdom CEO and publisher Daniel Aitken for supporting this project ever since I told him about it nearly ten years ago.

I dedicate this book to all of the sentient beings—human and
other-than-human—who are suffering now in the midst of the climate crisis.

Introduction

WHAT A TIME to be alive. Violence and war continue to wreak immense harm. Changing social conditions are making many of us feel vulnerable, left behind, or disrespected. Here in the United States, social divides are widening, white nationalism is on the rise, bizarre conspiracy theories are getting accepted by wider swaths of the population, and the terrorism threat is now more domestic than foreign. Many of us hurry through our days, feeling scattered as we multitask. We may see our lives as cluttered, with too many things on our calendars and too much going on in our heads. Some of us are lost in the hyper-individualistic world of consuming and self-branding. Even when linked through social media, we may feel disconnected from other people. Hanging over these issues are grave environmental problems, with climate disruption even threatening to destroy civilization as we know it.

In the face of all of this, many of us wish we could simplify our lives and find greater calm and contentment. We may yearn to be more connected with nature and the people around us. Some of us may even wish we were living more ecologically and doing more to mitigate climate disruption. Typically, though, we keep on doing what's familiar and find succor in food, television, films, shopping, sports, family life, and social media, without a clear sense of an alternative way of living that can reduce our negative environmental impact and help us get more engaged in solving problems like the climate crisis.

Recently, I've been trying to envision and practice a way of living that can help me slow down, stay grounded, and deal with all that is flying at me, and at the same time help me reduce my ecological impact and get more engaged in responding to the climate crisis. What I've come up with thus far is not something systematic, and certainly not a sure fix, but simply a way of living that is spacious, simple, embedded in nature, connected to others in community, and supportive of collective action. Though we may think that living ecologically and engaging in activism sacrifices our own enjoyment and happiness on the altar of doing the right thing, what I'm envisioning is a way of living that can actually be *more* fulfilling than typical ways of living. Rather than deprivation, it can bring us richness.

Though I'm still figuring this out and don't always do what I intend, I know that I don't want to become numb to what's been happening, and neither do I want to dwell in the distraction afforded by apps, videos, and the busy-ness I see all around me. I don't know if there is any truth to the metaphor about frogs failing to jump out of a slowly heating pot of water, but I don't want to ignore what's happening around me. If possible, I'd like to stay awake and help turn the burner off. To use another metaphor, I don't want to sleepwalk into a dystopian future.

Having spent much of my life studying and practicing Zen Buddhism while working as a professor of Religious Studies, I've been blessed with an array of resources from which to draw as I envision this alternative way of living. In workshops, lectures, and writings, Buddhist teachers have been sharing their tradition's resources to help people deal with climate anxiety and understand the cause of the climate crisis, and what they are offering has huge value at this time. While I have benefited greatly from their teachings, I've also found myself wanting to hear more about what I can actually do— what specific actions I can take to mitigate the crisis, and how those actions can be informed by Buddhism and perhaps even support us on our spiritual paths.

One reason I've created this book is to fill that void, at least partially. In the process of writing here about Buddhist resources for an alternative way of living, I've felt resistance within myself to suggesting specific actions and to using my own efforts as an example. I haven't wanted to run the risk of being overly prescriptive or coming across as virtue-signaling. But I do think that many of us are looking for some direction as we feel the impetus to do something—anything—in response to the climate crisis, and so I've assumed that risk in the hope that you can find at least some of what I share here to be beneficial to you, and in the hope that you may give me feedback as I try—and in many moments struggle—to live in a green and engaged way.

Much of what I am formulating here is a set of Buddhist ideas, practices, and values that can inform our attempts to live ecologically.[1] In sharing my attempts to put these resources into action, I move outward in a series of concentric circles, starting with myself and core relationships, then proceeding to the home, nature around us, local community, and broader arenas of activism. At the individual level, to deal with distraction, clutter, and ecological harm—or, to put it positively, to help us pay attention, simplify our lives, and free up time and energy to take action—I've been working with spaciousness in relation to mental, verbal, and physical action. I also deploy such Buddhist mental states as mindfulness, generosity, and contentment to envision a type of environmental virtue ethic. In the next concentric circle, as a support structure for spaciousness and the cultivation of these mental states, I offer some ideas about the home as a "place of the Way" (dōjo), with Zen monastic life as a model for this. Then I turn to how we can realize our embeddedness in nature and emplace ourselves in community with others, including other animals. Next, I offer some comments about how on this basis we can engage in activism to create a world that is more supportive of ecological health and spiritual fulfillment.

As you will see, much of what I explore here pertains more to people of privilege who bear more responsibility for the climate crisis than people who are struggling and may be disproportionately affected by the crisis. I'm pitching my comments to those who can—and need to—green their lifestyles and who have the time and resources not only to practice contemplative traditions but to get involved in activism to mitigate the crisis. That is to say, I'm assuming that many of my readers will be people with privilege deriving from their occupation, wealth, race, or gender, and hence are also people who can use that privilege to make a difference.

My explorations here build upon two of my previous books, *Zen on the Trail: Hiking as Pilgrimage* and *Meditations on the Trail: A Guidebook for Self-Discovery*. In those books I describe ways of connecting with nature or, more accurately, of realizing our embeddedness in nature *as* nature.[2] For many of us, this realization is a first step toward becoming more aware of what's happening to the beautiful planet we call home.

But this enhanced awareness is not sufficient. We must also figure out alternative ways of leading our daily lives. And not only that, but creative ways of responding to systemic issues. Simply put, this historical moment calls for lifestyle change at the individual level and structural change at the societal level. We need this dual focus, for to call only for a reduction of our personal carbon footprints is to lay responsibility for causing and solving the problem at the feet of individuals and thereby let our economic system and powerful players like the fossil fuel industry off the hook.[3] Advocacy of lifestyle change may also overlook the fact that many of us cannot afford to buy an electric car or equip our homes with heat pumps, better insulation, and weathertight windows, if we even own a home. And many of us don't have access to good public transportation or healthy, locally grown food with a minimal carbon impact.

In sharing this largely Buddhist approach here, I'm not viewing Buddhism as a panacea. Nor do I see its traditional beliefs and practices as sufficient for greening our way of living and bringing about structural change. Indeed, those beliefs and practices were formulated to liberate us spiritually, not to show us how to live in a healthy way with the earth and our fellow beings. Nevertheless, with its emphasis on restraining desire and cultivating mindfulness, insight, compassion, non-harming, and simple living, the fundamental Buddhist path *is* ecological. Practicing it now, with some of the tweaks and additions I offer here, provides a win-win scenario: this path, this way of living, bears both ecological and spiritual fruit.

I imagine that you, too, have thought about how to live in these times and have devised strategies of your own, and I offer this book to share what I've come up with thus far and to initiate a dialogue with you. Though the challenges we face are daunting, it is still possible for us to make changes, transform our world, and live fulfilling lives.

PART I

Identifying the Core Problems

1. Entanglement in Materialism

The habit of acquisitiveness is sustained by delusion:
psychological entrapment in the fantasy of lasting
happiness being achievable through the acquisition
of material goods, money, status, etc.
—STEPHEN BATCHELOR[4]

So where do we begin?
Many Buddhist thinkers start their analysis of our lifestyle and related environmental issues by criticizing consumerism and how it gets people entangled in wanting more and more things and causing more and more harm.[5] This focus is not surprising, for a core Buddhist doctrine is the claim that suffering is caused by desire.

THE TRAP OF CONSUMERISM

When people speak of consumerism, they seem to be thinking of certain behaviors, such as buying stuff we don't need; shopping as a form of recreation or a way to deal with feelings like boredom, sadness, and loneliness; crafting an identity around certain brands; purchasing trendy items to fit in with a group; and displaying certain consumer goods to convey a message about ourselves or our social status. Like every other -*ism*, consumerism also consists of a cluster of ideas, like the notion that the acquisition and possession of certain things will make us happy, or that a consumerist society offers the "good life." Along these lines, Sallie McFague defines consumerism as "a cultural pattern that leads people to find meaning and fulfillment through the consumption of goods and services."[6] In my teaching I've defined consumerism as (1) the belief that buying and having certain things and experiences will make a person happy, and (2) actions based on that belief, including certain consumer behaviors and the ascription of high status to those who possess wealth or desired consumer goods and experiences.

We see consumerism especially when people crave a recently invented thing or the newest model of an existing thing (like the newest iPhone), driven by the idea, "I've got to have it," even though they don't really need it. Of course, we get entangled in consumerism to differing degrees. Most of us don't believe the ideology of full-blown consumerism—we have no illusions that more stuff, or just the right combination of possessions, will actually bring us lasting happiness. But nonetheless many of us do buy unneeded things, especially when their price has been marked down. For me, this is especially the case with outdoor gear. Email messages from EMS and catalogs from REI arrive, and my eyes scan the fleece jackets, Gore-Tex rain shells, and hiking pants on sale. My mind starts offering reasons to place an order: "That fleece jacket would be helpful late on an autumn hike when the sun's going down, I'm still an hour from the car, and I need to put on a heavier layer over my polypro and light fleece quarter-zip"; or "My current winter shell isn't warm enough, and though I can wear a down vest under it, the Gore-Tex doesn't seem to be all that waterproof anymore. This shell in the catalog is marked down from $299 to $199, and I will use it for years. And unlike my current shell with its black and gray panels, this one is orange, which would be good to wear when hunters are out in the woods or if something goes wrong and I need to be spotted by searchers."

With justifications like these running through our heads, we accumulate unnecessary things, so much so that we may feel burdened by them. I see this much more now than when I was a child. Middle-class and wealthier Americans own many more things than they did in the past: a TV in each person's room, phones for all, gear clogging the garage. "Big box" stores and giant supermarkets tempt us with endless choices.[7] Those lucky enough to head off to college these days carry more than the trunk of clothes and copy of Webster's Dictionary that I schlepped into my dorm room fifty years ago: a smartphone, a laptop, an external monitor, and perhaps even a video game console are now de rigueur to many students. Not to mention all the clothes and accessories. Like many others, my students will often comment on how they want to cull some of their possessions. Nevertheless, I once saw an SUV with the bumper sticker, "He who dies with the most toys wins." This strikes me as one of the more perverse manifestations of the consumerism and hyper-individualism that is rampant these days.

Consumerism, of course, is not just about possessions. We also consume experiences, perhaps so we can respond in the affirmative when asked if we have seen a certain film, heard a popular musician perform live, tried bungee jumping, done hot yoga, or taken our kids to Disney World. I can get pulled into this when I hear friends talking about a new restaurant they've tried and feel a tug to check it out.

We're also in the midst of a commercialization of recreation.[8] When I was a kid, birthday parties were held at home and consisted simply of pizza or burgers followed by cake and a game of pin the tail on the donkey. Today, however, they have moved beyond the home to restaurants and other venues set up for parties. When traveling, we increasingly buy recreational experiences rather than experience things freely on our own. For instance, families with resources head to destinations like Disney World and Epcot Center where they can consume the experiences these resorts have for sale rather than create experiences while enjoying the simple and inexpensive pleasures of, for example, visiting friends in a nearby town or camping in state and national parks. Of course, opting for nature as our destination isn't free from commercialization, either: when heading outside, many of us are now more apt to do activities with price tags, like zip lining, river rafting, and climbing with guides.[9]

Then there's the spread of advertising. Over my lifetime I've witnessed not only more billboards but also more product logos on athletes' uniforms, sports arenas with corporate names, ads covering outfield fences, cross-marketing of films and fast food, and product placement in TV shows. A while back I was struck by how everyone in the White House on *The West Wing* just happened to like Starbucks and how often Nancy on *Weeds* swigged from cans of Diet Coke. States have even started offering opportunities for advertisers to buy the right to name or sponsor trails, benches, and trees.[10]

Living in a consumerist society, many of us slip into ascribing high status to those who possess what we desire, whether money or celebrity. We look up to business tycoons, and we even elected one president. We venerate movie actors, rock stars, and other idols in popular culture. In waiting rooms we read magazines about celebrities. We may spend our evenings watching shows about the lifestyles of the rich and famous. Ask an American teenager to name a famous rich person, popular singer, or sports superstar and names will flow. But when asked to name someone who has devoted their life to getting nutritious food to the hungry, setting up health clinics for those who cannot pay, or trying to keep our air and water clean, that adolescent will probably respond with silence. Of course, there's a flip side to celebrity: though we may look up to the rich and famous in envy, we also relish seeing them fall from grace when some sin or scandal knocks them off the pedestals on which we have placed them.[11]

So why is it that so many of us have gotten caught up in consumerism and, by extension, its dramatic ecological impact? Why do we crave unneeded new possessions? Why, in the midst of material abundance, do so many of us feel dissatisfied and unfulfilled? Why, in a country as materially rich as the United States, do we see so much malaise, illness, and violence?

One possible cause of our entanglement in consumerism is the dominant modern view of the human person: "The modern worldview," according to William Ophuls, "says that man [sic] is fundamentally a selfish hedonist. Concerned only with the satisfaction of

his own desires, he rationally pursues fame, profit, and position—
which inevitably puts him in conflict with others. Since this is so,
realism requires us to found our political and social institutions on
the fact of human selfishness."[12] Or as Simon James has put it, "One
could argue . . . that capitalism takes selfishness to be a fact of human
nature rather than a problem to be solved; that it encourages excessive consumption, rather than regarding greed as a vice . . . ."[13] Like all
fully ensconced ideologies, this view is something into which we are
born and, as we live our lives, something about which we are usually oblivious. To use a bit of contemporary theoretical jargon, it is
an unexamined set of ideas that are "always already" operating in our
cultural milieu and, by osmosis, in our minds.

CONSUMERISM AND THE THREE POISONS

The Buddhist tradition offers a cogent and sophisticated critique
of this way of viewing the world. Indeed, many of the core Buddhist doctrines and practices are concerned with calling selfishness into question, analyzing its causes and characteristics, and
providing a remedy.[14] The tradition claims that life as it is normally
lived is characterized by "suffering" (in Pali, *dukkha*), primarily in
the form of dissatisfaction, "dis-ease," unsettledness. This anguish
is caused by selfish desire, which consists of *craving* things that we
do not possess and *clinging* to things we do possess.[15] The historical Buddha taught that desire causes suffering because even though
the objects of desire—oneself, other people, certain objects and
situations—may give us a sense of identity and security, they will
inevitably change, and when they do, we will suffer to the extent
we were attached to them. Needless to say, desire can also wreak
havoc on the environment.[16] As an antidote to desire, Buddhists
cultivate generosity (*dāna*), primarily through acts of giving.

Buddhists have also noticed that when we cling to certain things,
we feel the negative counterpart of desire: ill will, anger, or hatred
toward whatever threatens our relationship with those things.
Insofar as I'm attached to my wife, Mishy, I may feel anger when

another man flirts with her. Insofar as I'm attached to my lifestyle as supported by my investments, I may get upset when the Federal Reserve tinkers with interest rates and causes a big drop in the Dow. We also see ill will in angry denunciations of progressive Democrats as "communists" or "Antifa" and conservative Republicans as "deplorables" or "fascists." We also see it in racially tinged arguments like "Look at what crafty China and overpopulated India are doing as they develop—they're not going to restrain their emissions of CO_2 and other greenhouse gases, so why should we?" It's us versus them, with various "thems": not only members of other political parties or nationalities but Jews, Muslims, "coastal elites," "rednecks," "illegals," "homophobic fundamentalists," "welfare queens". . . . If left unacknowledged, or if inflamed, ill will can lead to othering and worse. For many people here in the US, it's now okay to vent one's anger, call people names, and scapegoat them. As we face the climate crisis, ill will and othering make it all the more difficult to find common ground and work together to solve this huge and complex problem. Traditional Buddhism condemns ill will[17] and works to ameliorate it through the practice of extending loving-kindness (metta) or cultivating and expressing compassion (in Sanskrit, karuṇā).[18]

We can see desire and ill will as consisting of the basic binary of attraction and aversion, or like and dislike. We glom on to what we like and resist what we don't. Desire and ill will are the reactivity that leaves us feeling unsettled and anxious. We struggle. We're never satisfied or settled. We suffer.

In the background of desire and ill will is ignorance. The historical Buddha taught that we suffer because we're ignorant of the fact that all objects of desire are impermanent, and more broadly, we're ignorant of who or what we really are and what will truly fulfill us. For many of us, the most deeply rooted form of this is, as Sulak Sivaraksa terms it, the "delusion of the autonomous individual self."[19] What this renowned Thai Buddhist is getting at is the central Buddhist claim that insofar as everything is impermanent and interconnected, nothing has any enduring, separate essence. In human terms, there is no eternal, unchanging soul. A point of divergence between Buddhism and the other religious traditions of ancient India is the Buddhist doctrine of "no soul" (P. *anātta*, Skt. *anātman*). Buddhism understands each of us to be an ever-changing configuration of mental and physical elements that arises from the system of relationships in which we are embedded. Buddha argued that most of us are unaware of this, for we live with the mistaken sense of existing as a separate, enduring entity that only secondarily enters into relationships with other people and things. Typically I think, "I was born into the world in 1954, and ever since then I've been doing my thing here." It's as if I parachuted down into this world sixty-nine years ago and then started interacting with what I discovered here, whether my mother, my dad, the slats of my crib, my siblings, or the dog that licked me in the face.

Buddhism responds by arguing that interrelationship comes first. From this perspective, back in 1954 the processive web of interconnected events that constitutes this world generated, as one of its facets, the ever-changing configuration of energy that emerged in Marilla Ives's womb and nine months later was named "Christopher Avery Ives" by her and her husband, Bud. In this Buddhist way of looking at things, more than "I was born into the world in 1954, and ever since then I've been doing my thing here," it is more accurate to say, "Since 1954 the world, as a processive system of interconnectedness, has been doing its thing in and through me."[20] As Thich Nhat Hanh put it, "We are a living, breathing manifestation of this beautiful and generous planet."[21]

The ignorance of this fact of interrelatedness and embeddedness feeds our self-centeredness, our desire and ill will[22]—the hedonism flagged by Ophuls. In Buddhism, this ignorance, desire, and ill will constitute the three poisons,[23] the three mental states that cause our suffering.

These Buddhist insights into the interrelationship of desire, ill will, and ignorance suggest that the rise of consumerism has been

fueled to a large degree by an expansion and encouragement of
these basic mental states—especially when they are fed by advertising. Recent Buddhist thinkers have, indeed, made this argument.
For example, Stephen Batchelor writes,

> The impossibility of unlimited acquisitive growth in a
> world of finite resources is unlikely ever to be accepted
> by people still attached to the illusion that final happiness
> is found through compulsive acquisition—precisely the
> illusion fostered by the powerful worldwide advertising
> industry.[24]

Stephanie Kaza emphasizes the role of advertising in amplifying
these unhealthy mental states when she argues that "Advertising
deliberately promotes a climate of self-centeredness revolving
around material desires, setting up stereotypes that foster greed,
status envy, hyper-stimulation, and at root, a sense of psychological
dissatisfaction and inadequacy."[25] Needless to say, advertising does
not magically appear in a vacuum. "During the 20th century, corporate public relations and advertising specialists mastered the arts of
cultural manipulation to create an individualistic culture of greed
and profligate material consumption that serves well the short-
term interests of a financial oligarchy."[26]

The other day, while watching some advertisements for gas-
powered cars and trucks on television, I was struck by the irony of
how some of these carbon-spewing objects of desire were named
after facets of nature, like Tundra, the namesake of which is now
thawing at alarming rates and releasing scary amounts of carbon
dioxide and methane; Sequoia, currently threatened by warming
in California; and Tacoma, which derives from Tacopid, "She who
gives us the waters," an Indigenous name for Mount Rainier, whose
glaciers are quickly receding.

In part because of advertising, many of us who have our basic
needs met get caught in the "if only" trap: "If only I had that car, a
sexier partner, a bigger house . . . then I'd be happy." I know I suc-

cumb to that. Last week, when the Carbon2Cobalt catalog arrived, I said to myself, "If only I had a casual gray linen jacket like this one on page seven, my wardrobe would be complete." Though initially I didn't pounce, in due course I pulled out my credit card. The jacket is now in a FedEx truck on its way to our condo.

As Buddhism points out and most of us well know, acquiring things like a new jacket doesn't lead to lasting satisfaction. "Reflecting on what I learn observing my two children," writes Zen teacher Ruben Habito, "it seems that acquiring a specific object of one's desire brings but short-lived satisfaction. But more significantly, acquisition itself does not quench desire but only heightens desire for other objects not yet in one's possession and thus leads to increased dissatisfaction."[27] Simply put, consumerism breeds desire and strengthens our overall covetousness.

Entanglement in consumerism also stems, as I mentioned in passing earlier, from a desire to define and bolster the ego, to secure and display an identity, whether as a person of fine taste, a rugged outdoorsman, or an urban hipster. Sulak Sivaraksa writes, "Consumerism provides an artificial means to define our existence by suggesting that identity is realized through the process of acquisition."[28] Getting more specific, Stephanie Kaza critiques consumer identity, which is based on "brand-name preferences, material possessions, class status, social group, and market desires," and contrasts it with ecological identity, which revolves around a "sense of place, ecological concerns, and environmental values (such as respect, compassion, and reverence for life)."[29] Recently, I went to the local Toyota dealer to see if I could get a RAV4 that would not only be a hybrid with four-wheel drive but also give me good clearance whenever I drive up rutted and rocky dirt roads to trailheads. I found one, but my ego is a little unsettled about it. To get that clearance I had to buy the "sport edition," which with its spiffy eighteen-inch wheels doesn't fit my self-identity—a no-frills, eco-conscious guy—as much as would the other car I considered buying: a more modest Subaru Crosstrek.

Consumerism is also caused by concerns about our relative

status vis-à-vis others. We may find ourselves caught up in the rat race of striving to acquire the wealth and consume the objects and experiences apparently required for membership in a particular social class or affinity group. This seems to derive from fear, especially the fear of being left out. In a recent discussion of consumerism and technology, my students spoke of their fears of being out of the loop if they don't buy certain articles of clothing or stay on top of whatever's buzzing on social media. The accompanying desire to keep up with others—or, to use an expression straight out of white suburbia, "keep up with the Joneses"—may lead us to succumb to the most recent fad, or to work and "shop till we drop." In some cases, the goal of our consumption is not simply to keep up with the Joneses but to surpass them, not simply to fit in but to stand out and stand above others by having newer, better, or more stuff than they do. We can call this "competitive consumerism."

Consumerism may also stem from a desire to deal with emotions like sadness, as seen in "retail therapy." Most of us do feel happier and somehow more solid when we buy something. We can also find relief from our malaise in the buzz of "delivery delirium": my expression for the vague excitement I feel when packages are on their way to me—I've found enjoyment in going online to track purchases through the FedEx website as they move in my direction—or when I find them at the front door when I get home from a long day at work.

ANXIETY AND FEAR

I think, however, that there's something operating in us at a level deeper than these acquisitive behaviors. As far as I can tell, floating in all of us is anxiety about transiency, mortality, and possible insignificance. I've been feeling this as I approach seventy. Existential anxiety can lead us to buy unnecessary things—and more and more of them—in an attempt to find security in material possessions or to stand out and be recognized by others so we can grab our fifteen minutes of fame. David Loy examines this pattern through the

lens of "lack." Restating the Buddhist doctrine of no-soul, he outlines how, as a "self" that is conditioned and ungrounded, we are
left with "a sense of *lack*: the feeling that 'something is wrong with
me.'"[30] He adds, "Another way to describe this sense of lack is that
we don't feel 'real enough.'"[31] As a result, we attempt to fill this void
by, among other things, acquiring more and more possessions (in
a culture of consumerism) and gaining recognition if not fame (in
a culture of celebrity). "The problem is 'thirst'—not the emptiness
at the core of our being but our incessant efforts to fill that hole up,
because we experience it as a sense of lack that must be filled up.
The problem is not that I am unreal but that I keep trying to make
myself real in ways that never work."[32]

Because the void within us can never be filled, we are left feeling
dissatisfied. As Ruben Habito writes, "Our activities in the world
are motivated largely by the need to fill in this inherent lack we feel
at the heart of our being. And yet, the more we seek to fill this lack
by following our cravings to have more and more . . . the less we
are truly satisfied. . . . In short, this desire to have more keeps us in
a constant state of dissatisfaction."[33] This dissatisfaction is part of
dukkha, suffering.

Along these lines we can refine our understanding of *dukkha* by
recognizing that the suffering of which Buddhists speak may be
caused less by total ignorance of how everything is impermanent
than by having an inkling of that impermanence, which leads to
fear—fear of losing loved ones, of losing what we have, of losing
our lives, or of being insignificant in the larger scheme of things.
This fear, in turn, can lead us to deny our precariousness and to
engage in self-centered attempts to solidify our position, to use
our material stuff to build seemingly permanent, crenellated walls
around ourselves (desire) and react negatively (ill will) to anything
that threatens us or the objects of our attachment.

In other words, rather than muddling through life in total obliviousness of death, we know that we will die, but we tend to repress
our recognition of this brute fact and devote ourselves to working
on the protective castle. We build walls around our egos and shoot

arrows down from the ramparts at anything deemed threatening. We deal with the underlying fear by ignoring the impermanence that triggers it. We may seek distraction and try to stay busy, which is a mode of what we might call "ignor-ance": the willful ignoring of things that we'd rather not think about. As Pascal wrote in *Pensées*, we would rather be a pauper who is busy than a king who has nothing to do.

With all of this floating around in my mind, I've recently been thinking that we can develop the Buddhist analysis of the cause of suffering by expanding the poisons from three to four: the three traditional poisons plus fear. Or, perhaps more accurately, fear is the underlying root poison out of which the other three emerge.

Our existential fear gets exacerbated by demagogues who try to convince us that certain others are taking our jobs or threatening our safety. It seemed to me that after 9/11 the Bush Administration used fear—stirred by color-coded levels of safety and dire warnings—to enlist public support for their invasion of Iraq to secure the flow of oil coming out of the Middle East (which Alan Greenspan, former chair of the Federal Reserve, outed in his 2008 memoir: "I am saddened that it is politically inconvenient to acknowledge what everyone knows: the Iraq war is largely about oil"[34]). Some politicians get elected by stoking fear of Muslims and undocumented immigrants, or of "woke" agitators who are supposedly threatening traditional Christian values. This fear not only exacerbates desire and ill will (and a sense of grievance) but undermines the critical autonomy of citizens. David Domke writes, ". . . fear, more so than any other human emotion, is the enemy of democracy. Fear paralyzes people, engendering a sense of impotence in which any form of apparent strength gains appeal. Survival becomes the dominant concern."[35]

In the past, many people dealt with existential fear by participating in a religion or a tight-knit community. For many of us, however, such traditional structures of connection and support have crumbled, and our eagerness to acquire things may be an empty compensation for that loss. Stephanie Kaza claims that "the drive to consume has displaced the psychic space once filled by religion, family, and community."[36] Similarly, Ken Jones reminds us that in the past people valued "skills and knowledge, integrity and wisdom, as well as a rich and varied popular culture," but now we are left with "consumer culture in which this richness and diversity has been so diminished that the commodity market (which now packages experiences as well as things) comes to bear a disproportionate weight of the human need for meaning, significance, status, and belongingness."[37] Granted, if our family is abusive, or our religion oppressive, we may not want it to fill our psychic space; and in some cases, a withdrawal from community is necessitated by a need to work several jobs to pay the bills in an economy where solid middle-class career paths, or simply steady jobs paying a living wage, are disappearing.

MATERIALISM AND ITS IMPACT

A good number of Americans might say they're not dissatisfied, but having fun. We do enjoy satisfying—indulging?—our desires. Whenever gas prices dip, we flock to larger vehicles, relishing their bells and whistles but seemingly oblivious to the greenhouse gases spewed out their tailpipes. I sense that many of us think, "I've got the cash; I can afford the gas, so what's the big deal? It's a free country, and it was built on letting go of hesitation and going for it: cutting, plowing, building, eating." Small might be beautiful, but big is cool. It connotes power, success, status. Yet I wonder . . . at what point did the American dream become the American nightmare, at least as far as the planet is concerned?

Even if we have not bought in to the full-blown form of consumerism, many of us are caught up in a largely unexamined—perhaps subconscious—belief that certain possessions are necessary for our happiness. Many Americans are accustomed to having one or more cars in the driveway, personal computers and other gadgets, a large flat-screen television, air-conditioning in the summer, meat or seafood whenever desired, fruit and vegetables from around the world, and cheap airfares for frequent flights to "get away." We may fear losing these treats, or feel deprived when we have to cut back. I find it hard to imagine not having a car outside to use at my convenience, or not being able to turn on some air conditioning in the increasingly hot summer months.

In this way, we get attached to what we have. We cling to our lifestyle, whose environmental impact we often ignore. The issue then, may not be an active desire for more, but *a fear of having less*.[38] In Buddhist terms, our large ecological footprint may have less to do with craving than with clinging. Put differently, the issue is not so much consumerism as *materialism*, at least in the sense of being attached to certain material objects or to a lifestyle based on certain material conditions.

Of course, our consumption habits have impacts far beyond our own mental states—they also have an immense ecological impact. A while back in my course on Buddhism, nature, and environmental ethics, we took twenty minutes in class to visit one of the websites that takes information we input about our way of living and calculates how many planets would be needed if everyone on Earth lived like we do. As I recall, it came out to seven planets. Americans comprise about 4.7 percent of the world's population but generate 25 percent of the greenhouse gases.

Yet most of us don't want to take a hard look at our resource usage and pollution. This is especially true when it comes to flying, compared to which our energy use around the home is a drop in the bucket. "Wait a second," we might say, "flights are cheap. I have friends and family all over the place and I need to see them." Or, "I have to get out of winter to a warm beach in January." "I can't miss that bachelor party." "I can't say no to their invitation to their destination wedding in Mexico." "In my bucket list I have a thousand places to see before I die." I have a hunch that I'm not alone in being morally inconsistent. Though I drive a hybrid, consume minimal meat, and try to eat as a locavore, I have not yet gotten strict about flying, compared to which my green practices are negligible. A flight from Boston to San Diego and back a few years ago gobbled up 65 percent of my annual carbon allotment—the amount of carbon each human on the planet can put in the atmosphere each year and still keep the levels of greenhouse gases in the atmosphere steady. A month later I was invited to give a lecture in LA, and I said yes before checking about the possibility of doing it on Zoom. Many "progressives" readily talk about how they've greened their homes, workplaces, and driving, but they still fly all over the place. The annual difference between a Prius and a Hummer gets obliterated if the Prius driver takes one more flight a year than the Hummer driver does. (Granted, not all flights are created equal. A flight to a funeral, or a medical relief flight to Haiti, is not morally equivalent to a trans-Atlantic junket to play a round of golf in Scotland.) Taking stock of this, I sense we have a social taboo here: not to give each other a hard time for jumping on planes.

In any case, many of us Americans do, in fact, exhibit clinging insofar as we are attached to our lifestyle and are reluctant to simplify it to the extent necessary for a healthy biosphere. But regardless of the level of our attachment, insofar as we lead a highly consumptive, carbon-dense lifestyle—especially one that includes frequent flying, meat eating, and the use of fossil fuels for heating our homes—we each leave a large ecological footprint.

The material comfort to which we are attached comes at another price: pursuing jobs that pay well but are not rewarding, or simply having to work longer hours to sustain our cushy lifestyle. Many of us even get caught up in what I call "careerism." Bo Lazoff writes, "Career seems to have become the hub around which everything else revolves. We choose career over our health. We choose career over our mates and children. We choose career over our time to study, pray, walk, hike, meditate, or participate in community life."[39] Some of my fellow academics claim that in recent decades students have increasingly seen their undergraduate education as a way to secure a high-paying job rather than as a way to grow as a human being, figure out what sort of life is fulfilling, or find a way to help heal the world. This pertains even to students without debt on their backs.

Careerism is one facet of the broader phenomenon of *economism*, defined by Protestant theologian John B. Cobb, Jr., as the assumption that "the national good is measured by economic growth,"[40] because of which citizens come to believe that "our well-being is a function of total production or consumption."[41] Under economism, the broader culture gets subordinated to the economy, rather than economic activity existing within the broader culture alongside such other arenas as politics, artistic expression, religious life, and civic engagement. With the "subordinating [of] all other interests to the goal of economic growth,"[42] the pursuit of an ever-growing GDP takes precedence over justice and sustainability.[43] We can see this valorization of economic growth and a large GDP as a collective form of materialism.

Central here is the dominance of the growth paradigm—the belief that quantitative economic growth as measured by GDP over time is unequivocally good and sustainable—and a cluster of ideas related to it, which Joanna Macy and Chris Johnstone lift up as seven core assumptions in the "Business-as-Usual" approach:

- Economic growth is essential for prosperity.
- Nature is a resource to be used for human purposes.
- Promoting consumption is good for the economy.
- Life is unequal, and some lives matter more than others.
- The problems of other peoples, nations, and species are not our concern.
- There's no point in worrying about the distant future, as we'll be dead by then.
- What we do doesn't make any difference; we can't change the world.[44]

It is this approach—a kind of collective, selfish materialism—that has in large part caused the climate crisis and, at present, undermines our ability to mitigate it.

How is it that such harmful and fundamentally unsatisfying

patterns of consumption have come to dominate our lives? To answer this we need to explore the psychological and emotional landscape—the basic mindset—within which such materialist consumption has arisen and taken root.

2. Freneticism, Distraction, and Ignorance

The more alert and attentive we are, the more
the world will come alive, speaking or gesturing
to us in particular ways.
—Vajragupta[45]

WHAT WE'VE LOOKED AT so far helps explain the roles we play in causing the climate crisis, but we also need to consider why many of us don't seem sufficiently aware of the problem—or of the *magnitude* of the problem—and aren't taking the decisive action needed to mitigate it.

FRENETICISM

At this moment in history, most of us in the United States and other countries are saying that we're feeling harried and stressed out. Our days are cluttered, packed with things we "have to do." We scurry around, hurrying from one task to the next. Bo Lazoff writes, "Life is inherently joyful, yet we're not enjoying it. . . . Even the best, most loving people often seem to be working themselves into the ground, keeping up a frantic pace just to pay the bills and keep resolving each day's repairs, breakdowns, details, and little crises."[46] Pressed for time, we juggle our tasks, usually unable to devote sufficient time and focus to any one of them. Or we may try to do more than one thing at once: eating dinner while we text, check email, and carry on a fragmented conversation with someone across the table. Zen nun Yifa writes,

> We're so preoccupied, distracted, and multi-tasked that
> we can no longer work out what we want to do with our
> lives or really pay attention to people we care about. We're
> in such a hurry to get from one meeting to another, or one
> deal to another, that in those very rare moments when we
> have nothing to do and no one to meet, we panic: What
> are we going to do with ourselves? For one moment, we
> sit in a kind of daze. The next moment we reach for some
> kind of umbilical cord to the outside world: we log on,
> dial up, check in, tune out, and distract ourselves all over
> again.[47]

When hurrying and multitasking, we often do a half-baked job:
cutting corners, getting sloppy, leaving things unfinished, not
cleaning up after ourselves. Failing to do things mindfully, we subvert our own creativity and the joy of engaging fully in single tasks
one at a time. We fail to give ourselves—and our kids—a break from
constant scurrying, and we may not even know how to pull this off.
In this freneticism, we succumb to stress and the medical conditions it can cause. As Thich Nhat Hanh put it, "Many of us are lost.
We work too hard, our lives are too busy; we lose ourselves in consumption and distraction of all kinds and have become increasingly
lost, lonely, or sick. Many of us live very isolated lives. We're no longer in touch with ourselves, our family, our ancestors, the Earth, or
the wonders of life around us."[48]

Simply put, it often feels like there's too much going on and at
too high a speed. Granted, some of us have to work long hours and
multiple jobs just to pay the bills. But not all of us. Even those of us
with a financial cushion spend our days hurrying. Sometimes our
freneticism even gets a positive spin: scurrying, or at least telling
others about it, may serve to build up our image, as if to say, "I'm
plugged in, a player, doing things that are important. That's why I'm
always busy."

Living this way, many of us are devoting less time to family dinner conversations, recreation with loved ones, walks in nature,

contemplative practices, creative endeavors, and community involvement—the sorts of activities that make for fulfilling lives. Robert Putnam explored this trend in *Bowling Alone*:

> Television, two-career families, suburban sprawl, generational changes in values—these and other changes in American society have meant that fewer and fewer of us find that the League of Women Voters, or the United Way, or the Shriners, or the monthly bridge club, or even a Sunday picnic with friends fits the way we have come to live. Our growing social-capital deficit threatens educational performance, safe neighborhoods, equitable tax collection, democratic responsiveness, everyday honesty, and even our health and happiness.[49]

Granted, social media and movements like Black Lives Matter can offer new ways of being in community with others, but many of us are feeling increasingly isolated, if not alone, as we get busier and busier with little sense of being an engaged member of a larger community. We end up feeling disconnected—from our wiser selves, from other people, from our communities, from nature.

Freneticism, and the accompanying feeling that our lives are cluttered, are not limited to our physical actions and activities. They span each of what Buddhism regards as the three arenas of action or karma: physical actions, mental activity, and speech. The Buddha advised his followers to avoid what's known as the ten detrimental actions: the physical actions of killing, stealing, and sexual misconduct; the mental activities of covetousness, anger, and holding false views; and the verbal actions of lying, slandering others, harsh speech, and frivolous talk.

As we jump from task to task, screen to screen, our minds can get agitated. We may feel "wired," like when we get jittery from too much caffeine. Buddhism refers to this as "monkey mind": just as monkeys scurry through trees, grabbing branches and pieces of fruit, we latch on to thoughts and feelings as we obsess about this or that situation. This is mental agitation, one of the five hindrances in Buddhist psychology, which also include desire, anger, sloth, and doubt.

Our mouths can get frenetic, too. Many of us talk too fast. We repeat ourselves, interrupt others before they finish what they're saying or complete their sentences based on often mistaken assumptions about what they're going to say, weigh in on every topic or in response to each utterance, talk unnecessarily about minor things, or simply ramble on frivolously—the fourth type of wrong speech flagged by the Buddha. I'm guilty of all these forms of wrong speech.

When we're verbally frenetic, we also leave ourselves vulnerable to saying insensitive things, which relates to two of the other types of wrong speech laid out by the Buddha: harsh and divisive speech. These types of wrong speech derive not simply from ill will but from a lack of mindfulness, from not pausing before we speak and not slowing down as we speak. When we are hyperverbal, we may say unkind things that we later regret. Restraining ourselves from engaging in such harsh and divisive speech seems to be getting harder as we increasingly indulge in stereotypes and call each other names. I once heard a frazzled medical intern do this by referring to lonely, hypochondriacal people who repeatedly come to hospitals as "GOMERs": people they wish would "Get Out of My Emergency Room!" These types of speech may result in a full othering, even dehumanizing, of those we see as burdensome or threatening, who basically don't do what we want them to do, whether locally or internationally.

Freneticism in our physical actions, mental activity, and speech can lead to various forms of suffering, several of which my students have identified in recent semesters: feeling overload, stress, and burnout, and the medical conditions they generate; recklessly trying to squeeze in a text or phone call while driving; and doing rash, thoughtless things, like cutting in and out of freeway lanes. We may even succumb to what Carl Honoré has termed "time sickness": the obsessive tendency to feel that there is never enough time.[50]

As we all know, our freneticism can be exacerbated—and in some cases caused—by our ways of using technology. Technological developments, like the internet, e-mail, online shopping, texting, social media, and gadgets like smartphones and tablets, can all help people if used mindfully and with restraint. But that is usually not the case. Joanna Macy and Molly Brown write, "It is a painful irony that we who have more timesaving devices than any culture in history are the most time-harried and driven."[51]

In my own struggle with freneticism, the biggest tempter is my email in-box. It seems to call to me: "Come check your messages. See what's happening out in the world, in the circles in which you move. Don't get left out. Don't get left behind." I always make and break vows about keeping Outlook closed in the morning while writing, responding to urgent messages when I'm eating lunch, and leaving other messages until the end of the workday.

Our freneticism and related entanglement in technology also cause us to forget how to relax and do nothing. As Honoré puts it, in this "media-drenched, data-rich, channel surfing, computer-gaming age, we have lost the art of doing nothing, of shutting out the background noise and distractions, of slowing down and simply being there alone with our thoughts."[52] And when we get wrapped up in our consuming, our busyness, and our gadgets, we can easily start to feel disconnected from other people. Some of us text during family meals, or sit around in the evening with ear buds sending us to our own musical worlds and conveying the message, "Don't bother me." In some families, members text each other rather than walking down the hall and talking in person.

This social disconnection can exacerbate polarization, whether in families or in the political arena. Both ends of the political spectrum have been talking about class war, as seen in claims that the one percent and powerful corporations are waging war on the middle class and the poor by funding politicians to serve their interests and accumulating more and more wealth at others' expense, or claims that those who criticize the one percent, call for tax reform, and advocate getting certain regulations in place are waging class war as "socialists."

Sadly, such simplistic us–them dualisms have become a dominant frame for US political discourse in the form of the distinction between "red states" and "blue states." Setting aside the irony that "red"—previously a cipher for the communist powers—now refers to the more conservative, Republican-voting states, and bracketing the possibility that a more accurate distinction is between urban and rural areas, we can criticize the distinction between red and blue for eliding the fact that many "red state" conservatives, including members of the Christian Right, are as concerned about materialism, frenetic lifestyles, the negative effects of social media, and the impact of pollution on children as are "blue state" liberals. So if the red state–blue state distinction exaggerates political differences, whose interests does this dualism serve? Hard-right political candidates? Purist progressives who won't seek common ground? Blowhards on radio, TV, and the blogosphere? Powerful economic players whose interests would not be served if concerns spanning the red state–blue state divide were recognized, and people started working together to promote the common good as opposed what is good for the bottom line of corporations and their shareholders? The binary thinking engendered by America's increasing political polarization prevents many people from asking hard questions such as these and discourages citizens from finding the common ground necessary to tackle the social, economic, and environmental issues that affect us all.

DISTRACTION

When it comes to the climate crisis, there is a bigger issue in all of this. As we indulge in materialism, work long hours to secure the money and possessions we think will make us happy, dwell in the realities opened up through the "black mirror" of our phone or computer, and hurry through our days, we end up distracted. Popular culture and technology contribute to this distraction by offering us reality TV, myriads of cable stations, sports spectacles, shopping channels, consumer toys, video games, fun (and addictive) apps, and countless ways to lose ourselves on the internet. In those moments when we set our gadgets aside and actually spend time with others, many of us get engrossed in talking about our sports teams, the game last night, trends on social media, our favorite TV shows, and on and on, blissfully distracted from the crises around us.

Our use of technology is also affecting our cognitive abilities. Studies have been showing that we are becoming less able to engage in rational reflection, analysis, and argumentation. Whether it is a function of technology usage or high-school education being geared toward standardized tests, college students' ability to analyze texts, pose questions, and formulate rigorous and persuasive arguments seems to have been decreasing in recent years. David Loy argues that due in part to info-glut and shortened attention spans, we're facing a "challenge to our ability to construct narratives and logical sequences."[53] Some experts are also worried about our imaginations decreasing and our social skills getting stunted. Then there are the communication problems, such as misunderstandings that result from a reduction of face-to-face interaction that includes non-verbal cues, not to mention the growing problems of online lying, venting, and bullying. Moreover, with many of us writing only tweets and text messages, with little heed to grammar or style, we're not writing as well as people did in the past. Enclosing ourselves in our gadget worlds is also a main cause of something I will discuss below: disconnection from nature.

Many people today also suffer from what David Loy calls the "fragmentation of attention," in which we find ourselves less able to focus on one thing at a time.[54] Even when we can focus, we may notice that our attention span has gotten shorter. I recently heard that many teenagers can't focus on one thing for more than eight minutes. Unfortunately, however, what the climate crisis demands of us is sustained, focused attention.

Depending on how we use technology, we can also get lost in a deluge of information. Loy sees us as suffering from "info-glut": we used to be challenged by a scarcity of information, but now what is scarce is our ability to construct accurate knowledge from the flood of information available to us and to draw on that knowledge to make rational arguments, envision alternatives, and take informed action. Loy claims that we're also suffering from the effects of a deliberate "commodification of attention," in which corporations are attempting to control our attention and capture mindshare.[55] In such an environment, we may even lose the ability to distinguish between facts and falsehoods.

Distracted and overwhelmed in these ways, we fail to pay sufficient attention to the world around us. We're not fully present. About this distraction Bo Lazoff writes,

> We seem to be knocking ourselves out in pursuit of a vague image of success and meaning, while the real quality of our everyday life with our families and communities steadily declines. We're asleep at the wheel, swept up in a fitful, agitated dream, and we're missing some gorgeous scenery that only passes by once.[56]

Actually, some people are missing more than beautiful scenery, for they are oblivious to the ecological problems confronting us, or simply unable to give these problems the rigorous analysis and reflection they demand—not to mention the activism needed to ameliorate them.

IGNORANCE AND IGNOR-ANCE

This distraction and obliviousness are varieties of ignorance. Buddhism views ignorance as a central cause of suffering. The tradition construes ignorance mainly as our failure to discern impermanence, grasp what the "self" really is, and understand what true fulfillment entails. Ignorance also takes the form of failing to pay attention, or perhaps even *avoiding* paying attention to certain things: "ignor-ance."

Here in the climate crisis, we see a perfect storm of ignorance and ignor-ance, which can take many forms, including (1) ignorance of the problem; (2) believing false information or narratives; (3) distraction; (4) ignoring the problem by putting it out of our minds as we focus on other things; (5) ignorance of our causal responsibility; (6) the ignorance in which we ascribe causal responsibility to consumers and let players like the fossil fuel industry off the hook; (7) ignorance of what we can do in response to the crisis; (8) ideas that justify the continuation of our destructive lifestyle and economic system or that justify our doing nothing; (9) inaccurate ideas about certain groups of people; and (10) ignorance of our embeddedness in and dependence on nature. Let's look at these one by one.[57]

1. Ignorance of the Problem

Some people lack knowledge of the climate crisis, and this is a form of straight-up ignorance. They simply don't know about the problem, leaving them oblivious to the ecological impact of their individual actions and the economic system of which they are part. In some cases, this ignorance derives from our educational system and the media not providing sufficient coverage of the issues. It may also stem from information being withheld by the powerful. The White House under George W. Bush edited reports by the Environmental Protection Agency (EPA) to omit or downplay disturbing information. In Donald Trump's first term, the EPA removed most references to the climate or climate change from its website.

2. Believing False Information or Narratives

Sometimes, rather than simply being uninformed, people are ignorant because they are *mis*informed and come to believe incorrect information. We encounter this in unscientific statements about climate change that misidentify its causes or even question its very existence—statements like "There's no scientific consensus," or "Global warming is not caused by humans, and what we're seeing

is something that happens every ten thousand years or so." Sometimes the incorrect knowledge concerns the magnitude of the problem, as when people recognize the threat of the climate crisis but
minimize it by saying, "It's not a major problem," or "It's not going
to impact us that much." This mistaken understanding may derive
from the groupthink that arises in the echo chamber constructed by
climate-change deniers. Or it may be caused by disinformation and
lies that are spread, for example, by scientists on the payroll of the
fossil fuel industry at a time when the several hundred scientists on
the Intergovernmental Panel on Climate Change (IPCC) are in virtual unanimity about the causes and magnitude of the crisis. This
form of ignorance gets exacerbated when we lose a firm handle on
the difference between facts and fallacies (or facts and "alternative
facts").

3. Distraction

A key form of ignorance here is distraction, which, as I just discussed, is exacerbated by materialism, frenetic living, and entanglement in technology and entertainment.

4. Ignoring the Problem by Putting It Out of Our Minds as We Focus on Other Things

Ignorance can also take the form of simply ignoring the problem.
We are in a state of ignor-ance when we have learned about the
climate crisis but choose not to think about it. [58] Perhaps we have
glimpsed the magnitude of the problem but feel overwhelmed, and
as a result, we put it out of our minds and direct our attention to
other things.[59]

5. Ignorance of Our Causal Responsibility

Some people may know what is happening but are ignorant of their
own causal responsibility. If pressed on the issue, they might say,

"I'm not responsible; I don't drive a Hummer," or "It's totally the fault of the fossil fuel industry."

6. Emphasizing the Individual Over the Macro Level

Ignorance can also take the form of incorrectly seeing consumers as the biggest cause of the climate crisis and disregarding the much greater responsibility of the fossil fuel industry, the growth paradigm in economics, and other players and structures at the macro level. A correlate to this form of ignorance is the view that the solutions lie with consumers changing their behavior. But as Michael Mann writes, ". . . consumer choice doesn't build high-speed railways, fund research and development in renewable energy, or place a price on carbon emissions. Any real solution must involve both individual action and systemic change."[60]

7. Not Knowing What We Can Do in Response to the Crisis

We can also be ignorant of the range of constructive actions that we can take. In this case we may even hear people say, "There's nothing I can do." This stance is often coupled with ignorance of the impact we could make if we were to take action. We might say things like "It won't make any difference if I buy a Prius." Often lurking in the background of this ignorance is a denial of our responsibility to respond: "Dealing with climate disruption is the responsibility of Congress and folks in the EPA," or "I'm too busy to deal with the problem right now." In this way we shirk our responsibility, not in the sense of being responsible for playing a role in causing the climate crisis (being accountable) but in the sense of having a responsibility to respond to it (having a duty to act).

8. Ideas that Justify Doing Nothing and Keeping Things as They Are

Ignorance/ignor-ance can also take the form of ideas that justify continuing our destructive lifestyle or doing nothing, such as the notion that humans can adapt to climate change without any major loss of quality of life, or that we will reap a net benefit from the economic opportunities the crisis will provide (like starting companies to make sandbags for coastal cities or sump pumps for basements across the country), or that a technological fix driven by market forces will solve the problem, especially if we eliminate regulations that constrain corporations. This ignorance can take the form of ideologies at the national and international levels, whether belief in the economic-growth paradigm; belief that the free market will take care of the problem through the law of supply and demand; or belief in technology and our ability to come up with a technological fix. We may even get religious justifications: "Only God can affect realities as big as global climate systems," or "Christ is coming again soon and current global problems are part of the divinely ordained end of history that is outlined in the Book of Revelation, so rather than engaging in environmental activism you should focus on accepting Christ as your savior and convincing others to do so before it's too late."[61]

9. Inaccurate Ideas about Certain Groups of People

Related to this is ignorance in the form of ideologies that may pertain to subgroups, seen when we make assumptions (or succumb to stereotypes) about other types of people: "Those who work for oil, coal, and gas companies are greedy and immoral," or "Wealthy people are all selfish and don't care about the climate." Insofar as we succumb to such stereotypes with a self-other or us-them mindset, blurring our vision through rigid dualistic judgments about who is good or evil, we are caught up in ignorance. That is to say, we can construe ignorance as getting trapped in our views and, as a result, not being open, listening well, learning from others, refining our views, finding common ground, or working together to solve problems.

10. Ignorance of Our Embeddedness in and Dependence on Nature

One other form of ignorance is unawareness of our embeddedness in and dependence on nature. Spending much of the day engrossed in electronic media and virtual realities separates us psychologically from what lies outdoors (and what's happening in our bodies as another locus of nature). As Tyrone Cashman puts it, "electronic media insulate us from the environment" and cause us to become oblivious of the "web of life."[62] Anthropologist Helena Norberg-Hodge has pointed out that for many of us in the industrial world "it's easy to believe that we depend more on the technosphere than on life, or the biosphere."[63] Staying inside in front of computer and TV screens rather than going outside to play leaves many kids suffering from what Richard Louv has termed "nature deficit disorder."[64] Spending so much time in front of screens can also dilute our awareness of our *embodiedness*, and, by extension, our *embeddedness* in the physical universe.

This psychological disconnection from the rest of nature—from actual nature, not shows on the Nature Channel—is not caused solely by technology or our ways of using it. Many of us live in air-conditioned boxes in cities. Kids spend less time outdoors enjoying unstructured play. We are divorced from the source of our food, ignorant of how our electricity was generated and natural gas extracted, and oblivious to where our municipality gets water or where sewage goes when we flush the toilet. As a result, we have lost our lived connection to nature and the valuation of nature that usually accompanies that connection, while also losing out on the stress reduction and better health that studies have shown are gained by spending time outside.

A Zen Buddhist might add that our alienation from nature derives from causes deeper than urban living or changes in kids' activities. Stuck in dualistic modes of experiencing, we see ourselves as separate from nature. Nature is what we imagine to be "out there," and should this way of looking at nature get coupled with desire and ill will, we come to see nature as stuff, as "natural resources" to commodify and exploit, or as something dangerous, which we need to control if not conquer. (More on this later.)

Whatever the cause, it seems safe to say that many of us go about our daily lives ignor-ant of nature in and around us and, at a deeper level, unaware that we are part of nature and dependent on a healthy biosphere.

Perhaps the most dominant form of ignorance in most societies today is the notion that we can find happiness through acquisition. Studies have shown, however, that once basic needs have been met and we have some surplus assets for special occasions, levels of happiness—or, better yet, fulfillment—do not correlate signifi-cantly with ever larger amounts of wealth and possessions (though negative environmental impact does). This is an example of what economists term *marginal utility*, and the rest of us call the law of diminishing returns.

Many Americans realize—at least in certain moments—that a materialistic and frenetic lifestyle is not fulfilling. Though we'd rather not take our kids to theme parks or host commercialized birthday parties, we fear our kids will suffer if we don't. I might want to keep things simpler when dining out with friends and not go to the expensive trendy spot, but the fear of losing those friends keeps me from saying "no." This is not unlike adolescent boys doing dangerous things on a dare out of fear that not doing those things will get them labeled a "wimp" or, worse yet, get them ostracized from their pack of friends.

Simply put, I think it's safe to say that most of us want to figure out a way to slow down, pay attention, simplify our lives, lessen our environmental impact, and feel more fulfilled. We may have heard about studies that have identified the things that give us a sense of fulfillment: being loved, appreciated, and respected; feeling like we are part of something larger than ourselves; participating in a sup-portive community; helping others; finding a meaningful calling; and helping to create a caring and just society.[65] We may have even caught glimpses of a way of living that would lead us in that direction. But we may lack a model for such an alternative way of living, and hence may need pointers to help us start living that way.

Buddhism offers a way of rethinking "richness" and extricating ourselves from materialism, freneticism, ignor-ance, disconnection, and the ecological costs of such living. The Buddha offered a vision of fulfillment that is centered not on material possessions but on waking up, which involves working with the unhealthy mental states that lead to both psychological suffering and to the destruction of healthy communities and ecosystems. His vision generates a novel notion of wealth: "Buddhist wealth includes our mindful use of resources to enjoy life and to help others, and Buddhism teaches that our true wealth—love, compassion, and wisdom—are inexhaustible."[66] Phra Phaisan Visalo has written that the lifestyle of the Buddhist monastic community in Thailand provides the laity with examples that "point to the true value of life, indicating that development of inwardness is much more important than wealth and power, that the life of tranquility and material simplicity is more rewarding and fulfilling."[67] Or as Sulak Sivaraksa puts it, through meditation and other practices our orientation shifts from "more having" to "more being," which leads to greater contentment.[68] Living in this Buddhist manner can also help us shift from a consumer identity to what Stephanie Kaza calls an "ecological identity."[69]

This fulfillment is not simply a goal out in the future that is achieved after decades of pursuing a path, Buddhist or otherwise, for in key respects it's actualized here and now while on the path, in one's actions, in one's daily life, in a unity of means and end. To get a better sense of this alternative richness, let's turn to that path, to a way of living that is both spiritually rewarding in the here and now and ecologically beneficial over the long haul.

PART II

Slowing Down and Paying Attention

3. Mental Spaciousness and Presencing

*. . . our full presence is perhaps the best offering
we can make to our world.*
—JOANNA MACY AND MOLLY BROWN

WE CAN START extricating ourselves from materialism, freneticism, and ignor-ance by cultivating a way of living that is
less cluttered and more mindful. Easier said than done, you might
say. For me, it's more of a goal than an actuality, but it's good to
have an ideal to shoot for.

CULTIVATING SPACIOUSNESS

A foundation for this better way of living is what I call "spaciousness."
Spaciousness extends across the three types of action—mental, verbal, and physical—that we have discussed already. As a first step to
cultivating spaciousness and reducing our environmental impact,
we need to declutter our minds, speech, and bodily actions.

But before I go any further and share my struggles and strategies,
you might want to pause, consider the following questions, and jot
down what comes to mind:

- What might you identify as your **mental clutter**? What most
  typically fills your mind? Which thoughts and worries seem
  extraneous or excessive?
- Where do you encounter **verbal clutter**? In conversations,
  what gunks up the communication? Do you ever find

yourself being hyper-verbal, or anxiously filling the auditory space? Or do you get talked over by assertive people?
Do you ever find that those to whom you are talking don't
seem to be listening or really *hearing* you, because they're
talking or distracted as you speak?

- In your body, doing things in time and space, where do you
see **temporal clutter**? Do you ever find yourself oversched-
uled or overextended? How often are you multitasking and
scurrying from task to task or place to place?

- What about **spatial clutter**? Are there any rooms, closets, or
drawers that feel cluttered? With what sort of stuff?

Let me share some thoughts about each of the three arenas of
action and what I've noticed about myself, starting with the mind
and mental activity.

All of us are thinking and worrying beings. Some of our thinking
is practical, like when we remember something we need to do, or
when we are solving a problem or trying to make a good decision.
But much of what transpires in our heads isn't practical or helpful.
We often obsess about our actions, appearance, loved ones, financial security, or health. This mental activity may take the form of
regretting something we've done, perhaps while beating ourselves
up and obsessing about what we "woulda, coulda, shoulda" done.
Or we may find ourselves obsessively worrying about what might
or might not happen in the future, such as "Is the weather going to
mess up my day off?" "Will my sister be a jerk again at Christmas?"
"Is my friend going to recover from their illness?" "Will Congress
fail to pass significant climate legislation?" Though we often get
stuck in obsessing about one thing, sometimes we slip into thinking about all sorts of things. Our minds get scattered as we leap
from topic to topic in our hyperactive monkey minds. We get filled
with mental clatter and mental clutter.

Meditation can help us get some space from our busy mind, and
perhaps even quiet it down. In the case of Buddhist meditation,

we have lots of options. Over the past 2500 years, Buddhists have engaged in all sorts of meditative practices in an array of times and places. Nowadays, teachers also offer an assortment of mindfulnesses, as well as an extensive menu of practices to cultivate them.

My type of meditation is *zazen*, literally, "seated meditation," which is central to the Zen Buddhist tradition. I usually do it in a room off our bedroom in what used to be the attic. Two balcony windows offer views of the sunrise over the skyline of Boston. On the walls I've hung several pieces of Japanese calligraphy and some nature photographs, and in one corner is a low altar that Mishy and I set up, with beach stones, dried flowers, photos of loved ones we've lost, and a little statue of the bodhisattva Jizō, protector of travelers and children. The room is not a traditional *zendō* (Zen meditation hall), but it's simple and quiet.

Of course, thinking and worrying are tenacious, and we can't will them to stop. We weren't born with a switch to turn them off. So just as it's unhelpful to say, "Don't worry, be happy"—arguably the worst advice we can give a person who is anxious or depressed—it's not helpful to say to ourselves, "Don't think." What we can do, however, is shift our attention from thinking to breathing, as the first step toward disentangling ourselves from thinking and opening up our awareness. So, at the beginning of my meditation sessions, I simply try to follow my breath as it goes in and out. I breathe abdominally, feeling the sensation of my belly extending outward as I inhale and coming back in as I exhale. When it proves difficult to stay focused on my breath, I extend my outbreaths a bit. Another technique is to count exhalations, from one to ten and then from one again. If I'm feeling especially caught up in thinking, for a minute or two I imagine my in-breath as my empty mind being filled by the world, and then imagine my outbreath as my mind extending out across the world.

Another technique is to pour ourselves into the act of breathing. This is what Dōgen (1200-1253), founder of Japanese Sōtō Zen, called *gūjin*: doing something "thoroughly and exhaustively." It's the act of giving oneself as completely as possible to the activity at hand, whether breathing during meditation or performing tasks around the monastery. We may construe this pouring of ourselves into breathing as an exertion of the will, like when a weightlifter grits her teeth, grimaces, grunts, and strains to lift the barbell above her head. But it's actually more of a letting go. As Zen master Uchiyama Kōshō puts it, we "open the hand of thought"[70]: we stop grabbing onto thoughts, we let go of thinking and relax into the simple act of breathing.

Even when we're on a cushion in a peaceful meditation hall, we will likely find that thoughts continue to arise in our minds, like air bubbles floating up from the bottom of a glass of seltzer. When I notice that I'm thinking about something, I simply bring my attention back to breathing. That is to say, I don't try to label or track my thoughts and feelings. Rather, I just note when I've gotten caught up in thinking and then return to my breath. Coming back to breathing, back to the movement in my belly, again and again—this is the core practice.

By focusing on the breath we can gradually shift from thinking to awareness. Zen teacher Jan Chozen Bays writes, "The mind has two functions, thinking and awareness. . . . The mind truly rests only when we are able to turn off its thinking function and turn on its awareness function."[71] In this shift from monkey mind to calm attentiveness, we are cultivating mindfulness: "awareness without criticism or judgment."[72] With mindfulness we can thus rest in the present, free not only from incessant thinking but from desire and ill will. Andrew Olendzki writes,

> Mindfulness means being present to whatever is happening here and now—when mindfulness is strong, there is no room left for wanting something else. With less liking and disliking of what arises, there is less pushing and pulling on the world, less defining of the threshold between self and others, resulting in a reduced construction of self. As the influence of self diminishes, suffering diminishes in proportion.[73]

We can regard meditation, and this shift from thinking to mindful awareness, as opening up internal space in several senses. First, we open up space between our awareness and what's going on in our heads. Rather than being lost in thought, as we usually are in our cluttered "small" minds, we can get some separation from the train of thought, observe it from a detached place, and let go of it.[74] This is akin to the shift we see in a "rage-aholic" who initially is so caught up in his anger that he will angrily deny that he is an angry person, but then at a later date is able to get some space from the anger, observe it, become aware of it, and acknowledge that he has an anger problem.

Practicing meditation cultivates space in another sense: it opens up space between our thoughts or feelings and the actions they generate. The moral psychology of Buddhism sees meditation as opening up temporal space between unhealthy (or, to use other terms, detrimental, unskillful, unwholesome) internal mental states and the unhealthy external actions they can generate. The former includes the three poisons (ignorance, desire, and ill will) and the five hindrances (agitation, desire, anger, sloth, and doubt), and these mental states are the cause of suffering. When we purify the mind of these unhealthy mental states, we eliminate the cause of suffering and thereby nip suffering in the bud, bringing about a stoppage or cessation of suffering. In more positive terms, we attain nirvana.

The term "nirvana" derives from *vā*, to blow, and *nir*, out. Cognizant of this derivation, some British colonial figures in South Asia viewed nirvana is a "blowing out" of the mind, an interpretation that may have found expression in Hegel's statement in his *Philosophy of History* that Hindus (and, presumably in his eyes, Buddhists as well) are "driven to the creation of a dream-world and a delirious bliss in Opium"[75] and, by extension, in Marx's notion of religion as the "opiate of the masses." What is getting extinguished, however, are the "fires" of the unhealthy mental states. This metaphor is conveyed in the Saṃyutta Nikāya, where the Buddha says, "Bhikkhus [monks], all is burning. . . . Burning with the fire of lust [desire], with

the fire of hatred [ill will], and the fire of delusion [ignorance]."[76]
This should not strike English speakers as foreign, for we often say
things like "I'm burning with desire"; "I've got the hots for her";
"She's got a fiery personality"; "He's hot under the collar." Connoting the extinguishment of the fires of the three poisons, nirvana is
usually described in early Buddhist texts as an absence: the absence
of the fires of desire, ill will, and ignorance that cause suffering.

These unhealthy mental states can generate unhealthy external
actions. Examples of these actions appear in Buddha's sermons on
the eightfold path, in which he delineates right speech as refraining
from lying, divisive speech, hurtful speech, and frivolous speech;
right action as refraining from harming, stealing, and sexual misconduct; and right livelihood as refraining from occupations that
involve these actions that contravene right speech and right action.
The doctrine of the five precepts adds the use of intoxicants to
harming, stealing, sexual misconduct, and lying, as the five main
kinds of activity to avoid.[77]

As we become aware of our cluttered thinking and unhealthy
mental states and "get some space" from them rather than being
caught up in them, we are more able to restrain ourselves from
impulsively—and unwisely, and perhaps harmfully—acting on
them. When, for example, someone says or does something that
angers us, we will be less likely to say or do something immediately that we might later regret, like saying something hurtful or
physically harming the person. As I mentioned earlier, Buddhist
discourse about desire and ill will, or attraction and aversion, is a
way of talking about internal emotional reactivity, and by opening up some space between ourselves and those mental states and
becoming more aware of them, we can avoid reacting rashly when
those states arise. Sharon Salzberg talks of how we can "expand our
awareness and allow . . . feelings to come up," and how "[t]hat space
brings the wisdom that keeps us from getting lost in immediate
reactivity. That freedom is the essence of equanimity."[78]

This practice finds expression in an oft-quoted stanza of the

Dhammapada, a core Buddhist text said to be the words of the Buddha in verse form:

> Refraining from all that is detrimental,
> The attainment of what is wholesome,
> The purification of one's mind:
> This is the instruction of Awakened Ones.[79]

As we develop more inner space, we can more easily refrain from indulging the detrimental or unhealthy mental state and doing a detrimental action. This practice of "refraining from all that is detrimental" interrupts negative karma, and not simply in the exterior sense of "that which goes around comes around." Detrimental actions generated by detrimental mental states also act to deepen those mental states in a negative feedback loop. This is what we're getting at when we claim that a person who indulges in his anger is making himself a more angry and miserable person.

To help maintain the temporal space between thinking (or feeling) and acting, we can use a mantra: "Take one breath." That is to say, after experiencing what comes at you, take a breath before saying or doing anything in response, which will give you a chance to monitor your internal reaction to it. Thich Nhat Hanh advocated taking three breaths in such situations.

It is also important to note that just as meditation can help us restrain ourselves from doing detrimental actions, moral guidelines concerning those actions can help us meditate. If, for the moment, we view the components of the eightfold path sequentially, with the three morality components (right speech, right action, and right livelihood) coming before the three meditation components (right effort, right mindfulness, and right concentration), we can view the Buddha as, in one respect, teaching that before we can focus inwardly and meditate we have to restrain ourselves from doing detrimental external actions. As I put it to my students, we cannot meditate deeply (or at all) if we're running around indulging our desires as a "party animal" who always wants to eat, drink, and be merry, or engage in sex, drugs, and rock-and-roll like Steve Martin's character on Saturday Night Live: the "wild and crazy guy." We need to yoke the wild part of ourselves. This yoking is part of traditional "yoga." Indeed, "yoga" and "yoke" are said to have been derived from the same word in the family tree of Indo-European languages.[80] Though "yoga" may conjure up images of stretches and poses, in ancient India it also had to do with yoking the mind and the unruly detrimental actions generated by it, just as a farmer yokes a feisty draft horse to a plow. Or to use other equine expressions, we need to *rein* ourselves in so we don't *run wild* with our *unharnessed* energy and *unbridled* desire.

So, as the meditative components of the eightfold path help us practice the moral components by making us more aware of the detrimental mental states that we might be inclined to indulge through our actions, the moral components help us yoke ourselves from doing negative external actions and thereby support our efforts to redirect our attention inward and to meditate. This element of mutual support rather than sequencing shows how the eightfold path is less an eight-*step* path than an eight-*part* path, with each part supporting the others. I explain this to my students by asking them to flag eight things a college athlete might do during the summer to get ready for soccer tryouts in the fall. They mention doing drills, scrimmaging, stretching, sprinting, going for long runs, lifting weights, eating well, and getting ample sleep. Next I highlight that such an athlete will almost certainly not spend the eight weeks of training doing only one of these activities at a time, with, for example, a week of only intensive weightlifting followed by a week of just scrimmaging, then a week devoted to stretching, and so on. Rather, such an athlete would probably perform most of these various activities on any given training day, with each one supporting and complementing the others; it's hard to scrimmage, for example, if we haven't eaten well or built stamina with long runs. It's this sort of multi-component training regimen that I sug-

gest students keep in mind when they consider how someone practices the eightfold path.

As we continue meditating, we not only gain some space from
our thinking and worrying and between internal mental states
and external actions, but also start to observe the space between
thoughts. Though we often get caught up in trains of thought, in
meditation we can observe the gaps between thoughts and realize that the mind runs deeper than our thoughts and worries. As
Kittasaro puts it, "Be mindful of the space after the thought, before
the next thought arises. Mind the gap."[81] Over time, that gap may
grow wider. That is to say, the monkey mind may start to quiet
down. Fewer thoughts arise, with expanding space between them.
The mind settles down and gets emptied—at least of our obsessive
thinking with its clutter of thoughts that are repetitive and no longer have practical value. Internal space is getting opened up. This
seems to be what people are seeking when they declare, "I want to
clear my head."

As this happens, we calm down. The Japanese verb for this is
ochitsuku, literally, "drop down and adhere." A cousin to English
expressions that equate calming with downward movement,
ochitsuku can be rendered not only as "calm down" but as "settle
down" and "quiet down." In the physicality of Zen meditation, as
we breathe abdominally we bring our awareness from our cerebral
heads *down* into our belly, into what Japanese refer to as the *hara*.

As we drop down into calmer awareness, we become more able
to observe thoughts—or remnants of thinking—as they float up, lin-
ger, and, if we don't grab on to them, disappear. To use a Buddhist
simile, through meditation we get in touch with a mind that is open
and expansive like the sky, in which thoughts or bits of thinking
appear and then disappear like passing clouds, as opposed to our
being lost inside those clouds, caught up in our obsessing and worrying. Although we can experience this spacious mind, we cannot
objectify it. In the Zen metaphor of the mirror, the empty mind

clearly "sees" all things that appear before it and does not judge or react, but it cannot catch an image of itself. That is to say, the mirror can perform the act of reflecting but cannot reflect itself, just as a sword, to use another Zen metaphor, can cut things but cannot cut itself.

Deploying this notion of the spacious mind, contemporary Zen master Shōdō Harada teaches that our true nature is like the "huge expanding blue sky":

> Our ego-consciousness (at this moment or that moment) is like something which sends out puffs of clouds fluffily sailing across that huge blue sky. None of us looks up at that blue sky, sees those clouds, and thinks they are fixed and absolute. This is because we know the true nature of the blue sky. We know the clouds will at some time be blown away and disappear—that they are only moments of scenery up in the sky. . . .[82]

Zen is not alone in talking about this open, spacious mind that is like the sky. Tibetan teacher Tulku Urgyen Rinpoche says, "Whatever arises—concepts, feelings, your body, subject and object, everything—is like clouds in the sky. Your true nature, awareness imbued with love, compassion, and wisdom, is like the sky itself."[83] Aware of statements like this, Joseph Goldstein writes,

> The Tibetans use an image I have found useful. They liken the mind to a great clear sky, a cloudless sky. All the phenomena of mind and body are happenings in this clear sky. They are not the sky itself. The sky is clear and unaffected by what is happening. The clouds come and go, the winds come and go, the rain and sunlight all come and go, but the sky remains clear. Make the mind like a big clear sky and let everything arise and vanish on its own. Then the mind stays balanced, relaxed, observing the flow [of thoughts].[84]

With these notions in the background, many Buddhist teachers say that the goal of meditation is to wake up to this sky rather than try to eliminate thinking, for such elimination is impossible to attain—at least over extended periods of time—insofar as we are thinking beings, and thoughts will arise, as mental secretions,[85] as what Uchiyama Kōshō refers to as "the scenery of life."[86]

The Japanese character for "sky," 空, carries additional meanings that pertain to what we're considering here. When it has the meaning "sky," 空 is pronounced "sora." The character can also mean "empty," and in that case it's pronounced "kara." It can also connote space, as in the main word for "space," *kūkan*, where it's pronounced "kū." In short, this one character conveys the three core features of this calm, open awareness I've been discussing:

> emptied, spacious, and [like] the sky.
> *kara* (空)　　*kū* (空)　　　　　*sora* (空)

To denote this mental spaciousness I have coined a Japanese neologism, 空心, *kūshin*: emptied, spacious, "sky mind."

Because "empty" is one of the meanings of 空, Buddhists use this character to translate the key Sanskrit term *śūnyatā* into Japanese. This term is usually rendered as "emptiness" in English in the sense of each thing—or better yet, each *event*—being empty or devoid of any separate, permanent essence or soul. This lack of a separate, intrinsic essence is expressed in positive terms in the doctrine of conditioned arising (P. *paṭicca-samuppāda*; Skt. *pratītya-samutpāda*) of all event-things, in which we arise through inputs and influences from other events and now exist interconnected with those events in an ever-changing process and, hence, are "empty" of any separate, unchanging soul, core, or essence. With event-things being affected by and affecting each other moment to moment, some translate conditioned arising as "interrelational arising" or, as Thich Nhat Hanh puts it, "interbeing." Buddhists typically conceive of wisdom (P. *paññā*, Skt. *prajñā*) as an insight into conditioned arising.

We can also translate *śūnyatā* as a gerund, "emptying," which reframes it as a process rather than a thing and brings out the term's psychological connotations. Zen masters teach that zazen is a process of emptying or forgetting ourselves and waking up as the expansive "sky mind." In "Genjō-kōan" Dōgen writes,

> To study the Buddha Way is to study the self;
> to study the self is to forget the self;
> to forget the self is to be realized by the myriad things.

That essay includes the following sentence:

> Conveying the self to the myriad things to realize-in-
> practice[87] those things is delusion;
> for the myriad things to advance and realize-in-practice
> the self is satori [awakening].

What Dōgen seems to be saying here is that ordinarily the mind "conveys" itself or reaches out to the objects it experiences, discriminates them, and evaluates them positively or negatively as we feel attraction to them (desire, like) or repulsion from them (ill will, dislike)—as we react to them—based on our past experiences and mental constructs about them. Through meditation, however, we can "forget," or empty, ourselves. Fellow Sōtō Zen master Shunryū Suzuki has written, "The best way to perfect composure is to forget everything. Then your mind is calm, and it is wide and clear enough to see and feel things as they are without any effort. . . . Do not try to stop your mind, but leave everything as it is. The things will not stay in your mind for long. Things will come as they come and go as they go. Then, eventually your clear, empty mind will last fairly long."[88] Or as Chozen Bays puts it, "We teach the mind to empty itself and stand ready, alert but relaxed, waiting for whatever will appear next."[89]

In this emptying process of shifting from the thinking function of mind to the awareness function, to relaxed, open, alert awareness, we are cultivating mindfulness. You are then, as Chozen Bays puts it, "deliberately paying full attention to what is happening around you and within you—in your body, heart, and mind."[90] With our minds calmed down and opened up, we find ourselves fully present— simply paying attention rather than scrutinizing, judging, and reacting to objects of experience or getting caught up in thinking. This is what the Zen tradition calls the state of "mirror mind," which reflects things without distortion, discrimination, or judgment.

Expressed differently, when we are fully present in the present, we can be with things more calmly as they present themselves to us. Dōgen uses the term *genjō* for this "presenting"—or, we might say, "presencing"—of things. Zen teacher Okumura Shōhaku writes that when functioning as a verb,[91] *genjō* means to "manifest," "actualize," "appear" or "become," and "[a]s a noun it refers to reality as it is actually happening in the present moment,"[92] to "reality actually and presently taking place."[93]

THE PRACTICE OF PRESENCING

As we settle down in our breathing and open up mental spaciousness, we become more present; we are presencing ourselves, and in this awareness we can attend to the presencing of the sunset, the tree, the river, and everything else around us. To be present in this way, we need to "forget the self," or as Dōgen also puts it, we need to "drop off the body-mind." About this, Brett Davis writes, "Only through this ultimate experience of letting go and letting be does one become open to the self-presentation of things. The true self is an openness to the presencing of truth."[94] We can view this presencing as a vivid, alert attunement to what is unfolding in and around us. Though there may still be a subtle sense of experiencing something other than oneself, and hence an element of dualistic experiencing, one is experiencing that thing in and through open awareness—without normal mental chatter, attachments, judgments, or reactions—in a state of equanimity. Sharon Salzberg writes, "Equanimity can be described as the voice of wisdom, being open to everything, able to hold everything. Its essence is complete presence." She goes on to explain that in being present in this way, "we cradle both the immense sorrow and the wondrousness of life at the same time. Being able to be present with both is the gift equanimity gives us—spacious stillness, radiant calm."[95]

This presencing bears additional spiritual fruit. Sometimes when we are fully present, there is no sense of "I" or "me"—there is no "I" that is opening to something other, no sense of the "me" being filled by the presencing of the "not-me event." All such dualistic experiences of separation drop away. That is to say, in that moment there is simply presencing, or "reality happening." In Dōgen's terms, with the self forgotten and the mind opened up, things "advance" and fill our empty, spacious minds. What had been grasped as experiential objects "out there"—the mountain, the sunset, the sound of a warbler, the smell of mud emerging through the spring thaw—is simply what *is*, and what we *are*, in that moment. As Dōgen describes it, the "self" is realized by the "myriad things" insofar as we are waking up to a "self," to a mode of experience, in which we have no sense of existing separate from whatever "thing" is happening and filling us. In this mode of experience we are liberated, at least temporarily, from our mental struggles, including the estranged sense of being separate from the world.

Thomas Kasulis gives an example of such non-dual experience from batting in baseball:

> Although we can retrospectively look at a previous experience, analyzing its subject and object, that experience, while it was being lived, was not so divided. While it is correct in a certain sense to say that "I hit the baseball," . . . this expression, with its division into subject and object, is the result of retrospective analysis. At the moment of the original event, there is only an unbroken hitting-of-the-baseball.[96]

With no sense of separation from what is being experienced, a person might say, "In that moment I wasn't there—it was simply the swinging of the bat." In another context, someone might say, "During the piano recital the music was playing itself through me," or, "When its magnificence blew me away, it was just 'sunset!'" But this does not mean that the person had a sense of actually existing as a sunset, inside an orange, amorphous body twenty miles wide. Rather, the experience is perspectival, as Bret Davis flags with his expression, "egoless perspectivism":

> Perspectivism insofar as it [Dōgen's view] understands that reality only shows itself one aspect and focal point at a time. But while, on the one hand, in a deluded/deluding comportment to the world this aspect and focus get determined by the will of a self-fabricating ego. . . , in an enlightened/enlightening comportment to the world, on the other hand, things are allowed to reveal themselves through non-dual events in which the self has 'forgotten itself' in its pure activity of egoless engagement.[97]

The experience of non-separate, egoless engagement with the world helps us realize that we are part of a larger whole, that we exist as one node within an energy field. To use another metaphor, we begin to see that we are like waves on the ocean, which seem on the surface to be separate, autonomous things, but are really inseparable from the larger ocean. Likewise, when we shift our perspective from experiencing things dualistically, to a more integrated non-dual perspective, we no longer experience ourselves as simply a distinct thing separate from other things but carry a realization of the larger "ocean" of which we are part even as we function in our individual wave form. I am me, with a perspective, but I experience that "me" as the expression of something larger, which also finds expression in other things. This is the crux of Zen's metaphysical non-dualism: not two—I am not a completely separate thing or wave—and not one—I am not some oneness, some mass of water without any form as a wave. This non-duality is conveyed by the line in the *Heart Sutra* that says, "Form is none other than emptiness,

emptiness is none other than form." The wave is none other than the water, water is none other than [exists in the form of] the wave.

I once heard a story about a retreat at the Zen Center of Los Angeles that relates to this meaning of non-dualism as "not-two and not-one" and how the ultimate goal of Zen is not some sort of monistic oneness. About four days into a retreat there, Maezumi-rōshi, the Zen master, was giving a Dharma talk, and one of the retreatants suddenly exclaimed, "I can see it! It's all one! It's all one!" Without skipping a beat, Maezumi turned to the senior disciple who was sitting beside him and said, "Remind me not to send *him* out for groceries!"

Needless to say, the experience of non-separateness and non-duality, which I've been discussing here, can be realized in numerous ways, not just through Zen meditation. And it should also be recognized that Zen meditation yields numerous fruits. It has been my experience, however, that the practice of sitting meditation provides one of the most accessible and effective methods for helping us slow down, pay attention, see things more clearly, become less reactive, get in touch with our original spacious mind, and overcome our sense of being separate from the world around us— maybe so much so that, as Zen Buddhists put it, we "open up" to awakening (*satori o hiraku*).[98]

This opening up of spacious awareness is not all in our heads, for our hearts are affected as well. In Japanese, the term for mind, *kokoro*, also means heart (in the emotional sense, not the physiological sense), and the Sanskrit term *citta* carries this double connotation, too. Many Buddhist teachers claim that meditation opens up our heart and makes us compassionate and generous, as conveyed by such expressions as "open-hearted" and such statements as "I have space in my heart for him." With this spaciousness in our *kokoro*, our heart-mind, we are better able to deal with difficult people, including climate-change deniers, and forgive those who have wronged us. Often, though, our minds are too full to be open-hearted. We're overflowing with ideas about others, with labels, biases, and projections. This is especially true when we "other" certain people, such as those who march in the streets or those who are employed by the fossil fuel industry.

Meditation, and the spaciousness that it brings, can positively affect our relationships in other ways as well. When we fully presence ourselves, we are *being present*, in the *present*, and with a certain *presence*. This act of being fully present is a gift we give to others across all interactions.[99] It is also a gift that we can offer to the world around us. Thich Nhat Hanh, addressing Mother Earth, said, "I know that my true presence is the best gift I can offer you, the one I love."[100] Perhaps offering our presence as a gift to others and to the world is the foundational form of the Buddhist ideal of giving and generosity.

In my own experience, the gift of presence is especially important when we are sitting with people who are in pain, perhaps because of having to deal with loss, a scary diagnosis, or psychological issues. In some of those situations, we can provide more support and nurturance by simply being fully present than by knowing the right things to say, offering advice, or trying to fix things. At times when I've had to sit with the surreal shock of having lost a loved one, the condolence cards and food offerings have been helpful, but having loving people show up and simply *be* with me there in the room is what has supported me the most. Perhaps this is why we typically appreciate saintly people and spiritual teachers not so much because they follow certain vows or are morally pure, but for the way they tend to be fully present with us, for the way they sit with us and listen deeply, patiently, and compassionately. The same holds for mentors, skilled therapists, elders, and good friends as well.

When we are fully present with those who are struggling, they are more likely to feel heard, acknowledged, and supported. As one Zen teacher puts it, "Presence has no measurable product except positive feelings, feelings of support, intimacy, and happiness."[101] What we can detect here is a shift from morality to spirituality: a person goes from *being moral*—"having one's act together" and, hence, not doing prohibited things, whether swearing, fibbing, or avoiding responsibility—to *being present.*

But a part of me interjects here and says that paying attention and being present *is* something moral. As we all know, many conflicts are caused by people not paying attention or not being mindful: we bump into people, cause car accidents, impulsively say insensitive things, mindlessly divulge things that violate trust, or fail to pick up on cues or cries for help. When we pay attention and are present, we are less likely to commit these sins of commission and omission. I often point out to my students that Buddhist morality, with its grounding in paying attention (one facet of mindfulness), is less a matter of exerting one's will to follow accepted rules and commandments than it is about paying attention and being present, which allow one to better see what's going on in the situation (including one's unhealthy mental states), restrain oneself, and act in wise, compassionate, and skillful ways.

Perhaps we can think of mindful presence as a higher-order morality, in which we go beyond dos and don'ts and show up with a certain state of mind. Because many of our interpersonal problems are caused by not paying attention, rather than by one or more of the participants being "bad" or "evil," much good comes from paying attention, from being fully there for others. If the vice is being scattered and not paying attention, the virtue is being mindful and attentive. In the face of the climate crisis, we can all benefit from cultivating this virtue.

Presencing also helps us pay attention to little things, whether the face of a loved one, the miraculous taste of orange juice, or the early blooming of daffodils in a warming climate. This attentiveness shades into the related practice of appreciating beauty, including the restorative beauty of nature. During the unsettling days at the beginning of the COVID-19 pandemic in March and April of 2020, daily walks provided Mishy and me with a chance to savor flowers, bird calls, and budding trees of spring here in the Northern Hemisphere. Savoring this beauty helped us feel gratitude and count our blessings, even in the midst of a pandemic. It helped us appreciate the greatest blessing: being alive. Thich Nhat Hanh writes, "The first miracle of mindfulness is our true presence—being here, present, and totally alive."[102]

Many practitioners report that the benefits of meditation go beyond shifts in their way of experiencing things. Though years of meditation practice may not yield a singular, dramatic awakening like what the Buddha reportedly experienced under the Bodhi Tree, over time practitioners usually discover a deep, calm strength that helps them avoid getting rattled by challenging times, whether a late night in the emergency room with an ailing parent, a long day of listening to a depressed friend talk about their struggles, or a weekend of feeling rattled by the climate crisis. This strength is something we can actualize by taking deep breaths, similar to what people do in formal meditation. Kaira Jewel Lingo writes, "With all the tumult that may be in your life, still you can breathe in and out, with presence, recollecting yourself."[103] In crisis situations in my own life, I have found myself taking deep breaths and sitting up straighter, without consciously intending to do so. In the minutes, hours, and perhaps days of the crisis, I keep the slow, deep breathing going, all the while trying to stay present and meet the crisis with attentiveness, love, and savvy, or in Buddhist terms, mindfulness, compassion, and wisdom. In this I find strength.

Pouring ourselves into the breath in formal or informal meditation is not the only way to cultivate mental spaciousness. As I move through the day, I try to keep my tongue up against the roof of my mouth like I do in zazen, and it somehow brings me back to formal meditation on the cushion and to the calmness and focus I often feel there. For me, this simple touching of my tongue to the roof of my mouth is a kind of default stance for paying attention and being present, serving as a physical act of preparation and centering, like the ritualistic actions of a basketball player before shooting a free throw. As a kind of mantra, I say to myself "Keep your tongue on the roof of your mouth."

As another way to help me avoid getting lost in thought, some-times when I'm driving I chant, usually the *Heart Sutra* and the Fourfold Great Vow.[104] Through the day, I also do a practice that I call "stepping back." This takes the form of mini-breaks, during which I take several deep breaths, similar to Thich Nhat Hanh's "bell of mindfulness" practice, in which a bell reminds practitioners to pause and take three mindful breaths. For those of us who have to spend our days indoors, stepping back can also take the form of stepping *out*: going outside for a moment and taking in the sky and any trees or birds that might be out there.

Going Deeper

What I've been discussing here is not merely psychological. In wak-ing up to sky mind, we are getting in touch with a quiet place in ourselves that is deeper than our thoughts and worries. Normally we're caught up in what we like and dislike, trying to hold on to things that are pleasant while avoiding things that are unpleasant. We're stuck on a rollercoaster of highs and lows, or to use a differ-ent metaphor, we're stuck on a pendulum, feeling unsettled as we swing back and forth between pleasant and unpleasant, between good times and bad times. We wake up in the morning feeling great but fall apart later in the day when we get bad news. Or we feel down in the dumps and then someone says something that makes us feel better. At least temporarily. Then something comes along and knocks us off-kilter again, and after a while, something lifts our spirits. . . .

Realizing spaciousness can help us get off of the pleasant-unpleasant pendulum, or better yet, we can get in touch with a depth in ourselves that is always off the pendulum. Zen teach-ers have termed this place mind-ground, original mind, spacious mind, big mind, and sky mind. By waking up to a place in ourselves deeper than that pendulum, we shift from seeing Buddhism as a way to foster psychological well-being to Buddhism as *a religious practice*. Awakened to, and *as*, that deeper place inside ourselves, we can stay centered in the face of both desire and aversion, and the swings between them. We can meet whatever comes—pleasant or unpleasant—with equanimity, without being rattled, or at least not to the core. This is one way to think about faith and salvation: the ability to be okay, at the deepest level, with whatever life throws at us. Such equanimity is conveyed in a story about a group of bandits on horseback attacking a village long ago in Japan. At one point in the carnage, with villagers frantically trying to run away, the leader of the outlaws sees an old monk calmly drawing water from a well. The leader rides over, pulls back on his reins, and, looking down from his horse, waves his sword above the monk and says, "Don't you realize that I am the one who can run you through with a sword without batting an eye?!" In response, the monk slowly looks up at the outlaw and says, "Yes, but don't *you* realize that I am the one who can be run through with a sword without batting an eye?!"

Like that monk, we can free ourselves from the small mind that sees itself as a separate little critter (or wave) that will be obliterated someday, and wake up as something larger (the ocean). By letting go of the frightened self and identifying with the ocean, with nature, with reality, the problem of death as posited by that self is not solved—in terms of some afterlife or postmortem bliss—but *dis*solved. With this realization we can be liberated, we can be "saved"—not in the future, but here and now.

In addition to its psychological and spiritual benefits, presence is a crucial resource in the face of the climate crisis. It helps us extricate ourselves from distraction and ignor-ance so we can see our situation clearly. It helps us keep our eye on the ball—in its complexity and magnitude—without getting rattled and shutting down in some sort of psychic numbing. Though we may still feel anxiety if not despair, with spacious presence we can bear witness to what is going on, sit with it, understand it, and start figuring out skillful responses to it. Then, as we take action to transform the situation, spacious presence helps us stay calm when we encounter challenges, setbacks, and blowback. It provides a sanctuary where we can rest and replenish as needed, and it gives us fortitude and resilience as we continue to take action over time to mitigate global warming.

In Buddhist terms, presence is as a support mechanism for putting into practice the ten perfections of the bodhisattva, among which are patience, vigor, spiritual strength, determination, and skill-in-means—all of which are important attributes when acting to mitigate the climate crisis. Expressed differently, spacious presence is foundational to our "bodhisattva functioning"[105] in response to the climate crisis and other challenges we might face.

4. Verbal and Physical Spaciousness

Now more than ever, I feel that what matters most
is the practice itself: embodying the precepts,
practicing mindfulness, offering gratitude and
kindness, challenging delusion.
—STEPHANIE KAZA[106]

HAVING DISCUSSED the ways in which the mind and mental states can help or hinder our efforts to act skillfully in the face of challenges like the climate crisis, we now come to the second arena of action: speaking. Buddhism offers numerous guidelines around speech. As we saw earlier, one of the five precepts asks Buddhists to refrain from false speech, and the instructions on right speech in the eightfold path steer us away from false, divisive, hurtful, and frivolous[107] speech. The ten precepts of Mahāyāna Buddhism also include directions for right speech, asking us to refrain from discussing the faults of others; praising oneself while slandering others; and speaking negatively about the Buddha, Dharma, and Sangha, which together comprise the Three Jewels of Buddhist refuge.

Many of us, especially those of us who were brought up in monotheistic religions, construe right speech in terms of negative prohibitions, such as "Thou shall not lie." Put another way: don't swear, don't brag, don't say mean things. Buddhist precepts and the moral components of the eightfold path, however, while including some of this admonishment, are not understood to be negative commandments or lists of sins that result in estrangement from—and punishment by—a deity. Buddhist teachers typically say that the precepts function to make us more aware of detrimental, unhealthy actions, which, as we've seen, deepen our entanglement in the unhealthy mental states that underpin those actions and cause more suffering for ourselves and others.

Some Buddhist teachers view the precepts as reminders, as things to keep in mind, whenever we do something. This is one facet of mindfulness, for the Pali and Sanskrit terms—*sati* and *smṛti* respectively—that are usually translated as "mindfulness" literally mean "to recollect," "to remember," or "to bear in mind." This is why the Chinese used the character *nien* (念), "to remember," when they first translated these Buddhist terms from South Asia. I find it interesting how the character also connotes the more popular notion of mindfulness as paying attention in the present moment insofar as it combines the characters for "now" (今) and, below that, "mind" (心). Mindfulness as now-mind!

Other teachers portray the precepts and the moral components of the eightfold path as describing how an awakened person acts. In the case of speech, such a person not only refrains from lying, saying hurtful things, and rambling on, but speaks honestly, compassionately, and succinctly. To put it differently, we can say that such a person speaks skillfully, not unskillfully.

We can expand Buddhism's analysis of speech by shifting from the qualitative—*types* of detrimental or unskillful speech like lying, dumping on people, talking frivolously—to the quantitative, the *amount* of speaking we do. Of course, the unwholesome act of talking too much does not necessarily apply to people who have been silenced, censor themselves, are shy, or feel nervous about public speaking. But they, like the rest of us, are all too familiar with conversations that are cluttered.

When I reflect on the quantitative dimension of my own speech, I recognize a repetitive streak in me. This may derive from my being a professor and having spent four decades rephrasing things in the classroom to make sure that all of my students understand. I see this streak especially when I exert my will and try to control things, like I sometimes do when making plans with my wife, whether for what we're going to do on Saturday night or how we're going to orchestrate Thanksgiving. I also notice this tendency in myself when I repeat myself to assert—and reassert—my opinion about a topic in the news or an issue at work. At other times, even when not repeating myself, I can ramble on, wandering down digressive side streets. Close relatives have kidded me about the long voicemail messages I left for them back when we still used voicemail. Except in situations when we need to talk things out or "get something off our chest," excessive verbiage clutters conversations and ends up stealing the time and attention of others.

PRACTICES FOR UNCLUTTERING OUR SPEECH

How can we remedy the qualitative and quantitative parts of our cluttered, unmindful speech? I find it helpful to keep my tongue on the roof of my mouth when I don't really need to say anything and want to make an extra effort to restrain myself and declutter my speech. Another helpful practice is to take a breath before speaking, even after the other person has said what they had to say. This helps me contain my urge to express thoughts right away, whether to disagree, display what I know, exert my will, or move the conversation along. Sometimes it's good to take *several* breaths and bring a bit of silence into the conversation, thereby creating a momentary time-out that can help everyone collect their thoughts and sit with their feelings. Of course, silence makes some of us nervous, and when no one is saying anything we tend to rush in to fill the auditory void. But silent moments in our conversations can make us more thoughtful and careful in our speech and can give our conversations a depth that's usually lacking when we're talking nonstop.

In addition to the practices mentioned above, I follow several other guidelines to maintain spaciousness in conversations. One is to make an effort to speak succinctly. As we all know, sometimes less is more, and that certainly applies to speaking. In response to my hyper-verbal tendency, I've recently been trying to trim excess

verbiage from my utterances. At the very least, this opens up space
for others to speak, and reduces the frustration and fatigue that can
arise when others have to persevere with my long-windedness.

Speaking more succinctly—and less often—may also grant our
words more weight with others. When we shorten our statements,
people may be more apt to attend to what we say and take it more
seriously. We may feel more confident about what we're saying—
and even if we don't, conciseness conveys self-confidence. Either
way, it's good to keep in mind such expressions as "Those who
know do not speak; those who speak do not know," and "Silent
waters run deep." Or, as the Japanese adage goes, "The hawk with
talent hides its claws."

Another practice I try to follow is restraining the part of me that
wants to control things—particularly when making plans with
others. I remind myself that I don't need to weigh in on every detail
to ensure the event fits my picture of what will be enjoyable—or, in
a pandemic, safe. I resist the urge to preemptively assert myself to
set the rendezvous time early enough to accommodate the friend
who tends to run late. Instead, I can help maintain *space* for others
to contribute to the conversation, and if part of the plan seems mis-
guided or unhealthy, I can still speak up about it. Needless to say,
this approach can be especially useful when engaging in dialogue
or activism with others, situations in which people generally need
to feel that they have had a chance to express their ideas and have
been listened to respectfully in order to stay engaged.

I also try to be respectful and constructive when talking *about*
others. As I flagged above, one of the ten precepts in Mahāyāna
Buddhism asks us to refrain from discussing the faults of others,
while another asks us to refrain from praising oneself and disparag-
ing others. In light of these guidelines, I try to remember and repeat
little mantras I've created, like "Imagine everyone is in the room,"
and "Avoid negativity."

SPACIOUS LISTENING

As we all know, optimal communication with other people involves more than right speech. Right *listening* has a role to play, too. Greek philosophers and traditional liberal arts education celebrate the virtue of eloquence but say little about good listening. This is a serious omission, for many of us come up short as listeners. Poor listening derives from some of the things we're explored already in the above chapters. Rebecca Shafir summarizes the barriers to good listening when she writes,

> It's not just the noisy environments, megachoices at the mall, multitasking, information overload, or the intrepid remote control that challenge our ability to listen. It is the internal distractions that threaten our very existence and hopes for a better world—obsession with time, greed for speed and stuff, prejudice and aversion towards people and change, self-consciousness, ego gratification, negative self-talk, extreme preferences, dwelling in the past while obsessing about the future, and working so hard to sustain these beliefs. These are the delusions that endanger our ability to connect with each other, understand each other and live in harmony.[108]

Regardless of the cause, our poor listening clutters up the space of communication. Many of us find it hard not to interrupt others. If they're rambling or repeating themselves, we may grow impatient and feel that "Time's a wasting," which leads us to cut them off in an attempt to move the conversation along. We may even succumb to one of the most irritating forms of bad listening: finishing the other person's sentence, often incorrectly!

Even when we don't interrupt others, we may not be listening to them, or at least not attentively. We may be paying attention to something other than what the speaker is saying. We may be checking out other people or sneaking peeks at our phone. We may be sitting there figuring out what we want to say next rather than really listening to, and *hearing*, the other person.

One way to start cultivating deeper listening is to take breaths when others are talking and let them finish before speaking ourselves. Here, too, the restraint mantra—"Keep my tongue on the roof of my mouth"—can help. Next, we can try to be present and open when listening to someone as a way to help ourselves understand what the person is saying rather than listening selectively to what fits our preconceptions and opinions. As Chozen Bays puts it, we can see our ears as a sponge that soaks up all the sounds around us in a process of "absorptive listening."[109] Finally, after the other person has stopped speaking we can extend our deep listening by taking a breath or two before saying anything, and in this way we can let what they said sink in. Or, after the other person stops speaking, we can say nothing. Perhaps the deepest form of listening is not just listening intently but deciding not to say anything, especially if we are an assertive person with power or privilege. Allan Lokos describes the benefits of such silence when he writes,

> At times noble silence is the most skillful speech. For several years I facilitated a weekly sangha. The sangha rules were that no one commented on anything that was said by another member during the discussion period. We didn't even say, "I agree with Bob," or "My sister went through the same thing." All we did was listen. Over time, we realized how often our minds were busy preparing a response when we thought we were actually listening. Knowing that we would not respond dramatically changed the way we listened.[110]

Such an approach can foster spaciousness, opening up and preserving auditory space for others to express themselves, to be who they are, to be heard and appreciated.

If a person with whom you are speaking seems to be rambling

on, use it as an opportunity to be with your breath and monitor your reactions. This is a good practice for cultivating patience.[111] And if you feel impatient, see if there is anger, too, and maybe even fear.[112] Perhaps in the moment of listening patiently you will decide that what is needed is for the person to stop hogging the conversation, and the practice then is finding a skillful and compassionate way to contain that person and support them in talking less.

Ultimately, deep listening boils down to paying attention. Henry David Thoreau once wrote, "The greatest compliment that was ever paid me was when someone asked me what *I thought*, and attended to my answer."[113] Deep listening is also an act of compassion. As Thich Nhat Hanh writes, "Deep listening simply means listening with compassion. . . . Now you are a bodhisattva of listening. This is a practice of compassion."[114] Chozen Bays describes cultivating compassionate listening through a "recitation for invoking compassion": "We shall practice listening so attentively that we are able to hear what the other is saying—and also what is left unsaid. We know that by listening deeply we already alleviate a great deal of pain and suffering in the other."[115] Or as Rebecca Shafir tells us,

> Listening is the first step to making people feel valued. Mindful listening allows us to do more than take in people's worlds; it helps us better understand the how and why of their views. When understanding occurs, a sense of calm is achieved on both sides, even if no point of agreement is reached. From understanding, respect and trust for one another are possible; we are free to open our minds and widen the scope of potential solutions.[116]

As these writers make clear, deep listening involves much more than simply uncluttering our conversations. And given the need for us to reach across divides, find common ground, and mobilize in response to catastrophic climate disruption, the importance of deep listening looms large at this moment in history.

As we try to cultivate deep listening in ourselves, we can take

as our role model the most famous bodhisattva in Buddhist cultures: Avalokiteśvara. In South Asia and Tibet, this figure is seen
as male, and devout Tibetan Buddhists believe that the Dalai Lama
is an incarnation of him. In East Asia, this bodhisattva is considered female. In China she is known as Guanyin, and in Japan, as
Kannon. Books on goddesses in world religions usually include
her, and she functions somewhat like the Virgin Mary and female
saints in Catholicism. In Japan, people pray to her for such benefits as safe childbirth, finding a good spouse, recovery from illness,
and success in business. For our purposes, the key point is that the
two characters in the Sino-Japanese rendering of her name, 観音,
literally mean discerning or contemplating (観) and sounds (音). In
other words, this "discerner of sounds" is the person who *hears the
cries* of suffering beings.

Deep listening with our ears is something that can get lost in the
shuffle when, as is typically the case, we construe Buddhist meditative experience in terms of the sense of sight, as when we talk about
"seeing things just as they are," "seeing things in their suchness,"
"seeing the light," or "enlightenment." Highlighting the importance of right listening can provide a counterbalance to the usual
emphasis on seeing while also expanding the Buddhist construct
of right speech to include right listening. Or, better yet, we can offer
a new construct: "right communication," inclusive of speaking and
listening.

Right communication can help us as we try to reach across divides
and join with others to address the climate crisis. When talking
with people who are less concerned about the climate crisis or perhaps even in denial, we may slip into bombarding them with scary
facts about how climate disruption is causing floods and fires. But,
as Katharine Hayhoe has pointed out, ". . . fear-based messaging
can trigger awareness of our own mortality, invoking our finely
tuned package of defenses against the notion of considering our
own death—distraction, denial, and rationalization,"[117] all forms of
what I've discussed here as ignorance/ignor-ance. A more effective
approach is to start by focusing on something that the participants in

the conversation share, whether a value, concern, interest, or experience. Hayhoe writes, "Beginning a conversation with something that unites us instead of something that divides us means we are starting at a place of mutual respect, agreement, and understanding—which is pretty much the opposite of where most conversations about contentious issues like climate change begin these days."[118] Or, if you don't know much about the person, start by asking them questions— about their life, their passions, their place, and what may they have noticed about weather events or shifts in their local area—then listen carefully to their responses. If they don't respond—or if it feels manipulative to try to get them to talk about the weather as a tactic to make them more aware of how climate disruption is real, is affecting their life, and merits their attention—we can shift from listening to speaking, simply sharing what is important to us and what we are concerned about, and this can help open up a two-way conversation and foster connection. Hayhoe teaches that "sharing our personal and lived experiences is far more compelling than reeling off distant facts. Connect *who we are* to *why we care*."[119] Though I don't engage in many conversations with people who deny the reality or seriousness of climate change, when I do have such conversations I try to be present, go slowly, and speak and listen mindfully. Even if the conversation doesn't go anywhere, I can work on my ability to show up with presence, an open mind, and respect, and to, at the very least, try to connect with the other person at a basic human level.

Temporal Spaciousness

Spaciousness extends beyond mental and verbal actions to our bodily actions in time and space. Many of us feel constricted in our relationship with time. We complain about our calendars being cluttered, leaving us feeling frazzled and wishing we had enough time to do what we want. Of course, some of us have to work several jobs to put food on the table, but whatever our economic situation, most of us multitask, scurry from one thing to another, and get overextended, with all the stress, fatigue, and dissatisfaction that come along with this.

A first step in addressing this busyness and stress is to notice what's going on in our bodies when we're frenetic. How fluttery is my breath? Is my back tight? Jaw clenched? Do I feel like pushing someone out of my way? Then we can begin to slow down.

One way to slow down is by doing what I call "80 percent speed." I sometimes say to my students, "When you leave this classroom today, try walking at 80 percent of your normal speed as you head to your next class, the dining hall, your room, or maybe even the library." We can all try this in our daily activities. Shower and get dressed at 80 percent of your usual speed. When preparing a meal, slow your actions down 20 percent. Or when driving, try going at the speed limit, which for many of us is about 80 percent of our normal speed.

This slowing down works well with eating, too. Try to chew each bite more slowly, savoring the flavor and texture of the food. You may find that this will help you avoid the mindless snarfing that can leave us bloated, groggy, and overweight. The Japanese have an expression, *hara hachibu*, which can be translated literally as "gut—eight parts." The advice here is to slow down the act of eating, pay attention to what we're feeling in the stomach, and eat until we feel 80 percent full. If we stop at the 80 percent mark, even though we may feel like we still have space left in our stomach we'll soon feel satiated and our desire to keep eating will dissipate. In this way, we can pull back to both 80 percent speed and 80 percent amount.

Moving at what feels like 80 percent speed helps us pay more attention to what we are doing, allowing us to get *more* done, not less—and what we do will likely be of higher quality. We may also find ourselves doing everyday actions as something creative, and perhaps even feel joy.

I sometimes try to enhance temporal spaciousness by repeating to myself, "Just do one thing at a time, and pour into it, paying full attention." In other words, just walk; just cut the carrot; just wash the lettuce. While driving, don't make calls, and definitely don't text. Try not to multitask. We can support this by saying to ourselves, "I'm driving," or "I'm making a salad." As some Buddhist teachers tell us, mindfulness involves being fully aware of what we are doing: while driving, we're fully aware that we're driving; while making a salad, we're fully aware that we're making a salad. When we give ourselves fully to what we're doing—and just to that one thing—we naturally slow down and sharpen our attention. At the same time, if we are up against a deadline and need to do things quicker, doing just one thing at a time will help us avoid getting sloppy and making mistakes.

In Zen, the practice of pouring ourselves into the single action at hand is, as I mentioned earlier, what Dōgen called *gūjin*. Edward Espe Brown describes this practice, saying,

> When I asked my Zen teacher, Shunryū Suzuki Roshi, if he had any advice for working in the kitchen, he said, "When you wash the rice, *wash* the rice. When you cut the carrots, *cut* the carrots. When you stir the soup, *stir* the soup." Taking his words to heart, I found that they had the power to evoke what lies hidden in the depths of being. Something *awakens*. It is not self, not other, not me, not the world. To "be mindful while you work" carries a certain dryness, not to mention distraction: doing something—practicing mindfulness besides what you are doing. What Suzuki Roshi meant was more like "*throw* yourself into it" or "*immerse* yourself in what you are doing."[120]

Perhaps this is what Thoreau was getting at when he wrote in *Walden* that he wished to "live deliberately."[121] You may find that as you pay attention to what you're doing, you will experience the wonder and joy of being in a body—alive!—and able to do things with it. In that moment, you will likely feel gratitude as well.

We can apply this practice of *gūjin* to all of our actions. It can be especially useful with those actions that we tend to do in an unfocused or scattered manner, such as things we usually do while doing other things. For example, a good friend of mine usually calls me while she's driving, and I've yet to muster up the courage to ask her to hang up and call me after she's parked. In my case, it's writing by hand. I tend to hurry when I write things, scribbling as my mind moves on to the next thought. I recently started making it a practice to remind myself, each time I pick up a pen, to write legibly. Whether making a shopping list, jotting a comment on a student paper, or writing a check, I try to write slowly, legibly, and maybe even beautifully, approaching it as a kind of meditative practice. Not having good handwriting, or better yet, not being disciplined enough to slow down when I write, I find this challenging. But it does allow me collect myself[122] several times a day, and as I try to write better I also find myself wanting to add calligraphic flourishes to what I'm crafting. In this way, the act of writing becomes not only an exercise in cultivating mindfulness but a creative act. Now I just have to settle on one, and *only* one, signature and make it a thing of beauty rather than a chaotic squiggle that looks nothing like "Christopher Ives."

Another thing we can do to maintain spaciousness is to invert the 80 percent rule and *add* 20 percent to the time we set aside to do things. If you think it will take five hours to clean the house, add an hour so you can do it without hurrying. If you expect the ride to the airport or the clinic to take thirty minutes, add five or six minutes to give yourself some slack. Depending on where you're going, bring a book—not just a smartphone (unless your smartphone *is* your book). Getting to an airport gate or doctor's office early and having some time to read is a valuable gift to give yourself. You surely deserve it.

You can maintain spaciousness in your calendar by applying the 80 percent rule there, too. When you find that your commitments and activities have reached 80 percent of what you think you can handle mindfully, start saying "no" to yourself and others when you're tempted to put something else "on your plate" (an interesting metaphor linking tasks to food). Doing so will make for less scurrying and more enjoyable evenings and days off. Thoreau famously wrote, "Simplicity, simplicity, simplicity! I say, let your affairs be as two or three, and not a hundred or a thousand; instead of a million count half a dozen, and keep your accounts on your thumb nail."[123]

You can also try doing the same with technology. As a start, cut your time spent on the internet or watching TV by 20 percent (or more!). Use the opened-up space in your day to meditate, pray, talk with loved ones, read a book, shoot hoops, listen to music, or do an art project.

If you work away from where you live, give yourself, and ask for, space to land and time to transition when you get home at the end of the day. If at all possible, take a few minutes to empty your pockets, change your clothes, wash your hands, and brush your teeth. Then and only then, start engaging with your roommate or family members.

Another strategy for opening up temporal space is the practice of "pick and choose." We don't need to engage with every text, group email, family discussion, or interpersonal conflict. If we are clear about our values, priorities, and goals, we can get clear about what to do with our time. In response to invitations or requests, we can learn to say "maybe" and give ourselves time to consider the request, or we can say "no" as our default response unless the thing we are being asked to do excites us and feels like something we can do mindfully and joyfully. And when conflicts pop up around us, we can, as some people put it, "pick our fights carefully."

Another simple practice for cultivating temporal spaciousness involves pausing and taking three breaths when feeling frenetic or transitioning between activities. For example, when you sit down in your car and start the engine, take three breaths before putting the car in gear. (Your car will appreciate the chance to warm up, too.) Or when you take your seat on a bus, train, or plane, take three breaths before looking at your phone.

As I have learned from my students and friends, there are many other things we can do to cultivate temporal spaciousness:

- Do an inventory of your routines and make a note of which are unsatisfying and can be reduced or eliminated.
- Limit the use of your phone by turning it off or setting it aside at certain times of the day or week.
- Create a sacred time in your day or week, a sabbath, during which you can unplug, step back, and retreat from ordinary routines and stresses; this can be a special time to *be* and to *love*, not to *do* and *produce*.
- Do regular technology fasts, whether as part of a designated sacred time or simply as part of your day, week, or month.
- If you have kids, engage in slow parenting by pulling them back from too many scheduled activities, which will open up restful and creative space in their days. For example, give your child or children a break from TV and computer screens by limiting their time watching television, playing video games, engaging in social media, and surfing the web. You could also establish a habit of everyone in household having dinner together with no smartphones or other gadgets in the room.
- Remind yourself regularly that we are mortal and will die, maybe even today or tomorrow, and then ask yourself whether all of today's activities are really so important.

In short, slowing down and decluttering our calendars generates an array of benefits: less stress, greater ease, enhanced focus, more creativity, more joy in doing things, more appreciation of the little things and beauty all around us, more time with loved ones, and more time to help others. Describing his own experience of consciously slowing down, Stephen Altschuler writes,

> What's so important about living each moment, anyway? The answer lies in the effects I enjoyed from slowing down: less anxiety, more peacefulness, being clearer in thought and deeper in breath. Life sparkled with

more joy, interest, and appreciation, as if some part was returned—a part that, missing but unnoticed, made the whole feel unsettled, off-centered, incomplete.[124]

Slowing down and opening up space in our days can also help us respond to the climate crisis. When we hurry less, we can pay attention more. With more time in our days, we can look more into the carbon footprint of our diet or favored modes of transportation and investigate the feasibility of solar panels and heat pumps for our home (if we are lucky enough to own one). We can educate ourselves about structural issues, whether problems with energy policies or the ways in which elected officials have been co-opted by the fossil fuel industry. With greater spaciousness, we are more able—and inclined—to join an environmental group, write letters, attend hearings, go to protests. I know that when I'm busy and stressed, the last thing I want to do is take on something else, especially if it necessitates joining a group that has meetings in the evening and on weekends. But when I slow down and cull my less meaningful activities, I find it easier to get involved.

Reducing Spatial Clutter

Our bodily actions as the third arena of karma happen not only in time but in space. Just as our calendar and our days can get cluttered, so can the spaces in which we move our bodies. We can think of spatial clutter in two senses: messiness and too much stuff. Of course, messiness is in the eye of the beholder. Some people don't mind the clutter and always know where to find things in the midst of the apparent chaos. Some people with kids prefer living in a home with toys scattered about, and some people like what one of my students calls "creative clutter." Perhaps the question, then, is whether we can find things and function mindfully and creatively. Or, as Gary Thorp suggests, we can think of it in terms of striking a balance: "The objective is to find a balance between the wildness of the woodshed and the impractical sterility of the home as chemical laboratory, to find a place where there is both cleanliness and comfort, order and surprise."[125]

The feeling of being burdened by too much stuff is not simply a function of not having enough space in our abode. Possessing excessive stuff requires a whole array of activities: shopping, choosing, buying, unpacking, placing, moving, sorting, storing, maintaining, fixing, losing, finding, cleaning, and disposing.[126]

So how do we reduce spatial clutter? Needless to say, one way to do this is to acquire and possess less stuff. Thoreau wrote that a person is "rich in proportion to the number of things which he can afford to let alone."[127] In this regard, a useful practice for when we are on the verge of buying something is to ask ourselves, Do I need this thing, or do I simply want it? Another strategy is to give away one thing—or two things—in the class of objects into which an acquisition falls; if I want that new shirt on sale, I give away one of my current shirts. A student of mine said that she tries to buy one quality item that will last—an "investment piece"—rather than multiple cheaper ones. When giving a gift, we can offer an activity or experience rather than an object.

Once we have started restraining ourselves from acquiring and giving unnecessary things, the next step is culling unnecessary things we already possess. One tactic is to do an inventory at least once a year. Sort through your things and identify anything you have not used, worn, or eaten over the past twelve months. One of my students said that once or twice a year she goes through her clothes and other possessions and tries to fill two shopping bags with things she has not been using. You don't have to limit this winnowing down to once a year—you can do it whenever you notice that you have something that you don't need. Following the lead of Marie Kondo, we can identify and give away unnecessary things that no longer bring us joy. I also try to make it a daily practice to monitor for things that I don't use, are in the way, or seem redundant; as I notice such things, I set them aside to give away to people who need them.

It can help to set concrete goals, such as pledging to give away a certain percentage of our overall possessions or limiting how many we have of any one thing. At different times I've asked myself whether I could give away 20 percent of my possessions. Whether I, a bibliophile, can do what nature writer Paul Shepherd reportedly did and possess no more than twenty-five books at a time. Or whether I can be rigorous and start paring things down to the essentials. This, of course, prompts the question of what the essentials might be. Though not directly relevant to life at home, hikers take the "ten essentials" on day hikes.[128] As we'll see in the next chapter, monks are limited to a prescribed set of essential possessions.

With less stuff, it's easier to have less clutter, whether on your desk, on the floor, in the closet, on the dining room table, or in your car. It also makes it easier to feel less scattered. Chozen Bays writes, "Our mind seems 'cleaner' and our life less complicated when we've cleaned up the space and things around us."[129] Or as Ou Baholyodhin puts it, "By paring things down to the essentials, we arrive at a clarity which enables us to cope."[130] Duane Elgin echoes these Buddhist sentiments when he writes, "The hallmark of a balanced simplicity is that our lives become clearer, more direct, less pretentious, and less complicated."[131]

My notions of spaciousness at home have been colored by the Zen valuation of open space. What has drawn me to paintings influenced by Zen is the space that is left empty, or hazy, as seen in Sesshū's landscape paintings of mountains fading back into—or appearing out of—amorphous clouds. He seems to be conveying the relationship between form and emptiness: mountains and other things with form emerge out of formlessness, and the formed mountain dissolves back into formlessness, just as thoughts arise out of the formless depths of our minds and then dissolve back down. In traditional Zen monasteries, the zendō is largely empty, too, save for the meditation cushions, a sculpture of the bodhisattva of wisdom Mañjuśri, and the bells, gongs, and incense holders needed for directing meditation.

A close cousin of Zen, the Japanese tea ceremony takes place in an unadorned room of its own. Cushions to sit on, paraphernalia to make the tea, bowls to serve it in, sweets on a plate, and a scroll and flower arrangement in the alcove are virtually all that reside there. The simplicity, beauty, and tea smell are believed to purify the senses and, by extension, the mind, as the tea practitioner and guests let go of worries and settle down.

We can take Zen monasteries and Japanese tea houses as a model for limiting our possessions to things that are needed, appreciated, and used carefully and respectfully. One way to cultivate this is to set up a room, nook, or surface in your home as a sanctuary or altar that is free from chaos and clutter. In my case, that space is my zendō off of our bedroom. By uncluttering a small space in your home, over time you may find it easier to keep other spaces simple and uncluttered, too.[132]

Needless to say, reducing our clutter goes hand in hand with reducing our ecological impact. Usually, what clutters our space is stuff we don't need. These excess possessions usually have a negative environmental impact caused by extraction of the raw materials, the manufacturing process, shipping, usage (in some cases), and disposal. Unnecessary stuff, unnecessary damage. And when we buy less stuff, we can free up cash to do good, whether by helping others, covering the additional cost of organic food, saving for an electric car, or making donations to environmental groups.

PART III

Greening Our Individual Lives

5. Green Mental States and Green Living

A human being is a part of the whole, called by
us "Universe," a part limited in time and space.
He experiences himself, his thoughts and feelings as
something separated from the rest—a kind of optical
delusion of his consciousness. This delusion is a prison
for us, restricting us to our personal desires and to
affection for a few people nearest to us. Our task must
be to free ourselves from this prison by widening our
circle of compassion to embrace all living creatures
and the whole of nature in its beauty.
—Albert Einstein[133]

CULTIVATING MENTAL, verbal, and physical spaciousness helps us
slow down and pay more attention. It helps us become more
mindful of our actions and their effects, and it helps us simplify our
lives and open up space to become more engaged with issues like
the climate crisis. In this way, spaciousness provides a supportive
structure for greening our daily life and, at a broader level, for taking action to reduce greenhouse gas emissions (mitigation) and
learning how to live in the new and challenging conditions that are
upon us (adaptation).

But cultivating spaciousness is challenging. Untamed energy and
habitual actions can distract us and cause mental, verbal, and physical clutter. Those of us who have been brought up in materialistic,
hyper-individualist cultures may find it hard to restrain ourselves
from doing certain things. We may grab a hamburger, impulsively

turn up the AC, or jump on a cheap flight to the Caribbean without reflecting on the carbon effects of our actions. A worthwhile first step in dealing skillfully with this tendency to indulge our every desire is cultivating the virtue of restraint.

THE VIRTUE OF RESTRAINT

Talk of "virtues" may sound dated and stuffy, but as we make efforts to replace unhealthy mental states like scatteredness and greed with mindfulness and generosity, we are, in effect, replacing vices with virtues or, in Aristotle's parlance, "excellences" (Greek, *arete*). For many of us, our personal path centers on cultivating ourselves in relationship with others and—by extension—cultivating community, and this process hinges not on a single, dramatic peak experience that somehow transforms our character instantaneously, but on a lifelong process of growth as we try to learn from what happens (including mistakes and tragedies), engage in positive practices, and become more aware, generous, and loving in community with others. In the midst of the self-indulgence and anger that characterize many societies these days, restraint seems crucial, especially for those of us who are privileged and are adding a disproportionate amount of greenhouse gases to the atmosphere.

Restraint plays a particularly important role in the Buddhist tradition. The Buddhist precepts direct us to restrain ourselves from certain actions, as seen with the five precepts, which are typically "received" with a vow ("I vow to refrain from . . . ,") or a declaration ("I undertake the training-precept to abstain from. . . ."). More broadly, as Padmasiri de Silva has written, "Buddhism calls for a modest concept of living: simplicity, frugality, and an emphasis on what is essential—in short, a basic ethic of restraint."[134]

As Aristotle pointed out long ago, and as you may have discovered in your own life, at first it's hard to hold back from doing certain things, but if we stick with it, even with occasional backsliding, we can reach a point where not doing those things comes more easily, more naturally—it becomes second nature. You may have found this with cutting something out of your diet. You might have enjoyed bowls of ice cream in the evening and then decided to eat fruit for dessert instead. At first the transition was hard, but over time, reaching for fruit rather than ice cream became more habitual, and it became easier to keep the freezer closed.

Restraint also helps us hold back from actions and routines that plunge us into freneticism and distraction. I recently asked my students about strategies they deploy, and they mentioned such things as doing a "technology fast" for part of a day each week, in which they refrain from using their cell phones and computers. Several talked about making compacts with friends to put away their phones when socializing as a way to restrain themselves from constantly checking for texts or Instagram posts. One student said she gave up TikTok for Lent. Others spoke of making it a practice to hold themselves in check by waiting a day before responding to invitations to join clubs or take on leadership positions. This ethic of restraint is foundational for such other green values as simplicity and non-harming. Simplifying our possessions, for example, depends in part on restraining ourselves from acquiring unnecessary things in the first place. For many of us, the COVID pandemic provided an opportunity to cultivate restraint by holding ourselves back in social distancing—if we were fortunate enough to be able to stay six feet from others—and resisting the temptation to hoard when we went to a supermarket or pharmacy.

In the United States, celebrations of restraint may sound bizarre and perhaps even un-American. We are socialized to indulge our desires, to "Go for it!" and "Eat, drink, and be merry," so to our ears "restraint" implies a puritanical rejection of pleasure and fun. It also seems to connote a limitation of freedom. Whether as kids to our parents or as citizens to elected officials, many of us have said things like "It's a free country; I can do whatever I want," so "Don't tread on me."

But what I'm sketching here, and what Buddhism advocates, is restraint as something *liberating*. Externally, we restrain ourselves from actions that indulge our desire so we can free ourselves from that underlying craving and clinging, just as we restrain ourselves from angry and harmful acts so we can free ourselves from ill will.[135] This may take the form of taking a breath or two before acting, or it may involve simply slowing down. Internally, meditation enhances our awareness of desire and ill will, which in turn makes us more able to restrain ourselves from acting on them. More broadly, when we restrain ourselves from cluttering up space—whether auditory space in our conversations, temporal space in our calendars, or physical space in our homes—we help to free ourselves from scatteredness and bring greater calm, joy, and creativity into our days.

In this way, restraint generates the type of freedom lifted up by the German philosopher Immanuel Kant. He saw humans as filled with "inclinations": instinctual urges and personal desires that drive much of our behavior. Unlike other animals, however, humans can say "no" to their inclinations, and in this way we are not controlled by them. A child can restrain herself when she comes home from school and sees a chocolate cake on the kitchen table waiting for the birthday party that will be held that evening for her brother, but the dog she has just let in from the backyard may go straight across the room, jump up onto a chair, and start gobbling the cake. Ordinarily, the girl would not do this. In this respect, according to Kant, rather than being *free to* indulge our desires (a typical consumerist notion of freedom) humans have the potential to be *free from* those desires, in the sense of not being driven by them. We are able to avoid doing the wrong thing and suffering the negative consequences that follow, like being punished for cutting into the cake before the start of the party. This is not obscure rocket science, for we all know the importance of restraining ourselves from certain actions. Granted, we may do this more out of self-interest than a sense of duty to do the right thing, like when we restrain ourselves from screaming at co-workers and thereby protect our career over the long haul. But to Kant, once we have restrained ourselves and gained freedom from our desires, we can act morally. This parallels the Buddhist call to restrain ourselves from acting on desire and ill

will so we can free ourselves from them and begin to act more gen-
erously and compassionately.

Buddhism offers an array of structures beyond the precepts that
support us in our efforts to practice restraint and cultivate psychological freedom. Zen monastic life, for example, is replete with
forms to be followed. An elaborate set of guidelines directs monks
and nuns to do things a certain way while, in effect, restraining
them from doing those things in other ways. Their lives in the monastery are regimented, with detailed guidelines about how to sit
in meditation, perform rituals, cook food, eat food, serve tea, go to
the bathroom. . . . Then, over time, after restraining themselves, letting go of their personal preferences, and mastering these forms,
monastics feel the freedom that is so central to Zen. They can start
acting effortlessly and mindfully as they do actions—forms—from
the place of formlessness, from a spacious mind, not from the place
of ego with all of its preferences, agendas, and attachments to outcomes. They are now said to act from a formless place, perhaps
even as what lay Zen master Hisamatsu Shin'ichi called the "Formless Self."[136]

Some of us may find that prescribed ways of doing things are
confining or put a damper on our creativity. What I have found,
however—especially in the midst of the uncertainty, stress, and
anxiety of the COVID pandemic—is that having set ways of doing
things helps me in my attempts to stay calm and centered as I move
through the day. With a familiar way of making my coffee, I can
take a breath, collect myself in the moment, be present, and give
myself to the act of making the coffee. With that specific way to
make coffee—or get ready for class, cook supper, and so on—I find it
easier to bring breathing, mindfulness, and *gūjin* together, and this
in turn frees me, at least for a moment, from whatever anxiety or
stress I've been feeling.

The discovery of higher spiritual freedom through restraint and
surrendering to forms was lost on hippie fans of Zen in the 1960s
who, overemphasizing Zen's hermit and trickster elements, viewed

Zen as calling on us to become free by not con-forming, by letting go of forms, whether conventional etiquette or mainstream ways of living. They mistook Zen naturalness and spontaneity to be an iconoclastic "letting it rip" rather than the kind of spontaneity— effortlessness and expressiveness through the mastery of certain forms—that emerges from years of monastic training or apprenticeship in an art.

If hippies had realized that Zen practice is similar to the training of athletes, they might have avoided this misunderstanding of Zen freedom. Though Lebron James, when in the "zone," or in a state of "flow," might improvise and do an intricate layup worthy of being called a work of art, this is not because he is less uptight and more spontaneous than the rest of us. Rather, his ability derives from having spent thousands of hours in his youth on playgrounds and in gyms, dribbling the ball, taking shots, practicing fakes, and doing layups. He repeated these actions—forms of a sort—until they became "body memory," and it is on this basis that he is now able to improvise in amazing ways. Granted, some natural talent leavened his success, but his freedom and artistry on the basketball court derive mainly from restraining and disciplining his bodily actions as he practiced and mastered foundational forms. On that basis, the "space" opens up for him to work his magic. This is precisely what goes on with martial arts like karate, too, with an initial emphasis on practicing and mastering "forms" (*kata*). When this topic comes up in the courses I teach, the athletes among my students readily share their own experiences of being "in the zone" while playing their sport, and they often note how, paradoxically, they are performing at a peak level because they are *not* there, at least in the sense that while they are in the zone there is no thinking about what they are doing and no worrying about how they are performing.

The key for us, however, is not learning how to become a star basketball player or the next Bruce Lee but how, in *all* arenas in life, to restrain ourselves in ways that open up spaciousness in our minds, speech, and actions while, at the same time, reducing our negative ecological impact. As Stephanie Kaza writes in an essay about the Earth Charter,[137] "It is painfully clear, as the Charter points out, that the Earth is under assault by people's unrestrained actions. Unrestrained consumption by some, unrestrained reproduction by others, unrestrained hoarding of resources by still others. The net effect is more than the system can bear."[138] In this regard, the first step for all of us is to restrain ourselves from destructive actions, whether eating lots of meat, flying unnecessarily, or driving gas-guzzlers.

For me, restraint first comes into play—albeit at a trivial level—when I start craving chocolate or meat and my mind starts offering justifications for eating it. "I've been working hard and deserve some Ben and Jerry's ice cream." Or "I'm feeling depleted, and acupuncturists have twice suggested beef as a remedy for low energy, so it's okay to grill a steak for dinner." Today, after finding that my "There is no planet B" t-shirt is tight, I started poking around on Amazon and found one in a larger size. That led me to also start looking at "Leave no trace" t-shirts, then Appalachian Mountain Club t-shirts, then AMC beer glasses. At one point on my laptop, I had a window open with my Amazon cart and another with the AMC glass, until a voice of restraint chimed in and asked, "Do you really need the two t-shirts and the glass?" Eventually I closed the AMC page and settled on just the "Leave no trace" shirt. Not a role-model here, but at least I was able to practice partial restraint.

My wife and I have also been trying to practice restraint with travel, whether for work or for fun. Though I used to apply for and receive grants to go to Japan, largely to do research but also to see friends and keep my Japanese from getting rusty, I haven't done so for over a decade. Although my current scholarly work on Buddhism and environmental ethics hasn't necessitated going to Japan, there's a part of me that knows I could get funding to fly there and is tempted to do so. At other times, friends have recommended that we go to this or that cool spot in Europe, or accompany them on trips to the Caribbean that are "necessary" for mental and physical health during the long winter here in New England. Although my restraint has proven stronger around carbon-spewing travel than around unnecessary t-shirts, the temptation to vacation in far-flung places remains strong.

Given the challenge of restraining ourselves from any and all harmful actions, we might do well to follow the Buddhist approach to ethics and wed restraint to moderation—especially in our initial attempts to transform our way of living. If giving up all meat seems daunting or proves challenging, try giving it up on certain days of the week. If giving up air travel altogether seems like too much initially, try instead to restrict your use of air travel for pleasure to one trip every two years. Or don't set the thermostat quite so low when you turn on the air-conditioning.

THE VALUE OF SIMPLICITY

Practicing restraint and moderation can help to simplify our lives, and simplicity, coupled with such mental states as non-covetousness and non-attachment, lies at the heart of Buddhism. The ten precepts in Theravāda Buddhism add five additional precepts to the five precepts mentioned earlier, directing monastics to reject luxury in the form of sleeping on extravagant beds, adorning themselves with jewelry and scents, enjoying entertainments, handling gold and silver, and eating after midday. Buddhist monks and nuns are instructed to possess only the "four requisites": food, clothing, shelter, and medicine, or, as early Buddhist texts put it, alms, rags, a tree, and urine. (I'm glad that monastics now have access to modern medicine.) In Theravāda monasteries, individual possessions are typically limited to three robes, a belt, a razor, a needle, a filter for straining organisms out of drinking water, and a bowl for begging alms.[139] In Japanese Zen, according to master Morinaga Sōkō,

> When setting out for a monastery you take a *bunko*, a satchel-sized box which contains your monastic robe. A pair of bundles hung from your shoulders holds your

other possessions: eating bowls, chopsticks, a whetstone and razor for shaving, sutra books, undergarments, and a raincape. You wear the traditional outfit of leggings, straw sandals, and wicker hat, tucking up the robe with a band.[140]

Though laypeople like me may not be able to simplify as much as monastics do, trying to live simply can be liberating—and not only for ourselves. Living simply can help us share more with others. The thirteenth of the fourteen mindfulness trainings crafted by Thich Nhat Hanh and others in the Order of Interbeing includes the line, "We are committed to living simply and sharing our time, energy, and material resources with those who are in need."[141] In this and other ways, we can, as the saying goes, "live simply so others can simply live."

A key value in all of this is what I've called "enoughness."[142] Zen celebrates the value of shōyoku chisoku: "with few desires, know what's enough." Once we get clear about what's enough, we can better focus on our needs without being overpowered by our wants. This focus doesn't have to be spartan; we can see our needs as extending beyond what is required for physical survival and include special holiday meals, celebratory gifts, the arts, and occasional travel, all of which we can enjoy in moderation.

Zen also asks us to use the things we already possess as much as possible before replacing them. D. T. Suzuki once wrote of a "secret virtue" cultivated in Zen, saying that "It means not to waste natural resources; it means to make full use, economic and moral, of everything that comes your way; it means to treat yourself and the world in the most appreciative and reverential frame of mind."[143] To convey this practice, Zen teachers have deployed the expression, mono no shō o tsukusu, "to use completely the nature of things." In other words, get the most out of each thing. Use it as long—and in as many ways—as possible. As your shirt loses buttons, sew on new ones. Patch the elbows. Stitch frayed hems back into place. And when the collar splits and the cuffs open into tassels, use the shirt as a rag. By paying attention to the object, tracking its wear and tear, and imagining novel ways to use it when it can no longer perform its original function, we can cultivate frugality as one dimension of simple living. In her study of traditional lifeways in the Indian trans-Himalayan region of Ladakh, Helena Norberg-Hodge notes how frugality becomes "fruitfulness," insofar as Ladakhis find uses for worn-out things.[144] Many of us already practice this facet of simplicity when we repair, repurpose, and recycle things.

The value that Buddhism places on simplicity accords with the approach of writers on simple living such as Duane Elgin, David Shi, Cecile Andrews, and Michael Schut.[145] For instance, championing "voluntary simplicity" and sounding like a Zen master, Elgin writes,

> To live more simply is to live more purposefully and with a minimum of needless distraction. The particular expression of *simplicity* is a personal matter. We each know where our lives are unnecessarily complicated. We are all painfully aware of the clutter and pretense that weigh upon us and make our passage through the world more cumbersome and awkward. To live more simply is to unburden ourselves—to live more lightly, cleanly, aerodynamically. It is to establish a more direct, unpretentious, and unencumbered relationship with all aspects of our lives: the things we consume, the work we do, our relationships with others, our connections with nature and the cosmos, and more. Simplicity of living means meeting life face-to-face. It means confronting life clearly, without unnecessary distractions. It means being direct and honest in relationships of all kinds. It means taking life as it is—straight and unadulterated.[146]

To Elgin's way of thinking, this is "outwardly more simple and inwardly more rich"[147] and, in this respect, it isn't painful self-sacrifice. He writes,

> A conscious simplicity . . . is not self-denying but life-affirming. Voluntary simplicity is not an "ascetic simplicity" (or strict austerity); rather it is an "aesthetic simplicity" where each person considers whether his or her level and pattern of consumption fits with grace and integrity into the practical art of daily living on this planet.[148]

Simply put, living simply in community with others—as monastics have been doing for centuries—is not deprivation but wealth, a higher-order spiritual wealth.

Likewise, the Buddhist call for simplicity is not a call to be self-denying and miserable, for it is coupled with the virtue of contentment—being happy with what we have once our basic needs have been met. The *Dhammapada* refers to contentment as the "highest wealth,"[149] and the *Saṃyutta Nikāya* sings the praises of the monk who is content with his robes, any kind of alms food, any kind of lodging, and any kind of medicine.[150] This contentment is exemplified by the forest-dwelling monk who "has abandoned worldly desires and is content with little."[151] We don't have to live as austerely as forest monks do in order to cultivate contentment insofar as we recognize that happiness derives mainly from non-material sources like having good relationships and helping others.

Contentment may, of course, be a threat to those who want to foster high levels of consumption as a driver of economic growth. Pibob Udomittipong tells us that the Thai government in the 1960s "prohibited Thai monks in Thailand from preaching *santutthi*, the teaching of austerity or contentment with what one has. . . . The reasoning behind this decree was that the government believed that the teaching of *santutthi* was opposed to the ideals of economic growth, and hence opposed to development."[152] Robin Wall Kimmerer recognizes how contentment can be subversive when she writes, "In a consumer society, contentment is a radical proposition. Recognizing abundance rather than scarcity undermines an economy that thrives by creating unmet desires. Gratitude cultivates an ethic of fullness, but the economy needs emptiness."[153]

Practicing Generosity

For many of us, a first step toward a simplified way of living is giving unneeded things away. This practice and the other ways of reducing clutter that I discussed earlier accord with a core virtue on the Buddhist path: generosity and giving (*dāna*). As we saw, Buddhists strive to restrain themselves from doing external actions that are generated by detrimental, unhealthy mental states and, ultimately, to cleanse their minds of those mental states by cultivating the healthy mental states that are their opposites. So, for example, the three poisons—desire, ill will, and ignorance—are countered by cultivating their opposing positive states: generosity, loving-kindness, ·and wisdom, respectively. It is through fostering such positive mental states as antidotes, that Buddhists "purify the mind."

Given the Buddha's initial emphasis on desire, most Buddhists take their first steps on the path with a focus on replacing desire with generosity. To initiate this shift, Buddhists engage in acts of giving. In the Theravāda Buddhism of Southeast Asia, this giving has traditionally taken the form of giving food to the monks in the morning when they come around with bowls to beg for alms. In this daily interaction between the monks and the laity, the monks are performing an act of giving, too, for they are giving laypeople a chance to offer food and thereby gain karmic merit. For this reason, monks are referred to as the "field of merit"—the fertile ground in which the laity can plant karmic seeds, not unlike the biblical notion of people reaping what they have sown.[154] Through acts of giving, the giver can also start cultivating the mental state of generosity.

The traditional Buddhist practice of giving has been reinterpreted in modern times to address new issues and pressures. For example, the Sarvodaya village-development movement,[155] begun in Sri Lanka in the 1950s, has expanded the scope of giving beyond the traditional practice of giving alms to the monks. It construes *dāna* as the act of sharing not only one's material possessions but one's time, energy, talents, and labor. Sarvodaya leaders organize this giving in collective actions called *shramadāna*, from *shrama*,

labor, and *dāna*, giving. These actions range from weeding in irrigation ditches to teaching people how to read.

In Mahāyāna Buddhism, the perfection of *dāna* is the first of the
ten perfections cultivated by a person on the path of the bodhisattva. Similar to the Sarvodaya approach, Mahāyāna Buddhists
broadly construe *dāna* as encompassing all generous actions that
help liberate others from suffering. This can extend from giving
food to offering the teachings of the Buddha.

This core value of giving and the generosity it fosters can play a
central role in our attempts to green our lifestyles. Cultivating generosity can help us resist the urge to claim, grab, and possess. It can
help us to let go of the desire to acquire unnecessary things, thereby
reducing the ecological impact that comes from the production,
shipping, usage, and disposal of these things. When generosity is
coupled with compassion, we can offer other-than-human animals
the gift of protecting and restoring the habitats that support their
flourishing. And we can more readily give our time and energy to
working with others to generate the change needed to protect our
shared ecosphere.

As we have all likely experienced, the rewards of giving extend
beyond freeing ourselves from clutter and reducing our environmental impact. When we are feeling down, rather than pulling back
into solitary depression we can go out and help someone or do a
good deed, which gets us engaged with our surroundings, lifts our
spirits, and gives us positive feelings about ourselves as people
who contribute to the world. This happens for me when I wake up
in a "gloom-and-doom" cloud but then spend the day helping my
students; by evening I'm feeling lighter and more hopeful.

In practicing giving, one can also realize that, as Dale Wright
points out, "My giving depends on many factors behind and beyond
me," and the only reason we might be in a position to give is the
"contingency of our fortune."[156] By realizing all the factors that have
enabled us to give our offerings, we deepen our insight into our
basic interconnectedness. And when we recognize our dependence

on other people and how much we have received in our lives, we are more apt to share. Zen teacher Taigen Leighton writes, "When we receive and experience generosity . . . we are moved to acts of generosity ourselves."[157]

Expressing Gratitude

The simple act of pausing to say a prayer before we eat can help to deepen our appreciation of our interconnectedness. When we acknowledge all of the inputs into our meal, we can recognize the countless people, things, and processes that support us, and realize our indebtedness to all of these blessings. The Japanese term for blessings and indebtedness is *on*, and Buddhism traditionally cites four main sources of blessings for which we are indebted: the ruler, one's parents, all sentient beings, and the Three Jewels. We could expand this schema by adding *nature* to this list—or substitute it for the ruler!

Recognizing our blessings and our indebtedness usually generates a feeling of gratitude. When I discern the people, the labor, and the parts of the natural world that went into the creation of my food or my prized possessions, I feel gratitude for those inputs. As I sit here at my desk taking sips of coffee, I feel thankful for the clay, the potter (Todd Pike), and the kiln that came together to form my dragonfly mug. When I savor this mug or other possessions, I try to express my gratitude by handling them more mindfully. Chozen Bays writes, "When we wash, dry, sweep, fold, and put away our things with mindfulness, it becomes an expression of gratitude for their silent service. . . ."[158]

Another worthwhile practice is to take a minute at the end of the day, or any time that you're feeling down, and recognize the things for which you are grateful, and perhaps even thank them in your mind. We can start with the simple fact of being alive. Joanna Macy and Molly Brown write, "for all our woes and worries, our existence itself is an unearned benefaction."[159] And then there's the biosphere, which gave us life and has sustained our life since we were born. What parts of the biosphere have been supporting your existence today? Think of the food you ate. Think of—and thank—the rain and sunshine that made the ingredients in that food possible. I find that keeping gratitude in my heart and mind helps me find some inner positivity on days when it seems like the world is falling apart. Such gratitude also helps me appreciate the natural world that supports me and, by extension, motivates me to reciprocate by trying to protect the natural systems that have given me so much. Feeling grateful also helps me settle down and stay present. As Macy and Brown put it, "In times of turmoil and danger, gratitude helps to steady and ground us. It brings us into presence...."[160]

RESPECTFUL VALUATION

In expressing gratitude for certain things, we may even come to feel a kind of respect, even reverence, for them. We can appreciate how each thing that supports us has its own attributes and capabilities. The maple tree shading the south side of our house, the wooden desk at which I sit, the laptop on which I am writing this book: like us, each of these things appeared here in its complexity through a vast network of inputs and influences, and it functions as part of the larger whole of which we are part. In this way, we can honor each thing as another being with its own integrity, and out of this recognition, respect it. Zen teacher Norman Fischer notes that being "present with and respectful of all material things, as if each and every one of them were a sacred object, is a primary practice and primary value."[161] Though I do not agree with Fischer that "all material things" are sacred objects deserving my respect—a COVID-19 virus particle, or the melting radioactive core of one of the Fukushima reactors, seems to be in a separate category from a spring rain or a useful hammer—for the most part he is flagging a valuable approach to the objects around us. All too often, we throw our clothes in a heap, waste food, chip dishes, and let tools rust. But as Gary Thorp points out, "Buddhist teachers have always counseled their students to keep things simple and in repair, to keep them sharp and shining and ready to achieve their intended purpose in a carefully chosen place."[162] As my way of showing respect, I try to appreciate my possessions and take care of them like people do with old, favorite objects—whether a favorite mug, a patched pair of jeans from high school, or a '65 Mustang convertible.

The Zen emphasis on settling our minds, which we discussed earlier, supports the valuing of each thing, whether that thing is in a monastery, a tea hut, or our home. Approaching our world with a calmer mind helps to create space for things to present themselves, allowing us to see them in their suchness, in their as-it-is-ness, "just as they are" (J. *sono mama*). A calm, clear mind allows us to discern each thing in its uniqueness, to recognize its distinct beauty and dignity, and to acknowledge the role it plays in our daily living—as *this* shirt, *this* bowl, *this* screwdriver, *this* table. This, in turn, helps us to not take things in our life for granted or treat them carelessly.

We can extend this reverential attitude to nature around us, and couple it with wonder and awe. By showing respect to the things in nature that support us in all of their complexity, we become less likely to harm them. It can even help us resist what we humans have been doing to our planetary home in general. Sister True Dedication writes, "Cultivating reverence for the simple wonders of life is, in our times, a powerful act of resistance. Choosing to step outside, to open our eyes, ears, and hearts to the presence of this beautiful planet takes courage and freedom. Society has conditioned us against it."[163]

NON-HARMING

This brings us to a cornerstone—if not *the* cornerstone—of Buddhist ethics: non-harming. This value appears as the first of the five precepts: "refraining from harming living beings." Pulitzer-Prize-winning Zen poet and ecological visionary Gary Snyder has written that the core ethical guideline in Buddhism, and presumably in many other traditions, is "Do no unnecessary harm." Together with loving-kindness and compassion, non-harming provides an antidote to the "poison" of ill will, and hence, like generosity—the opposite of desire—it plays a central role in the Buddhist path, other parts of which—such as restraint, simplicity, contentment, generosity, gratitude, and respect—help us put this core Buddhist value into practice.

Coupled with these other virtues, the practice of non-harming not only purifies our minds but provides a foundation for a less destructive way of living. At this point in history, with all of the devastation happening around us, the least we can do is to pursue our lives with a commitment to keeping harm to a minimum. As Richard Hayes points out, "the Buddhist ideal of a life of simplicity, non-violence towards all living beings, and non-acquisitiveness is one that human beings must learn to follow very soon if they have any interest in the continued survival of their own and countless other species."[164] We can think of non-harming as a negative prohibition, "Don't make things worse," and we can couple it with compassionate action (and activism) as a positive guideline, "Make things better."

Of course, to be alive is to cause harm to some degree—we can't avoid it. Each time we drink or eat something, microorganisms are killed by the acid in our stomachs. To ride in an automobile during the summer is to participate in the killing of insects. But we can at least make non-harming our guiding star. As Rita Gross points out, Buddhism has always had "the practical recognition that non-harming is an ideal toward which we strive and that the practice is minimizing the harm inflicted on other beings in order to survive."[165] As Snyder suggests, we can strive to reduce the *unnecessary* harm we cause. Perhaps we will not follow those in India who sweep in front of themselves as they walk along a path, strain their drinking water, and live only on fruits and vegetables whose harvesting causes no lasting harm to the plant. But we can at least try to avoid harm by, for example, slowing down and not talking on the phone while we drive; while this may not reduce the impact on bugs, it will surely make pedestrians and other drivers safer.

Or we can try to switch from meat to plant-based meat substitutes. Or only eat things that don't feel pain, which, as my friend Bill Kite once put it, are "things that don't scream when you put them in the pan," like clams or oysters, not to mention tofu and nuts. This ideal also pertains to our livelihood, as seen in the *Sigālovāda Sutta* guideline that "a householder should accumulate wealth as a bee collects pollen."[166] Our non-harming can be informed by what environmentalists call the "precautionary principle," meaning that if we are not sure whether an action will hurt living beings or the environment, we should take precautions, like not releasing a genetically-modified organism into nature and not using a chemical whose environmental impact has yet to be determined.

Perhaps we can boil all this down into a maxim: "Focus on needs, not greed; mindfully restrain our actions; and act in ways that cause minimal harm and help sustain or regenerate healthy ecosystems."

When we consider the pain that most cattle, pigs, chickens, and dairy cows experience, as well as the pain that even free-range animals feel when slaughtered (or their fear when they realize that they and their fellows are getting slaughtered, even if painlessly[167]), it seems a no-brainer to move in the direction of veganism, unless we can determine the provenance of our milk, cheese, and eggs and verify that the animals generating those foods are being treated well and are not harming the environment, in which case we can opt for vegetarianism. That being said, it does seem morally acceptable to eat roadkill and animals that have died a natural death, even though they may be much less appetizing.

Of course, the production of meat causes other harms insofar as it typically generates major amounts of greenhouse gases and other negative environmental impacts. Eating meat can harm our bodies in various ways. The *Mahāparinirvāṇa Sūtra* even claims that "One who eats meat kills the seed of great compassion."[168] Given the harm to animals, to nature, and to our bodies, it doesn't seem all that hard to make the moral argument that whenever we have access to alternative sources of protein we should not eat meat.

Although Buddhist societies have not always put non-harming fully into practice, an optimal Buddhist society would. Such a society would reject the acceptance and valorization of violence—not just the violence involved in factory farming but in sports, entertainment, interpersonal relations, models of masculinity, and other arenas in which violence is often celebrated. It would also place a just-war theory in the center of its foreign policy, with clear criteria for initiating military violence (*ad bellum*) and for waging that violence (*in bello*).

THE VIRTUE OF COMPASSION

Though the call to reduce harming may sound like a restrictive prohibition, especially if we like our steak and fried chicken, we can view it in positive terms as a call for loving-kindness and compassion toward other sentient beings around us—both human and other-than-human.[169] The thirteenth of Thich Nhat Hanh and the Tiep Hien Order's Fourteen Mindfulness Trainings declares, "Aware of the suffering caused by exploitation, social injustice, stealing, and oppression, we are committed to cultivating loving kindness and learning ways to work for the well-being of people, animals, plants, and minerals."[170] Perhaps one of the biggest tasks before us is to feel compassion for other-than-human animals who have been suffering because of human dietary preferences, habitat loss, and all of the negative effects of global warming: higher temperatures, wildfires, droughts, floods, or the spread of diseases.

And we can choose to approach the climate crisis from a place of compassion and love rather than react to it primarily from a place of fear and shame. Kathrine Hayhoe highlights how rooting our activism in love can empower us and make our efforts more effective, saying,

> Love starts with speaking truth: making people fully aware of the risks and choices they face in a manner that is relevant and practical to them. But it also offers

compassion, understanding, and acceptance, the opposite of guilt and shame. Love bolsters our courage, too;
what will we not do for those . . . we love? And finally, it
opens the door to that most ephemeral and sought after
of emotions, hope.[171]

Compassion and love can also prompt us to take greater action.
As we've seen in our own lives, when we feel love or compassion
for someone, we are more inclined to do things to help them, and
this active love often extends beyond fellow humans to certain
other-than-human animals like our beloved pets and to certain
places like our home towns or neighborhoods.

In our efforts to cultivate and express compassion, we can
take inspiration from the thousand-arm form of the bodhisattva
Avalokiteśvara, who lends a helping hand (a thousand hands!)
to others. In paintings of this bodhisattva, each palm has an eye
of wisdom in it, and this combination of loving outreach and discerning insight into what suffering beings might need represents
the skillful means to assist others. While our caring actions may be
more modest in comparison, through them we can begin freeing
ourselves from ill will and cultivating the compassion and wisdom
that are woven into bodhicitta, the "mind of awakening" that aspires,
like Avalokiteśvara does, to liberate sentient beings from suffering.

The compassion that accompanies wisdom is not just empathy
or a feeling of the pain of others (com-passion, "suffering with"),
for it also implies an earnest wish for that suffering to end and an
inclination to take steps to ameliorate it. Zen thinker Abe Masao
argued that the compassion realized in awakening to emptiness
prompts us to make vows to help others and then engage in helpful
actions. In this respect, Buddhist compassion is active compassion.
This characteristic is reflected in Jay Garfield's advocacy of translat-
ing karuṇā as "care" rather than "compassion." This rendering cov-
ers two facets of compassion: compassionate concern as in caring
about others, or being a caring person, and compassionate action
as in caring for others, or taking care of them. Cultivating compas-

sion also supports us in our efforts to respect other beings and feel a sense of connection to them. Marc Bekoff writes,

> Each time we nurture the seeds of compassion, empathy, and love, we deepen our respect for and kinship with the universe. All people, other animals, human communities, and environments benefit greatly when we develop and maintain a heartfelt compassion that is reflexive as breathing.[172]

We can further augment Buddhist compassion and wisdom by lifting up something that we don't hear much about in traditional Buddhist discourse: moral imagination. I have found that hearts open and people take action when they use their imagination to get a stronger sense of what it might be like to be, for example, a refugee at the US-Mexico border who has fled violence in their country, or an Andean farmer who has had to come down into city slums from traditional plots of land after the glaciers that had provided water for irrigation started to disappear, or a polar bear whose Arctic ice habitat is disappearing. Some Buddhists claim that wisdom and compassion automatically give us a sense of other peoples' plight, but I wonder whether these two mental states are enough. Perhaps the perfections of a bodhisattva can be augmented by using one's imagination to get a more specific, vivid sense of what is being experienced by others, whether human or other-than-human. This in turn leads to a greater sense of connection and solidarity. Shantigarbha writes, "Ethics is really to do with feeling solidarity with all life. It's a direct recognition of the life in us, in others. This is clearly a kind of imaginative act, a kind of imaginative empathy."[173]

PATIENCE

Given how immense, complex, and systemic the climate crisis is, we need to cultivate another virtue: patience, the ability to stay committed while maintaining one's poise and, in this way, avoiding frustration, burnout, and anger. Patience (Skt. *kṣānti*, which we can also translate as "forebearance" or "perseverance") in its perfected form is one of the ten perfections (*pāramitā*) in the Mahāyāna tradition, and even if we don't attain the perfection of patience needed for countless lifetimes of bodhisattva functioning to end suffering, we will certainly need emotional stamina for long-term social activism.

One way to cultivate patience and perseverance is through an ongoing meditation practice. Meditative mental states like calmness and presence enhance our patience. Dedicating oneself to a regular meditation practice can foster patience in another way. As many meditation teachers tell us, we need to stick with our practice, without having expectations or being attached to desired outcomes. This commitment calls on us to sit every day, and to sit through boredom or pain until our timer goes off or the person running the meditation session rings a bell to end it. By hanging in there, through each session and over time, we are cultivating stick-to-it-ness, or expressed differently, patient perseverance.

The traditional Buddhist healthy, wholesome, and skillful mental states that I've been discussing here as virtues provide a triple benefit. First, they are the opposites of the three poisons and other detrimental, unhealthy mental states, and insofar as we cultivate these virtuous mental states—and thereby eliminate the opposite "vices"—we are rooting out the cause of our suffering. Positively put, these mental states move us away from suffering and toward liberation. Second, in addition to that spiritual benefit, the cultivation of these mental states bears ethical fruit, for one has now acquired a virtuous character. This is not unlike the approach of Aristotle, who saw the full cultivation of virtue as the means to achieve excellence and flourishing (Greek, *eudaimonia*). Third, these mental states, as we have noted, have clear ecological ramifications insofar as they encourage and enable us to restrain ourselves, consume less, limit harm, and feel gratitude, respect, and compassion, all of which reduce our environmental impact and make us more apt to take action.

The virtue ethic of Buddhism, parts of which we've just discussed, provides a promising starting point for a Buddhist environmental ethic. Damien Keown writes, "A Buddhist ecology . . . simply
calls for the orientation of traditional virtues towards a new set of
problems concerned with the environment."[174] The virtues he has
in mind are the four "divine abodes" (loving-kindness, compassion,
sympathetic joy, and equanimity), non-greed (P. *arāga*), mindfulness (*sati*), skillful means (Skt. *upāya-kauśalya*), generosity, contentment, non-covetousness, and non-harming. Similarly, Simon P.
James claims that "certain character traits—primarily insight, compassion, non-violence, selflessness, and mindfulness—are environmental virtues."[175] As I have tried to do above, we can work with
these Buddhist virtues to slow down, pay attention, green our lifestyles, and lay a foundation for activism.

Gary Snyder sets forth a cluster of virtues and values that over-
laps with what we're highlighting here:

> Practically speaking, a life that is vowed to simplicity,
> appropriate boldness, good humor, gratitude, unstinting
> work and play, and lots of walking brings us close to the
> actually existing world and its wholeness. . . . No expecta-
> tions, alert and sufficient, grateful and careful, generous
> and direct. A calm and clarity attend us in the moment we
> are wiping grease off our hands and glancing up at the
> passing clouds.[176]

Needless to say, Buddhists are not the only ones lifting up virtues
and other components of character as a basis for living differently.
Climate activist Bill McKibben emphasizes five characteristics—
durable, sturdy, stable, hardy, and robust—about which he comments, "They conjure a world where we no longer grow by leaps
and bounds, but where we hunker down, where we dig in. They are
words that we associate with maturity, not youth; with steadfast-
ness, not flash. They aren't exciting, but they are comforting—think
husband, not boyfriend."[177]

Cultivating these sorts of mental states, virtues, and traits is not a path of deprivation. With spaciousness and simplicity, we are calming down and opening up space in our minds, our days, and our homes. We are making it possible to extricate ourselves from clutter and frenetic living, to be more mindful and present, to be more joyous and creative, and to engage the climate crisis more robustly. In short, positive mental states such as generosity, gratitude, compassion, and patience provide both spiritual and ecological benefits, right now and in the future.

6. The Home as a Place of the Way

... while many of the problems we face are global,
some of the most imaginative, powerful, passionate
solutions come from home. Home is a place we can
act. Home is a place we can take care of. Home is a
feeling that can inspire us. Home is a way for us to
rethink and reimagine and remake our lives.
—Madeline Ostrander[178]

EVEN WHEN we recognize the spiritual and ecological benefits
of restraint, generosity, contentment, simplicity, non-harming,
and compassion, it's hard to cultivate and practice these values
on our own. Most of us aren't monks or nuns in a monastery, with
guidelines that foster these values, such as eating a vegetarian diet
or having few possessions. Even when we affirm their importance
and have good intentions to put these values into practice, we may
find that our efforts are unsuccessful. I've found that what I need
are structures that support me in my efforts.

Vows

One such structure is vows. By making vows, we can strengthen
our intention, and with them in the back of our mind we can stick
closer to our principles when having to make decisions. And insofar
as we share our vows with others, we also become more motivated
to fulfill them, if for no other reason than to avoid embarrassment
should we fail to do so. At the very least, Buddhists typically follow

the vows contained in five precepts to avoid harming, stealing, sexual misconduct, lying, and intoxicants. Some authors have reformulated Buddhist precepts in ecological terms.[179]

I work with the five precepts in direct relation to the climate crisis. Here's how I do that, with a focus on intention:

1. Killing/harming: I intend to refrain from actions that unnecessarily increase carbon emissions.
2. Stealing: I intend not to steal from future generations by doing things that have long-term negative environmental impacts.
3. Sexual misconduct: I intend not to give in to immediate desires and lose sight of the long-term consequences of my actions.
4. Lying: I intend to resist misinformation about the climate crisis and to share what I've learned.
5. Intoxicants: I intend not to numb out through distraction in all of its forms.

Whatever their specific contents, precepts and vows provide a structure, a background framework, that can support us in our efforts to stay grounded in core values on our path.

A related support to putting restraint and the other values into practice is using mantras, or simply reminders, which we can derive from our vows. As I mentioned before, depending on the situation I repeat to myself such phrases as "Take three breaths," "Act at 80 percent of my normal speed," and "Do one thing at a time." For actions related to the climate crisis, I try to keep in mind guidelines like "Do no unnecessary harm," "Contribute to the solution," and, following Thoreau, "Simplify, simplify, simplify." In your own life you can come up with reminders that work for you.

RITUALS IN THE HOME

Another support for putting values into practice is our home and the rituals we can do there. You may ask, What kind of home? What sort of rituals? Where can we find pointers, or perhaps even a template, for making our homes a green sanctuary and a springboard for action?

Though we can't turn our homes into traditional monasteries, we can at least take Buddhist monastic life as a model for spacious and ecological living. In my case, the model is Zen monasticism. I have always felt drawn to the simplicity, the rusticity, the minimalist aesthetic, the emphasis on the physicality of sitting in meditation and doing chores, and the emplacement of monastic buildings in natural surroundings that characterize Zen monasticism. In describing Zen monastic life, Gary Snyder writes, "Its community life and discipline is rather like an apprenticeship program in a traditional craft."[180] I think Snyder is referring to the discipline involved in the repetitive practices of meditation and working with tools and materials, sticking with the activity over the long haul, pushing through physical pain and frustration, and cultivating the ability to do things well. Snyder also comments, "The arts and crafts have long admired Zen training as a model of hard, clean, worthy schooling."[181] This "hard schooling" has a lot to do with the physicality of Zen life. Reflecting on his years in Daitoku-ji Monastery in Kyoto, Snyder writes, "Sleep was short, the food was meager, the rooms spare and unheated, but this (in the sixties) was as true in the worker's or farmer's world as it was in the monastery."[182] Not easy, but a path that joins the practical, the aesthetic, and the spiritual, replete with benefits. As I try to follow this model in a modified form as an older person, I recalibrate the physical demands and make the schooling less hard than it was when I was younger: I no longer sit zazen in full- or half-lotus; I keep our condo comfortably warm in winter; I do chores more slowly; I pull back from pain rather than try to push through it; and I no longer lift heavy things like couches or large rocks in the garden.

With Zen monasticism as my template, I sometimes refer to our condo, the second and third floors of a three-story house, as my "home-monastery"—not in the sense of a place of silence and seriousness, though they do play a role, but as a sanctuary and as a *dōjō*, literally "Way place," a place for practicing my Way, my path. I try to make our home a place of practice in two senses: (1) training or cultivation, like when we talk about practicing the piano; and (2) putting something into action, as when we say, "Practice what you preach!"

To promote practice in the former sense, it's helpful to set up an area to meditate, pray, or do yoga. Maybe it's a separate room, or the corner of a room that's big enough to accommodate a meditation cushion or yoga mat. My meditation space is a room with balcony windows off our new bedroom in what used to be our attic. Whatever your space, try to keep it tidy and beautiful to your eye. Set up an altar, whether on a shelf or the top of a dresser, on which you can place a sacred image, a vase with flowers, or objects brought back from pilgrimages into nature, such as stones I've picked up on hikes in the woods and strolls on ocean beaches. Sitting there on the altar I've set up, those stones are available for one of my other personal practices: to remind myself of the spaciousness I have felt on a trail or beach. Before I leave home I put into my pocket one of those stones, usually a flat one with an indented side that I can rub my thumb against as I hold it while teaching or sitting in a meeting.

For many of us, even if our homes are not a sacred space, they're at least a sanctuary, a calm, safe space to which we can retreat from stressors out in the world. Of course, at the same time they're a place of endless tasks such as cooking, washing dishes, vacuuming, dusting, doing the laundry, putting the laundry away, maybe even mowing a lawn and pulling weeds. Lucky for us, Zen monastic life gives us a model for turning these "chores" into forms of meditation rather than burdens to be dealt with so we can get on to the "important" things like meditation, watching TV, and frolicking on social media. Zen monks and nuns engage in an array of tasks to maintain their monasteries: sweeping, raking, sewing, cooking, wiping verandas with wet rags, ladling out the outhouse, and spreading that human "waste" in the vegetable garden. This labor around the monastery is called *samu*, and it is done as a meditative practice. Just as they give themselves fully to the act of breathing while in meditation, monastics pour themselves into these activities. In East Asia, doing tasks as a form of meditation, and thereby breaking down distinctions between religious practice and mundane chores, harks back 1,300 years and finds expression in such famous Zen statements as "A day of no work is a day of no eating" and "Chop wood, carry water."[183]

Modeling ourselves on Zen monastics doing *samu*, we can pour ourselves into activities at home: cooking, cleaning up after meals, fixing things, creating things of beauty, and taking mindful care of our tools and other possessions. We can also give ourselves to such tasks as paying the bills, applying for a job, or calling the landlord. When I feel anxious, pouring myself into doing tasks fully— and doing them as a form of self-expression and as an offering to others—focuses my attention, calms me down, and gives me the satisfaction we all feel when we finish "a job well done." It also helps me stay grounded and present as I encounter the things that cause anxiety, whether a physical pain at one end of the spectrum or the climate crisis at the other. It helps lift me out of the gloom-and-doom funk that weighs on my psyche. I think that this effect derives from the physicality of pouring myself into tasks, the way my body and senses are constructively engaged with the physical world around me, leaving me feeling vigorously alive in the present rather than anxious about imagined futures.

I'd wager that we've all experienced what it's like to do a task as *samu*, as a form of spiritual practice. Think of the last time you had the necessary spaciousness in your schedule (and mind) to focus on a single task, and how you poured yourself into it. Maybe you were making a tasty meal, setting the table for guests, or rearranging a

room to make it more cozy. You might have been braiding someone's hair, knitting a scarf, mowing the lawn, or changing the oil
in your truck. Perhaps it happened while you were folding laundry
and attending to each item: your favorite t-shirt, your child's pants,
an old dish towel. You may have lost track of time and perhaps even
entered into a state of "flow." At the very least, the task likely felt
more creative and rewarding than usual. And being fully immersed
in the present, you probably felt more alive. Perhaps for a brief
moment you were freed from your worries as well. You may have
even experienced joy.

Needless to say, the tasks that keep a home running may seem
endless and daunting, and it isn't easy to follow this Zen model and
transform those tasks from nagging burdens into spiritual practices. It can help to apply the 80 percent rule by consciously performing the task 20 percent slower than might otherwise be your
pace. Then, as you begin doing the physical actions—washing the
dishes, plugging in the vacuum cleaner, or tucking in the sheets and
blankets—try to attend to your body, to the physical sensations in
your hands or back. Take time to check in with your other senses
as well and then transition to practicing *gūjin*: pour yourself into
the actions you are performing, one at a time. If you find yourself
distracted or daydreaming, pause, take a few deep breaths as if you
were sitting on the cushions in meditation, and then go back to
doing the actions, giving yourself fully to them.

Whatever the task, when you do it, do it precisely, thoroughly,
and as well as you possibly can. Try not to do a half-baked, messy
job, even if you don't want to do the task. The Japanese have an
expression for this, *kichinto suru*, basically "do it right." Michael
Carroll seems to be getting at something similar when he writes,
"being awake at work is engaging our work precisely, genuinely,
and directly as it constantly unfolds, moment by moment, without
bias or pretense."[184]

As we give ourselves fully to what we're doing, we can better
savor each moment as something precious (at least those moments

that are not painful). Tea masters use the expression *ichigo-ichie*. A direct translation of this expression is "one moment, one encounter," and it connotes appreciating each moment in its uniqueness as an event that will never be repeated. Even if the moment seems mundane, savor it. This appreciation can help us act with gratitude and grace, like the gentle demeanor of the host of a tea ceremony. To move gracefully is to move lightly, disturbing little, leaving no trace, or at least as small a trace as we can.

In Zen, "leave no trace" (*mu-seki*) refers to doing something without attachment to the outcome, to what one has created, or to being recognized and celebrated for it. It asks you to give yourself to the action, do it thoroughly, do it well, and move on to the next action at hand. At the very least, we can leave no trace by cleaning up after ourselves. Chozen Bays writes, "Our mind seems 'cleaner' and our life less complicated when we've cleaned up the space and things around us."[185] This Zen way of leaving no trace thus goes beyond the focus of the "leave no trace" ethos of backpackers and climbers,[186] for it aims to cultivate a mind that can flow free of self-centered attachment. Zen master Shunryū Suzuki once said, "When you do something, you should burn yourself completely, like a good bonfire, leaving no trace of yourself."[187]

A spacious way to practice this in our lives is to prepare for each moment,[188] do one's best, and then let go. Who knows if my family will like the supper I've prepared? I've tried to cook a delicious meal, it is now out of my hands; I need to let go of any attachment to a desired response from them and just see what happens. Maybe my family will like it. Maybe not.

Being intentional and present, without becoming attached to the results of our actions, allows us to deepen our commitment to meeting each moment fully, with our whole body-mind without getting stuck. We make that effort, moment to moment, then move on to the next thing that needs doing. In this approach, as I mentioned above, spiritual maturity and wisdom are not some ability to eliminate sadness, setbacks, and struggle—basically, how to

keep bad stuff from happening—but are about learning how to deal
with what comes at us, or at least to not be *totally* rattled by it. The
embodied presence with which we do actions and stay grounded as
we meet what life throws at us is central to the responsiveness and
resilience we need in our encounter with the climate chaos.

Rituals, too, can support us in our efforts to pursue our eco-spiritual
path at home. When I teach about rituals, I begin by asking my students if they have a "morning ritual." After several students share,
we note how a morning ritual consists of our doing the same
actions, in the same way, and in the same order, each morning. Formal *religious* rituals additionally feature trained officiants, whose
actions and utterances are not only formulaic and repeated but
formal, symbolic, archaic, and directed to a sacred entity like God,
Lakṣmī, or the deity believed to reside on Mount Fuji.

Perhaps you are already doing rituals in religious services you
attend or on your own, such as personal prayer, meditation, chanting, or yoga. When I sit zazen in my zendō upstairs, I put my hands
before my sternum, palm to palm, in what is termed *gasshō*, and
bow before I enter the room. Then, keeping my hands in that position, I walk the several steps to my cushions, turn away from them,
and bow. Next, I sit down, cross my legs, light a stick of incense, set
a timer for twenty-five minutes, ring a small bell, and put my hands
into the position I use. Doing this series of actions the same way
each time I practice zazen helps me direct my attention away from
daily concerns and focus on the meditation.

We can also introduce ritual action at home during what for most
families is the main communal activity: meals. Saying some words
of thanks—"saying grace"—before a meal is one of the most widespread rituals of communal eating. Pausing before eating helps us
collect ourselves and be more present with the food and with the
other people around the table. Depending on the words, saying
grace can also strengthen our realization that we live in an interconnected world. We can acknowledge and express gratitude to
all of the beings and forces that made the meal possible: the soil,
the sun, the rain, the farmer, and so on. We can augment this prac-

tice by going around the table and offering brief comments about something that supported us that day for which we feel thankful.

Out of our gratitude and our recognition of interconnectedness, we can also reflect on the actions that the meal will make possible. At Zen Mountain Monastery in the Catskills, practitioners recite the following "Short Meal Gatha":

> We receive this food in gratitude to all beings
> Who have helped bring it to our table,
> And vow to respond in turn to those in need
> With wisdom and compassion.

Building on this vow, we can go around the table, with each person completing the phrase, "I want to use this food to support me in my efforts to. . . ." This practice can help us focus our intention to serve others, perhaps by taking steps to mitigate climate disruption. In its "Five Contemplations," Thich Nhat Hanh's Order of Interbeing has pulled together these various facets of saying grace and connected them to the climate crisis:

1. This food is a gift of the Earth, the sky, the universe, numerous living beings, and much hard work.
2. May we eat with mindfulness and gratitude so as to be worthy to receive it.
3. May we transform our unwholesome mental formations, especially our greed, and learn to eat with moderation.
4. May we keep our compassion alive by eating in such a way that we reduce the suffering of living beings, preserve our planet, and reverse the process of global warming.
5. We accept this food so we can nurture our brotherhood and sisterhood, strengthen our Sangha, and nourish our ideal of serving all living beings.[189]

Beginning meals with a statement of gratitude and intention can catalyze a learning moment for children, especially if people at the table talk about which foods are healthy, how plants can be grown in an ethical and regenerative manner, the farm-to-table carbon footprint of the ingredients, and other dimensions of the primal act of eating.

In Zen monasteries, ritualization goes beyond the act of saying grace and extends to the meal itself. Ritualized Zen eating is centered on prescribed ways of using three bowls (ōryōki), including how to lift up these bowls to receive food, how to handle the bowls while eating, how to wash them when done, and how to wrap them in a cloth at the end.[190] Though we may not want to mimic the intricacies of Zen meals or eat in silence or as quickly as Zen monks do, we can still ritualize our communal eating by slowing down the serving process, saying grace, expressing gratitude, and acknowledging the network of relationships that made the meal possible, and in this way bring everyone's attention to the present moment of sharing the meal. Needless to say, to support this ritualized way of cultivating gratitude and awareness, we need to ask everyone to leave their smartphones in another room, turn off nearby televisions, and stay at the table until everyone is done eating. Nothing particularly new or Buddhist about this—just good old-fashioned manners.

Our approach to eating and meals can also help us cultivate compassion and generosity. In the segaki ritual performed at Zen monasteries, each monk or nun places a bit of their food on a wooden platter, and the collected food is left outside as an offering (se) for "hungry ghosts" (gaki).[191] Though we need to be careful about giving human food to animals (salt!), we can come up with our own version of segaki by leaving food outside—unless that attracts "pests"—or we can make it a practice to set something aside before each meal for those in need of good food, whether a can of healthy soup, a box of pasta, or some money for a food bank.

We can augment our meal rituals with the Buddhist practice of extending mettā, loving-kindness. The wording for this ritual appears in the Mettā Sutta:

Whatever living beings there are,
whether frail or firm, without omission,
those that are long or those that are large,
middling, short, fine, or gross;
whether they are seen or unseen,
whether they dwell far or near,
whether they have come to be or will come to be,
may all beings be inwardly happy!
No one should deceive another,
nor despise anyone anywhere.
Because of anger and thoughts of aversion
no one should wish suffering for another.[192]

I do a *mettā* practice with wording that is shorter than this passage. I usually say something like "May all beings become free of suffering and wake up." Traditionally, *mettā* practice starts with wishing happiness to oneself. Then one extends this wish to one's immediate loved ones and then to others, radiating outward in concentric circles of intimacy. This loving-kindness is even extended to people we find difficult, dislike, or even hate. This is usually done as a silent visualization exercise in our mind, but during or right after saying grace I sometimes extend *mettā* out loud.

I also weave this *mettā* practice into traditional Jewish observances on Friday evening at the beginning of the Sabbath. After lighting two candles and saying a blessing, Mishy and I use our hands to extend light to those who need it: sick friends, people who have suffered a loss, refugees, those who are stuck in places of violence, sentient beings suffering from climate disruption, and anyone else we can think of who could use some support. Then, as we drink a cup of wine and eat the braided challah, we express gratitude for the bounty in our lives and express our intention to share it with others. To introduce a Buddhist element into the ritual, I use my hands and voice to send loving-kindness out along with the light. In addition to making the Shabbos ritual more meaningful to me with my Buddhist inclinations, extending loving-kindness in this way makes *mettā* practice much more physical and real for me.

Establishing a healthy morning ritual offers us another potentially powerful way to transform our daily lives. I find that when I wake up feeling lethargic, anxious, or depressed, having a familiar and habitual routine gives me something I can plug into as I start the day. While attending to my breath (unless I'm half asleep), I go to the bathroom, wash my hands, brush my teeth, put water in the kettle, get out the coffee pot, put the filter holder on the top, place a cone filter in it, take out the canister of ground coffee, pour some into the filter, sprinkle some cinnamon on top, and then stand there by the counter looking out at the backyard while waiting for the water to boil. Because I repeat this every day I can give myself to the actions without standing around thinking about what I need to do. Like the skill of athletes, this draws upon body memory. And as I do something constructive like making a cup of coffee, more often than not, I start feeling better—or, at the very least, I free myself from inertia and inaction. In some ways, the morning routine is like a train that I can board while feeling groggy or depressed, and it can get me "rolling down the tracks" into my day.

The power of morning rituals to help us get on with our day even when we're feeling lousy echoes the approach of Japanese psychologist Morita Shōma, who claims that to live a fulfilling life we don't need to eliminate anxiety or discover its source, as people do in talk therapy with realizations like "I lack confidence because when I was a kid my father always told me I was a loser. " Rather, if you're feeling anxious as you wake up in the morning, simply get up and do what is needed: brush your teeth, get dressed, make the coffee. If you have to do something that makes you anxious—like giving a speech—acknowledge the pressure in your chest and the shaking of your hands, prepare well, and then just give the speech . . . while feeling anxious. This approach can serve us as we try to respond to the climate crisis but find ourselves immobilized (and un-mobilizable) by anxiety or despair. When we feel hobbled or overwhelmed by the magnitude of the crisis, taking small actions can help get us moving. They can be something simple at the level of lifestyle change, like turning down the heat in winter or avoiding meat on certain days of the week, or something at the level of structural change, like calling the office of a politician and urging them to vote for a certain piece of legislation.

BEYOND THE HOME

In addition to routinizing the first constructive actions of our day and/or sitting in meditation before breakfast, we can add structure and meaning to our morning by crafting practices we can do on the way to school, work, or wherever we might be headed. Whether we go by our own car, wheelchair, or public transportation, we can use the time spent driving, wheeling, or waiting for the bus or train to check in with our senses: What am I hearing, smelling, and seeing? What's the taste in my mouth? Toothpaste? Coffee? Burned toast? What is my body feeling? How do my shoulders feel as I maneuver my wheelchair, steer the car, or take a seat on the bus? Getting in touch with sense experience, with our body interacting with the world, is a good way to get out of our heads.

If you walk at least part of the way to work, you can ask yourself questions such as, What does it feel like as my feet touch the ground with each step? How cold is the breeze that is hitting my cheeks? What's going on in my head? If you can, perform your walking as a walking meditation, which Japanese Zen monks call *kinhin*. Focus on your breathing and feel your feet touching the ground with each step, your thighs lifting up your foot for the next step, and your body moving forward.[193] As Thich Nhat Hanh explains it, "When walking you just walk, giving one hundred percent of your awareness and attention to your walking. In this way, you will be present for the ground beneath your feet, for the plants in front of you, the clouds above you, and the people around you."[194] If you are in a wheelchair, see if you can synchronize your breath with the actions you do to move forward.

I drive to work, and right after I start the car I take a few breaths and feel my body sitting in the driver's seat and my hands grasping the steering wheel. (At least I try to remember to do that.) As I drive, I try to practice extending my awareness out around me to the other vehicles and road signs. I also try to remind myself that my purpose is not to get to Stonehill College as quickly as possible but to get there safely and, at each moment along the way, to be in *this place* fully, even when "this place" is barren, oil-stained asphalt that is changing moment to moment as I cruise along the freeway. I sometimes augment this practice by chanting the *Heart Sutra* or the Fourfold Great Vow.[195] These rituals help me pay attention and stay present. Though I may listen to WBZ for Boston traffic reports or to NPR for the news, I turn the radio off if I find that my mind is getting lost in the broadcast.

At the end of my commute, when I arrive at my destination and park in a lot at Stonehill College or in our garage back here at home, I take a moment to prepare for the interactions I'm about to have, whether with my colleagues, my students, or my wife. I may recite a mantra, like "Keep your tongue on the roof of the mouth," or "Listen deeply, take a breath, and then speak." I may also remind myself that "No one is intentionally trying to be a jerk," and couple that reminder with a moment of extending *mettā*: "May all beings become free from suffering and wake up."

Sometimes, if I remember and repeat these practices and mantras during my commute, my mind starts feeling cluttered. In those moments, I draw from the Sōtō strand of Zen, which historically has focused on getting in touch with and manifesting the awakening that is within us all along, and distill my intention down to an overarching guideline and mantra: "Manifest your buddha nature in each moment." In other words, show up as your wiser, kinder self. Or, to riff on bumper stickers about Jesus, ask yourself, What would Buddha do? I find that negative prohibitions—Don't interrupt! Don't keep eating once you feel 80 percent full! Don't eat meat! Don't do things that unnecessarily spew carbon!—need to be balanced with affirmations that resonate in our hearts and inspire us.

Perhaps the most important support structure as we try to put ecological mental states into practice is community. Many of us may not currently be part of a community that is committed to supporting its members in reducing their ecological impact. We may not be members of a formal Buddhist sangha, or of a church, synagogue, mosque, or temple. We may not even be an active participant in a secular group such as a neighborhood committee or other local organization. Either way, a key part of the task before us is finding— or cultivating—a community of kindred spirits who value restraint, generosity, non-harming, and compassion, and who are committed to living in a more spacious, ecological, and engaged way. When we are actively involved in such a community, we can more easily pursue the way of living I'm sketching here in this book. We will delve into this process of community building in chapter nine below. But first, I think it's important to explore our relationship with nature.

PART IV

Connecting to Our Place

7. Realizing Our Embeddedness in Nature *as* Nature

We are here to awaken from the illusion of our separateness.

—Thich Nhat Hanh

O NE FORM of ignorance, as I mentioned earlier, is our sense of disconnection from nature, our obliviousness to how we are interconnected with the natural world and depend upon it for our survival. Zen and other strands of Buddhism offer an array of resources for helping us realize our embeddedness in nature as nature.

Zen Aesthetics

When I reflect on how Zen monastic life might provide a template for an alternative way of living in our homes, my mind inevitably wanders to Zen aesthetics. When I lived in Kyoto, I saw firsthand why Zen temples were prime tourist attractions: most of the buildings, the objects in the buildings, and the gardens around the buildings are works of art. And what always struck me was the simplicity of their beauty. It's a beauty without clutter. It's minimalist—just this sprig, just this rock, just this bowl of tea, presented in a way that supports our savoring that one object. This aesthetic appears in the interface between Zen and the tea ceremony. The tea-house aesthetic is one of simple, elegant beauty, and one part of being a guest at a tea ceremony is appreciating the beauty of the space and the objects in it.

Of course, as we share our home with others, including active children, it's unreasonable to expect that we can create a home with the refined beauty of a Zen temple or Japanese tea house. Clothes get tossed in a corner, dishes pile up in the sink, kids scatter toys, and surfaces get covered with keys, phones, and mail. But if we want to live mindfully, appreciating and respecting each object, person, and moment in our homes, it helps to reside in a home informed by the Zen aesthetic. We can achieve this by keeping things uncluttered and clean, with at least one space of simple beauty, whether an entire room or just a corner of a room. Reducing the number of objects and pieces of furniture makes it easier to take respectful care of our possessions as well as reducing the mental scatteredness we often feel in cluttered rooms, not to mention the economic hit we suffer—and the ecological toll we exact—when we fill our rooms with unnecessary stuff.

Another way to cultivate beauty in the home is through food, especially how we put it on plates and present it to others. Paying attention to the presentation helps us slow down and appreciate the elements—the color and texture of brown rice, a cherry tomato, a clam in its shell. Or the bowls in which we serve them. This doesn't take all that much effort. Pausing to take a breath or two while pulling the meal together can help us make the process more mindful, creative, and enjoyable.

The Zen aesthetic informing these practices centers on *natural* beauty. We see examples of this in tea bowls whose sides remind us of lichen-covered boulders, alcoves with flower arrangements in rustic vases, sliding fusuma panels depicting bamboo, and ink paintings of natural scenes—whether a lone crow perched on a pine branch or an angular cliff shrouded in clouds. Temple compounds are replete with evergreens and other trees. They also feature multiple gardens, some depicting natural landscapes in abbreviated form, as seen in the gardening style called *karesansui*, which we can translate as "withered trees, mountains, and waters."

The Zen appreciation of natural beauty is both informed and enhanced by meditative practice. As we saw before, many Zen teachers have talked about how when we empty our minds of thoughts and worries in meditation, or at least free ourselves from getting entangled in thinking when it arises, we can get filled by what we experience. And when we experience things in this way, with our analytical minds quieted down, we can better see things "just as they are," presencing themselves in their vibratory suchness. This, in turn, helps us appreciate the beauty of things in their particularity.[196] We may even get a sense of what Rabbi Abraham Joshua Heschel was getting at when he wrote, "Our goal should be to live life in radical amazement, to look at the world in a way that takes nothing for granted. Everything is phenomenal; everything is incredible; to be spiritual is to be constantly amazed."[197] (Though I resonate Heschel's statement, I do find myself wondering whether he felt this radical amazement when he saw destruction wrought by war or refugees struggling to find food and shelter.)

The Zen engagement with the beauty of nature is not simply a matter of artistic appreciation. Though Plato separated aesthetics (beauty) from ethics (the good) in his philosophy of the three transcendent Forms—truth, goodness, and beauty—it's worth our while to give some thought to how appreciation of the beauty of nature might go beyond aesthetics and bear ethical fruit. As Zen Buddhists—and nature writers around the world—have claimed, natural beauty can lift us out of our narrow selves and fill us with awe and wonder. Typically this leads to greater appreciation and valuation of nature. British scholar Simon James has noted that for "Zen there is no clear line between a moral concern for nature and an aesthetic appreciation of it."[198] This is not limited to Zen. Theravāda ethicist Padmasiri de Silva has written that it is the "aesthetic dimension that reinforces our move toward conservation."[199] And beyond Buddhism, Aldo Leopold's focus on the integrity, stability, and beauty of ecosystems has prompted David Barnhill to write, "our moral love and respect for nature is based on an aesthetic appreciation of the beauty and value of the land."[200] Or, as I once said in a debate with a colleague eager to sacrifice religion and feeling on the altar of rationality, "For every person who becomes an environmentalist after crunching numbers about ecological degradation, there are ten who become environmentalists after a powerful experience of beauty out in nature." As an aside, I recall how when I said this I was struggling to find wording that doesn't reinforce the society-nature binary by positing nature as something "out there."

DISCONNECTION AND RECONNECTION

Zen can also help us deal with the contemporary problem of feeling disconnected from nature. As I flagged earlier, modern living has pulled many of us away from wilder natural environments. Increasingly, we live in cities and spend our days indoors. Enchanted by our gadgets and apps, we escape into virtual realities. "We are enclosed," according to Joan Halifax, "in a psychocultural cocoon; the outer world no longer flows into our being."[201] Cut off in this way, we lose out on what psychologists have identified as the mental and physical benefits of spending time outside in a forest or on a beach. We may even suffer from nature-deficit disorder. Moreover, as Claire Dunn tells us, "Disconnection from the natural world makes it easier to treat it like a commodity."[202] This disconnection also feeds our ignorance and ignor-ance of the damage we are doing to biological and climatic systems that sustain life as we have known it. It subverts our sense of reciprocity within the living system of which we are part. As Daniel R. Wildcat puts it, "Although our own lives depend on a complex web of life, it is hard for humans to respect relationships and responsibly reciprocate in this web when so many of us take it for granted and seldom directly experience it."[203]

To remedy this disconnection, we need to put down our devices, get outside, and start paying attention to the natural world in and around us. We need to break down mental boundaries between "me in here" and "nature out there." We need to realize that as embodied beings woven into a vast system of interbeing, we are always existing in nature *as* nature.[204] This realization of how we are part of nature can play a vital role in extricating ourselves from the precarious situation in which we now live. "To have safe homes in the twenty-first century," Madeline Ostrander writes, "we cannot keep acting as if we are isolated individuals. We are not just consumers. We are not just a collection of independent bodies with separate carbon footprints. There are no sharp boundaries between our lives and the lives of others. There are no clear borders between the safety of our households and our bodies and the health of the land and the ecosystems around us."[205] For many people, waking up to how we are part of the web of life is the first step to recognizing how we are impacting nature and how the degradation of nature is affecting us. It can motivate us to become more humble and respectful as we participate in the more-than-human world. It may even prompt us to take action to protect this world.

Zen offers helpful resources for realizing that we are part of nature. Though we need to be wary of claims about Zen intimacy with nature that are overstated and fraught with cultural nationalism,[206] the tradition offers several ways of freeing us from feeling separate from nature. With their depictions of facets of nature, Zen paintings, tea bowls, and flower arrangements bring nature indoors.[207] Wall panels can be slid aside to extend interior spaces out across verandas that overlook gardens. Some of those gardens are positioned to integrate distant mountains on the horizon as part of the garden landscape in a technique termed *shakkei*, "borrowing scenery." Rural Zen temples as a whole are usually *nestled into* a natural setting, whether a forest or a valley, not *towering above* it. With vague or non-existent boundaries between the compound and its surroundings, temples seem to blend into the landscape, so much so that the Japanese character for forest often appears in the names of temples, and major monasteries are sometimes referred to as "mountains," as in the Five-Mountain system of prominent monasteries in China and Japan in the twelfth through fourteenth centuries.

Many temples, especially those with monks in training, foster closeness to nature by cultivating vegetable gardens. Through physical labor, monks connect with fields, plants, sky, rain, and frost. For fertilizer, they ladle human "waste" from latrine pits and spread it on the vegetable garden, thereby plugging themselves into a sewage-soil-food-sewage-soil cycle. Monks further connect with their natural surroundings by, as we saw earlier, setting aside a few morsels from each meal to be left outside for "hungry ghosts" and consumed by birds, squirrels, and other critters around the monastery. I have tried to emulate these practices (though not the fertilizer one) by planting a garden each summer with tomatoes, lettuce, and basil, and by putting vegetable scraps out on our compost pile, which is visited daily by birds, squirrels, and the occasional possum.

The Zen tradition also values going into nature as a good place to practice, far from the "dusty world" of towns and cities. Hermit-monks, like Hanshan (ninth century) in China and Ryōkan (1758–1831) in Japan, stand as exemplars, and their poetry is replete with images of intimacy with their surroundings. In one poem Hanshan declares,

> Here in the wilderness I am completely free,
> With my friends, the white clouds, idling forever. . . .
> On a bed stone I sit, alone in the night,
> While the round moon climbs up Cold Mountain.[208]

In an apparent affirmation of non-separation, Hanshan takes his name from the name of the presumably chilly mountain on which he has built his hermitage: Hanshan or "Cold Mountain." Engaging in Zen practice outside has also been advocated by Nelson Foster, the Zen master of Ring of Bone Zendo in the foothills of California's Sierra Nevada, who has conducted mountains-and-rivers retreats that take the form of backpacking trips in the wilderness of California and other western states.[209] I have written about how we can draw from Zen to make hiking and other outdoor activities forms of pilgrimage and meditation that help us overcome our sense of separation from nature.[210]

Perhaps the most powerful way that Zen helps people realize their embeddedness in nature is the practice of zazen. Sitting quietly, we can get out of our heads and attend to our bodies and to what is coming to us through our senses, and in this way we can make more immediate contact with the world around us. As we open up our more expansive sky mind, we can witness nature as it presences itself to us in its suchness. In this intimate contact, we can see nature more clearly, savor it, and feel awe and wonder at its complexity and beauty. In our open attentiveness, we can also attend to how things interact and change, and we can feel ourselves woven into that process. We can realize that in one respect "I am nature doing its thing through me," and thereby let go of the false notion that "I am a separate entity doing its thing in nature." With this liberating insight into conditioned arising (interbeing), we can realize that, as Joanna Macy and Molly Brown put it, "We are not closed off from the world, but integral parts of it, like cells in a larger body."[211]

Zazen can also free us from dualistic modes of experience that leave us feeling that nature is an object or a world apart from ourselves. It can facilitate a shift from appreciating nature to being so filled with it that any sense of the subject "me" appreciating the object "nature" drops off.[212] As Zen master Kōdō Sawaki Rōshi says, "What is the true self? It's brilliantly transparent like the deep-blue sky, and there's no gap between I and all living beings."[213]

Though such direct experience may be mediated at a preconscious, pre-reflective level by concepts,[214] in that moment there is no thinking, self-reflective "me" apart from nature out there, but simply raw, immediate experience. It is not that we are *having* an experience *of* an event but, in that immediacy, we *are* the experience, we *are* the event as it happens, at least psychologically. And in that moment, all that exists is the event, reality, nature: the mountain rising up into the clouds, the flower in all of its intricate beauty, the call of the meadowlark, the glorious colors of the sunset. As we said earlier, in the immediacy of this experience it is simply "Sunset!," or "Mountain!"

Though this experience may last only for a moment and be beyond the power of words to describe it, afterward we might be inclined to join Yangshan (807–83) in saying, "I came to realize clearly that mind is no other than mountains and rivers and the great wide earth, the sun, the moon, the stars."[215] Or we might reflect on the experience and say, "In that moment, I was the mountain and the mountain was me." (Perhaps this is why Hanshan named himself after the site of his hut.) This may be what people are trying to convey when they talk of "becoming one" with nature, or what Thich Nhat Hanh is getting at when he writes,

> If you are a mountain climber or someone who enjoys the countryside or the green forest, you know that the forests are our lungs outside of our bodies. . . . We should be able to be our true self. That means we should be able to be the river, we should be able to be the forest. . . . That is the non-dualistic way of seeing."[216]

But, it is not the case that we are somehow inside the trees and having actual physical sensations of existing as multiple root systems, trunks, and branches. Rather, in that moment all there is is the forest, the event.

EMBEDDEDNESS AND INTERCONNECTION

Of course, we don't need to be a Buddhist meditator to sense this oneness with nature. We may get a taste of this by relaxing and being so open to what we are experiencing that any sense of separation drops off. And this is not simply some interesting blip in our stream of consciousness, for it impacts us at a profound emotional level. About such experiences, Vajragupta writes, "The door swings open and a whole glorious world is waiting. Losing myself in that world, I find love and connection, gratitude, wonder and reverence."[217] These feelings in turn help free us from selfish desire and subvert our objectification and commodification of nature.

Our insight into our embeddedness in nature and interconnection with other parts of it also helps us, as Vajragupta mentions, to feel gratitude for the myriad things that shape and support us and, by extension, helps us value them. This realization of how we are woven into the web of interbeing also prompts us to recognize how our actions have countless effects on the world around us, and how many of those effects rebound on us. In this way, we can realize that, as Chatsumarn Kabilsingh puts it, "When we abuse nature we abuse ourselves."[218] This realization deepens our recognition that it is in our interest to preserve and protect the natural world, and it nudges us to give greater thought to the possible impacts of our actions on the world around us and to act in less harmful ways.

In identifying with, realizing our connection to, and valuing the things, spaces, and beings around us, we are not only less apt to harm nature but more apt to care for it, just as we might care for our own bodies. Arne Naess, who coined the term "deep ecology," writes that ecological "care flows naturally if the self is widened and deepened so that protection of free nature is felt and conceived of as protection of our very selves."[219] In Buddhist terms, non-harming operates here as a marriage of compassionate concern about the suffering that can be caused by our actions and the insight that our actions can also harm us. These realizations and transformations also foster a greater sense of responsibility, not just in the moral or legal sense of being accountable for our actions but in the sense of an impetus, or an obligation, to care for someone or something, as in the claim that "Parents are responsible for the well-being of their children."

In sum, eco-Buddhists often argue that as the "self" expands, self-interest expands as well, to the point where the protected self is no longer the clinging, acquisitive ego but an expanded self, which is ultimately nature in and around us. This expansion of identification and interest is said to transform the person's outlook from egocentricity to *eco*centricity.[220] Or, as Joanna Macy puts it, the culturally conditioned sense of self gets "replaced by wider constructs of identity and self-interest—by what you might call the ecological self or the eco-self, co-extensive with other beings and the life of our planet. It is . . . 'the greening of the self.'"[221]

PRACTICES FOR REALIZING OUR EMBEDDEDNESS IN NATURE

Over the years I've developed an array of practices that comple-ment zazen and other Zen ways of overcoming our sense of separa-tion from nature.[222]

Slowing Down and Paying Attention

The first and most general step is to do whatever it is that helps us to be more fully present. For most of us, this starts with slowing down and attending to what's around us. I have found that using the 80 percent rule—consciously slowing down certain activities to 80 percent of our normal speed—to be an effective support for cultivating more attention to the present moment. By paying close attention, we can begin to realize how we are woven into a system of interrelationships, affecting things and being affected by them.

Attending to Sensory Experiences

Attending more closely to our sensory experience offers another way to cultivate attentive presence and connect with our surround-ings. Sometimes in zazen, as I give myself to breathing, I direct my attention to settling back into my sensory field; it's as if I'm sitting back in a comfortable chair and tuning into what my body is sens-ing around me. You can practice a similar sensory attentiveness off the cushion as well. When I go outside, whether on my front steps or at a trailhead, I find it's useful to check in with each of my five senses. I go sense by sense, taking note of what I'm seeing, hearing, smelling, tasting, and feeling in and on my body. This practice helps me get out of my head and into my body, into my sense experience, into closer contact with my surroundings. It also makes me more aware of my interactions with nature. I recognize that I bump into things, and they may respond by attaching pollen or sticky seeds to my legs. I might notice that my consciousness gets affected by hot, humid air, or that my body starts shivering as I walk outside on a cold winter day. A sudden, startling sound helps me understand that I, too, am a critter, similar to other animals, in interrelationship with them, in a food chain with them.

So much of the time we are stuck in our heads, out of full sensory contact with our surroundings, and not fully alive in our bodies here and now. Regularly reconnecting with our sensory experience helps bring us back to the present moment. Sister True Dedication describes the power of our sensory experience to awaken us to the present moment when she writes,

> As a meditator our task is to become fascinated with what the present moment *feels* like. I remember at first thinking that I need to access the present moment with my mind. But I've slowly understood that I can access it most directly with the senses: the smell of the woods, the edge of the breeze, the sound of the rain, the rumble of humanity through the asphalt. I've learned to cut through the noise and open up space to connect with a moment with my whole being.[223]

Giving and Receiving with Plants

We can also attend to our exchange of gases with trees and other plants. As you inhale, imagine oxygen coming to you as a gift from the trees around you. As you exhale, imagine your outbreath, replete with carbon dioxide, as an offering back out to the trees. Feel yourself in a loop: you inhale the oxygen you need to live and exhale carbon dioxide, and the trees inhale the carbon dioxide through stomata under their leaves and needles, grab the carbon, and exhale the oxygen back to you. Sit for a few minutes breath-ing, feeling yourself in this exchange of gases with the trees, in the interbeing that is happening with each of our breaths. You may even come to feel that you are "being breathed by life, sustained in a vast living breathing web."[224]

Reminding Ourselves

One other practice is to constantly remind ourselves that nature is not happening only "out there" in the woods or nearby desert. It's happening in and around us, wherever we are. My stomach grum-bles to remind me that I need to eat some lunch. My head turns suddenly in response to the growl of my neighbor's dog. Ants walk along the kitchen counter. Fruit flies hover above the ripe bananas. Make an effort to attend to all of this. Outside on the front steps, how cool or warm is the air? What's up there in the sky overhead? What plants are growing? Are there any animals out and about? As Scott Russell Sanders puts it, "Nature does not halt at the property line, but runs right through our yard and walls and bones. Possums and racoons browse among kitchen scraps in the compost bin. Moss grows on the shady side of the roof, mildew in the bathtub, mold in the fridge. Roots from our front yard elm invade the drain. Mice invade the cupboards."[225] The biome in my belly includes more living beings than there are people on Earth.

As I work with these practices, I have come to think that the key ecological resource offered by Zen is less a oneness with the world that obliterates any sense of self than a deep sense of interconnec-tion and belonging, or what I have been calling embeddedness. When we feel ourselves in intimate community with nature in all of its forms around us, we care about it and become more inclined to care *for* it as well.[226] We can enhance our sense of connection by "rewilding" ourselves, which Marc Bekoff describes as "encourag-ing, honoring, and growing our inherent connection to nature and nonhuman animals."[227]

A New Paradigm

As we cultivate our ability to be present and our feeling of embeddedness within nature, we need to find ways for these fruits to generate a lasting shift in our way of thinking and our way of being in the world.[228] Philip Clayton and Wm. Andrew Schwartz provide a glimpse of such a way of being in the world, envisioning an ecological civilization "in which human beings are fully aware of themselves as part of the natural world, and aware of their close kinship to the other creatures who constitute that world."[229] We can foster this awareness by imagining and embracing a worldview that avoids core elements of the perspective that has dominated for so long here in the West. As Clayton and Schwartz put it, we need "a conceptual framework that fully overcomes the dualisms of modern thought: mind versus matter, human versus nature, and value versus value-free."[230] We can find this conceptual framework not only in Zen but in Indigenous cultures that view us as living in "a nature-culture nexus" and recognize "the fundamental connectedness and relatedness of human communities and societies to the natural environment and the other-than-human relatives they interact with daily."[231]

We should note here that although this daily interaction with the natural environment may generate the sense of being connected to "the natural world" writ large, this interaction happens in the *particular*—with our *local* environment—not with some generic, broad "Nature." I would argue that, more often than not, our caring for "the natural world" begins with caring for a particular place that we know and love, whether the woods in which we played as a child, the pond where our family vacationed, or the beach on which we hung out with our high school friends.

In the next chapter, we will look at Gary Snyder's vision of *reinhabitation* as model of how to cultivate this caring—both in the sense of valuing and in the sense of nurturing and protecting the world around us.

8. Reinhabitation

Reinhabitory refers to the tiny number of persons who
have come out of the industrial societies . . . and then
start to turn back to the land, back to place. This comes
for some with the rational and scientific realization of
interconnectedness and planetary limits.
—GARY SNYDER[232]

UNFORTUNATELY, few of us feel like we live in a "nature-culture"
nexus. Most of us spend our days indoors. We get entranced
by the black screen in front of us. We're largely ignorant of the natural systems enveloping us. We have little sense of place. In the
United States, people tend to move around—in search of education,
employment, and love—and end up dis-located and dis-placed.
Gary Snyder writes,

> One of the key problems in American society now, it
> seems to me, is people's lack of commitment to any given
> place—which . . . is totally unnatural and outside of his-
> tory. Neighborhoods are allowed to deteriorate, land-
> scapes are allowed to be strip-mined, because there is
> nobody who will live there and take responsibility; they'll
> just move on.[233]

In some respects, however, our disconnection from a specific
place is *inside* of history, at least *recent* history. Daniel Wildcat writes,

In the increasingly geographically mobile world humans inhabit at the beginning of what Western civilization calls the twenty-first century, fewer and fewer people have tangible lifeway relationships to the places in which they live. Humankind's diets, clothing, dwellings, and everyday lives are increasingly shaped by social forces such as corporations and marketers that attempt to transcend the unique features of the peoples and places of the planet.[234]

This recent historical development has left us with "one monolithic global consumer culture that makes a sense of place—or more properly, natural landscapes—irrelevant in its homogenizing logic."[235] And being dis-placed, we may not pay close attention to what is happening around us, whether pollinators disappearing, songbirds becoming scarcer, or insect-borne diseases spreading. In this way, our awareness of climate disruption gets stunted.

Reinhabitation

In response to our dis-placement, Snyder has drawn from his youth on a farm, extensive time in wilderness areas, monastic practice of Zen in Kyoto, commitment to his region in the foothills of the Sierra, understanding of Indigenous traditions, scientific knowledge, and a range of other sources to offer a vision of how we might live more fully in our place and take care of it in community with others. He advocates that we discern "the web of the wild world"[236] and "make intimate contact with the real world, the real self."[237] Here, he seems to be drawing from the Zen idea that we do not exist apart from the world and that, in the depths of practice, we can realize our non-dual relationship with it. Unfortunately, however, our moving around and mental disconnection from nature has made us, in Snyder's view, "an unsettled and disenfranchised people."[238]

This pattern of unsettledness and disconnection certainly pertains to me. On the one hand, I grew up in one house and spent much of my youth down at the river across the street. I came to love the pools where I fished, the hemlocks and ferns on the banks, and the tall grasses and wildflowers in the abandoned cow pastures through which my brothers and I walked on our way down to the river and back. My body was intimately engaged with that place, as evidenced by the mosquito bites I sported on my legs each summer. I felt wonder as I watched the trout in that river and the fireflies above those fields at night. My love of that place is in my bones, as is the grief I feel over recent changes that have been wrought by our disrupted climate: the dwindling trout population as the river warms, the disappearance of those fireflies, the inability of kids to scamper through those grassy fields without getting deer ticks on their legs, and the stark fact that the delicate mosquitoes that used to leave me with those familiar bumps on my legs can now hammer me with West Nile virus and eastern equine encephalitis.

Though I fully inhabited that place with my youthful body and spirit, across the thirty years between leaving there for college and moving to Massachusetts my residence changed every year or two. For much of that time, I knew little about the watersheds in which I lived, and I rarely got involved with the local community. Granted, in certain moments I felt connected to the nature around me, but my knowledge of it was limited.

To be in nature more fully than just experiencing rare moments of intimacy with our surroundings, we need to "turn back to the land, back to place."[239] And do so for the long haul. Snyder once said, "First, don't move, and second, find out what that teaches you."[240] As we stay put, "we must honor this land's great antiquity— its wildness—learn it—defend it—and work to hand it on to the children (of all beings) of the future with its biodiversity and health intact."[241] Settling down in my current semi-urban place has been hard for me at times, for there is a part of me that wants to move out into the country, with some land, and maybe some forested acres to cut wood for a fireplace. But I stay here in our condo on the edge of Boston, at times frustrated but cognizant of the carbon emissions caused by heating with wood and enjoying a fire, not to mention the effect that the wood smoke would have on my wife's asthma.

In our turning back to the land, we have to reinhabit our local place. We have to grasp how our homes are nestled in a specific ecosystem, in a watershed, and, more broadly, in a bioregion. This necessitates a detailed understanding: "Bioregional awareness teaches us in *specific* ways. It is not enough just to 'love nature' or to want to 'be in harmony with Gaia.' Our relation to the natural world takes place in a *place*, and it must be grounded in information and experience."[242] Through this information and experience, we acquire knowledge of our place as a particular locus of interconnection. As Snyder puts it, "You should really know what the complete natural world of your region is and know what all its interactions are and how you are interacting with it yourself."[243] Charles Strain argues that Snyder is in this way emphasizing "the practice of mindful concentration, *samadhi*, refocused as the kind of attention to the detailed variations of climate and soil, to what will flourish and what will not in this *place*...."[244]

To this end, we need to study the geological history underneath and around our dwelling. We need to get a handle on the constitution of the bedrock and the composition of the soil. My geological knowledge of the area where I live is limited, but I do know that it was under a mile-thick layer of ice during the last ice age, and that nearby Walden Pond is a kettle pond, similar to those on Cape Cod, which formed when the ice melted back from south to north.

It is important to know what has happened here since that melting, including the lifeways of the different peoples who have lived here, whether Indigenous or invasive. We also need to identify bugs and other animals living on our block or in our backyard, as well as the plants growing around the buildings. We need to learn how water moves through this place in a hydrological cycle. Scott Russell Sanders writes, "When we figure our addresses, we might do better to forget zip codes and consider where rain goes after it falls outside our windows."[245] In the place where I live, known by its original inhabitants as Pigsgussett—present-day Watertown,

Massachusetts—much of the rain flows into Quinobequin (the Charles River), as it does in other nearby towns, at times pulling sewage into the river and resulting in the cancellation of one of my favorite activities in the early summer: participating in a one-mile swim race in the Boston section of the river before it flows through a dam by the Museum of Science and into the harbor. We also need to learn how our local ecosystem changes with the seasons.[246] We need to come up to speed with how land is being used and perhaps damaged in our town or city, and how local government is—or is not—regulating what is being done.

As part of this inquiry into the places where we live, those of us who are non-Native can learn from the Original peoples who have complex knowledge systems derived in part from their enduring connection to land, waterways, animals, and all forms of life, and who have their own ways of being in these places.[247] Snyder writes that Original peoples can be "a great instructor in certain ways of tuning into what the climatic cycles, plant and animal communities, can tell us of where we are."[248] At the very least, as pointed out by Daniel Wildcat (Yuchi, Muscogee), "Tribal lifeways can remind us of the imperative to reconstitute a life-enhancing nature-culture nexus in the places where we live."[249] I might add that white Americans like me who descend from colonial settlers must also acknowledge the genocidal history that has "taken place," taken *land*, in the places where we live.

Practices for Reinhabiting the Places Where We Live

In addition to securing this knowledge in our heads, we need to get outside and, in our bodies, interact with the things and processes surrounding our homes. We can engage with these particulars of place through our sense experience and physical actions, through our "body, commitment, time, labor, walking."[250] If you can, grow some vegetables. Each year we plant lettuce, basil, parsley, and tomatoes in the beds that we created with my cousin Don in our small backyard. Track the "weeds" and "pests." If you live in North America, plant milkweed for migrating monarch butterflies. If you have a lawn and are able to mow it, do it yourself—waiting to mow it in the spring until after the spring flowers have bloomed in the grass. Or, better yet, turn your lawn into a native-plant garden. Rake leaves in the fall to use as mulch. Forage for edible plants. Drip sweat onto the land; get its dirt under your fingernails; maybe even get stung by the honey bees that help it flourish (or, in my case, by the yellow jackets I disturbed last summer). And, as Snyder writes, "if you are gathering milkweed, fishing, picking berries, raising apples, and tending a garden[,] it shouldn't be too difficult to realize that you have some relationship with nature."[251] This relationship is a physical, sensory, working relationship in which we can plug into our place with all of our senses and come to understand and love it. As David Orr writes, "I do not know whether it is possible to love the planet or not, but I do know that it is possible to love the places we can see, touch, smell, and experience."[252]

To (re)inhabit our place, we also need to educate ourselves about the origins of our water, our electricity, and, if we have a furnace, our heating fuel. We need to find out where things go when we flush the toilet or put our garbage and recycling out on the curb. Here in Watertown, our water comes from the Quabbin Reservoir in the center of the state, and our sewage is treated in Boston Harbor on Deer Island, which during Pometacomet's Resistance (1675–78)—otherwise known as King Philip's War—was the location of a concentration camp to which colonists forcibly transported and abandoned hundreds of Native people at the beginning of winter in 1675, with no food, water, or shelter, resulting in great suffering and loss of life.

Those of us who do have food and water can pay attention to what's on our table. What's the field-to-table carbon footprint of the ingredients? Can we become more of a locavore? Is there a farmer's market nearby? My wife and I participate in Farmers to You: each weekend we go to a website showcasing vegetables that are being harvested in Vermont, as well as honey, pasta, bread, and other foods, and then place an order, which we pick up on Wednesday afternoon in a nearby bank parking lot from a refrigerated truck that has been driven down from Vermont that morning. Of course, in some cases the carbon footprint of each potato brought from Vermont to Boston in a small truck may be greater than that of a potato shipped here from Idaho in an 18-wheeler. Be that as it may, we can view knowledge of the carbon footprint of our food as part of the right livelihood component of the eightfold path and as one way to follow the first precept of non-harming.

Through all of this, we can grasp in our minds and bodies how we are plugged into and dependent on larger systems and cycles. Each time we take a bit of food—a tomato, a lettuce leaf, a grain of rice—we're ingesting a focal point in a vast web of causes and effects consisting of the sunshine that triggered photosynthesis, the dirt in which the plants grew, the rain that watered the crops, the farmer who worked the fields, the truck driver who transported the harvested crop, the people who built the truck, the gas in the truck, the plants that died millions of years ago and became oil and then that gas, the clerk in the store where we bought the produce.... As Thich Nhat Hanh would say, we can see the whole universe in each bite of food. With this insight, we can begin to get a firmer handle on how our diet is woven into the system of interbeing in which we are embedded, and with a bit of inquiry we can also discern how certain agricultural practices and choices we make about our food contribute to the climate crisis and other environmental problems.

Reinhabiting Cities

With all this focus on agriculture, we may wonder whether Snyder's vision applies to people living in cities. We might interpret him as advocating that urban dwellers move to rural areas. This seems to be the implication when he writes, "If man [sic] is to remain on earth he must transform the five-millennia-long urbanizing civilization tradition into a new ecologically-sensitive harmony-oriented wild-minded scientific-spiritual culture."[253] As I understand it, however,

Snyder's "turn back to the land" is not directing us to move out to the country and start homesteading. Luckily for me, as someone who lives in a semi-urban location, he wants us to turn back to the land on which we find ourselves, even if it's only a quarter-acre lot or a city block. Indeed, Snyder explicitly includes cities in his exposition, as when he says,

> No amount of well-meaning environmental legislation will halt the biological holocaust without people who love where they are and work with their neighbors, taking responsibility for their place, and *seeing to it*: to be inhabitants, and to not retreat. We feel this to be starting in America: a mosaic of city neighborhoods, small towns, and rural places where people are digging in and saying "if not now, when? if not here, where?"[254]

And regardless of our location, we need to "get back in touch with people, with ordinary things: with your body, with the dirt, with the dust, with anything you like, you know—the streets."[255] Indeed, city streets are as much a part of the hydrological cycle as mountain ravines.

In this process of getting in touch with our surroundings, we realize that "nature" is not *over there* apart from cities. Cities are part of ecosystems, and though cities don't offer us "wilderness," we can find the "wild" and "wildness" there. We've all seen plants vigorously sprouting up through sidewalk cracks and between buildings. Aldo Leopold writes, "The weeds in a city lot convey the same lesson as the redwoods."[256] Moreover, many cities were built in bountiful spots along rivers where Indigenous people lived for millennia and still do, such as Manahatta, the island in the homeland of the Lenni-Lenape that the Dutch colonized and later called Manhattan. As I mentioned earlier, my city is situated along Quinobequin (the Charles River), where the Pequossette band of the Massachusett Tribe used to build fish weirs to catch the alewife that returned to the river from the ocean to spawn upstream.

Some of the stewardship that Snyder advocates has found expression in "green urbanism" and the biophilic city movement. "Biophilic cities," according to Marc Bekoff,

> . . . incorporate a variety of approaches: building green rooftops and green walls, planting native vegetation around homes and buildings, reducing the spatial footprint of buildings, implementing nighttime lights-out campaigns, restricting the use of highly reflective glass and glass facades that disorient birds, enforcing noise restrictions, and developing nature corridors where human and nonhuman animals can mingle freely.[257]

As we work to create such cities, we may find that the distinction between urban and rural will start to break down, as will the distinction between culture and nature, and we will be called upon to reimagine how all of us, both in cities and in the countryside, are, in different ways, woven into nature.

Bioregionalism

This process of reinhabiting our place and more deeply realizing our embeddedness in nature is one facet of bioregionalism, which, as Snyder explains, centers on "commitment to this continent *place by place*, in terms of biogeographical regions and watersheds. It calls us to see our country in terms of its landforms, plant life, weather patterns, and seasonal changes—its whole natural history before the net of political jurisdiction was cast over it."[258] I identify with the Quinobequin/Charles River watershed and participate in the activities of the Charles River Watershed Association. To be a member of a bioregional natural community, according to David Korten, one should seek not only to benefit from it but to contribute to it:

> Earth's biosphere localizes decision making by segmenting itself into self-reliant, self-regenerative bioregional

communities, each engaged in the constant locally self-reliant capture, sharing, reuse, and regeneration of locally available nutrients, energy and water to maintain the health and vitality of all its resident organisms. Each community member contributes; each in turn benefits.[259]

For us humans, this contribution can take such forms as removing invasive species, protecting forests, creating wildlife corridors, and getting plastic trash out of streams. Mishy and I have participated in actions organized by the Charles River Watershed Association on Earth Day, such as picking up plastic in and alongside Quinobequin. With people contributing in these and other ways, bioregionalism gives prominence to "[w]atershed imagining, bioregional ideas of governance, the actual existence of communities that include the nonhuman in their embrace, dreams of ecological justice, and the faint possibility of long-term sustainable land and culture. . . ."[260]

Despite Snyder's focus on taking action locally, he does not advocate focusing exclusively on one's home region. We should not get stuck in a parochial bubble, with our focus, concern, and action only extending to our regional surroundings. Snyder writes, "No one ever said that the old bioregional slogan 'don't move' means you can't go on trips"; instead, we are now called "to be ecologically and culturally cosmopolitan, hip to the plant and weather zones of the whole world, as well as to those of cuisine and architecture."[261] In other words, while grounding ourselves in our local places, we can be cosmopolitan as well, tracking and responding to what's going on around the world. Granted, rising sea levels, droughts, and agricultural breakdown are making it hard for some of us to remain in our places, and in this way climate disruption is presenting huge challenges to (re)inhabiting certain locations.

Responding to Snyder's call for reinhabitation can benefit us in multiple ways. If we reinhabit our place, we reap the physical and psychological fruits of getting our bodies outside and more in touch with nature. Regardless of our place—Montana or Manhattan—by reinhabitating, we also gain an understanding of how we arise together with, and are affected by, local natural processes. We may even come to feel a deep connection, if not an identity, with our place. Scott Sanders describes this as being "firmly grounded—in household and community, in knowledge of place, in awareness of nature, and in contact with that source from which all things arise."[262] In this respect, reinhabiting the places where we live helps us realize that we are part of something larger, a realization that many see as the hallmark of "spirituality."[263] In Buddhist terms, through reinhabitation we can deepen our realization of how we are indeed part of something larger, how our local place exists in a vast network of conditioned arising. This realization fosters the wisdom that liberates us from ignorance and, by extension, from suffering.

Over time, this intimacy with our place will lead us to cherish or even love it. From this love emerges an urge to take care of it. In this way, reinhabitation enables us to see more clearly what is happening in our place because of climate disruption, and pushes us to take effective action—locally, nationally, internationally—to protect that place. Moreover, the attention to what is happening locally also accords with what some have argued is an effective way to wake people up to the climate crisis: helping them see its local effects—the droughts, fires, floods, warmer winters, and newly arrived insects in their bioregion.

The social dimension of reinhabitation—getting to know one's neighbors, working together with them to steward the land, mobilizing with them politically—also offers the benefit of feeling connected to others and discovering the satisfaction and happiness that come from social bonding. Moreover, as we all face the climate crisis, the sort of local community that Snyder sketches strikes me as an essential support for taking action to reduce the magnitude of the crisis (mitigation) and for developing the resilience needed to adjust to climate disruption (adaptation). In the next chapter, we will discuss the role of community in confronting the climate crisis.

PART V

Taking Action in Community with Others

9. Community

All I'm saying is simply this, that all life is interrelated,
that somehow we're caught in an inescapable network
of mutuality, tied in a single garment of destiny.
Whatever affects one directly affects all indirectly.
For some strange reason, I can never be what I ought
to be until you are what you ought to be. You can never
be what you ought to be until I am what I ought to be.
This is the interrelated structure of reality.
—MARTIN LUTHER KING JR.

AS WE SAW in the previous chapter, getting to know our neighbors and building local communities are core components of reinhabiting our places in a more regenerative and fulfilling way. In seeking to foster deeper connections with those around us, we should not limit our efforts only to other humans. We need to expand our sense of kinship to other inhabitants of the more-than-human world. In this chapter we will investigate the ways in which we can understand and honor our innate interconnectedness with other beings—plants, animals, and other humans—and how interconnectedness and community can empower us in our efforts to respond to the climate crisis.

EXPANDING OUR CIRCLE OF CONCERN

Expanding our circle of concern to include all the beings that share our world is crucial at this moment in time. When we pay attention to the damage caused by climate disruption—whether floods, fires, or droughts—our focus is usually on the damage done to humans, whether loss of life or loss of property. The media will report on these human consequences following fires and floods, but we rarely learn how many animals died. This summer, as fires erupted across Canada, I wondered how many owls, elk, and bears were killed or maimed. Then there's animal hunger and starvation as droughts impact plants. And animal diseases. Global warming has caused an uptick in avian malaria. Many animals are also suffering increased levels of heat stress. Because of recent higher temperatures in northern parts of the US and in southern Canada, a brain worm that is typically found in white-tailed deer but can cause a neurological disease in moose has increased in those areas and infected more moose.[264] Separate from climate disruption, we rarely hear news reports about how animals are affected by habitat destruction due to urban sprawl and deforestation.

So as we reflect on the suffering caused by the climate crisis, we need to ask ourselves whether our compassion encompasses the suffering of other-than-human animals beyond our beloved pets, the chickadees at our feeder, or the family of ducks crossing the street in front of our car. How often do we use our moral imagination to try to get a sense of what other animals—including those that are less cute than chickadees and ducks—are experiencing as climates get disrupted? Does our compassion extend to them? Do we care about and care for *all* of our fellow sentient beings, who also feel pain? When we make decisions, whether at the policy level or in our individual lives, do we take their pain and suffering—their interests—into consideration?

Given the Buddhist tradition's emphasis on loving-kindness—in effect, wanting sentient beings to be happy—and, on the flip side, compassion—wanting sentient beings not to be unhappy—we might expect Buddhists to be at the forefront of caring about animal suffering. However, Buddhists historically have had a limited understanding and mixed view of other animals.

As we have seen, a main concern of the Buddhist tradition is to help people extricate themselves from the delusion that they are a separate, enduring entity and from the dualistic mode of experience that accompanies this sense of self. This extrication is brought about by waking up to conditioned arising and, by extension, to the fact that the "self" exists as an ever-changing event that is getting shaped by other events. This process of deconstructing our normal sense of self can elicit experiences of non-separation that are spiritually liberating and can foster ecological insight into our embeddedness in nature, but the traditional focus is on the experiencer and their mode of experience rather than on the *content* of those experiences.[265] As a result, though Buddhists may see natural things around us—animals, trees, misty mountains—as events manifesting or *presencing* themselves and filling our emptied minds, historically they have offered little analysis of those things, apart from some basic classification schemes[266] and some debates about which other-than-human entities—sentient and non-sentient— have buddha nature.[267]

This lack of detailed examination of the natural world is one reason why Buddhist views of other animals over the past 2500 years have been a mixed bag. Buddhism has usually seen animals as fellow sentient beings who, just like us, are trapped within the continuous cycle of living, dying, and being reborn that is samsara. We see this fellow feeling expressed, for example, in a passage in the *Lankāvatāra Sūtra* that says, "In this world among the sentient beings living and dying in transmigration through this long course of time, it is not easy to find a being that has not been either one's own kindred or relative."[268] Eco-Buddhists have argued that the doctrine of transmigration, when coupled with the claim that all animals, as sentient beings, have buddha nature and hence the potential to awaken, establishes an intimate connection between humans and other animals, and this connection provides a basis for ascribing value—perhaps even intrinsic value—to animals. At the same time, however, the Buddhist tradition views animals as intellectually and morally inferior to us insofar as they cannot cultivate wisdom and are unable to restrain themselves from acting on desire and ill will. In Buddhist iconography, ignorance is represented by a pig, desire by a rooster, and ill will by a snake. Perhaps early Buddhists didn't know that pigs are actually intelligent animals. It's also interesting to note that once again in the realm of religions, snakes get a bad rap.[269] Be that as is it may, with animals having an inferior status, rebirth as an animal is seen as an unfortunate, unhappy state to which humans may be subject as a natural consequence of immoral actions that they have committed.

In traditional literature, such as the Jātaka Tales, Buddhism does ascribe such positive qualities as compassion, wisdom, and generosity to rabbits, monkeys, birds, and other animals. I assume that many of us would agree with this ascription. We may have experienced pets being attuned to what we are feeling, showing what seems to be compassion by nuzzling or cuddling when we're feeling depressed, and, as I often felt with my childhood cat Rusty, they may exude a kind of wise, observant calmness if not full-blown mindfulness. Perhaps the writers of the Jātaka Tales had picked up on these traits. Rafe Martin writes, "The Jatakas help us sense that animals have their own lives, their own karma, tests, purposes, and aspirations."[270] The virtuous animals in the stories, however, are usually said to be the Buddha in a past lifetime.[271] Hence these stories are not attempts to plumb the psyches of actual rabbits or monkeys and do not necessarily reflect human practices vis-à-vis those animals.

Buddhist valuation of animals does find expression in texts that advocate extending loving-kindness to them, but this practice is often advocated as a way to protect oneself *from* animals rather than as a way to express concern *for* them (or protect them from us!). And while early Buddhist texts do include calls to protect animals, and while vegetarianism is widespread in East Asian Mahāyāna monasticism, early Buddhism did not prohibit monastics from eating meat unless it was "seen, heard, or suspected" that the animal had been killed specifically to make a meritorious donation of meat to the monastic. Moreover, most lay Buddhists have not been vegetarians.

As a final example of the Buddhist tradition's mixed view of animals, although Buddhists have regarded other-than-human animals as "sentient beings," they lump them together in a distinct category of beings, as seen in the "six paths" scheme of rebirths where they are aggregated as *chikushō*, which we can translate from Japanese as "beasts," existing above the realm of hungry ghosts (*gaki*) but below that of humans. There are, however, several exceptions to this lumping: certain early texts give large animals greater moral standing than small animals, privileging certain species like elephants, and as we saw, denigrating pigs, roosters, and snakes by having them represent the three poisons in Buddhist iconography.

So, although Buddhism highlights certain animals in this way and takes the elimination of suffering as its central concern, most Buddhists have spent little time considering the exact nature of the sentience and suffering of specific animals. To enhance our understanding of and compassion toward other-than-human animals who are suffering because of climate disruption, we can take a closer look at animal sentience in dialogue with zoologists, Indigenous peoples, and animal-rights thinkers.

The Transformational Power of Being Present

Zen values our being present and caring in the moment. When we cultivate presence and sustain that presence in the open awareness of sky mind, we can pay greater attention to other things and beings presencing themselves around us and see them as worthy of our care and concern. By developing greater presence—on the meditation cushion or out in the woods—we can begin to realize facets of reality that we probably haven't noticed before. David Abram powerfully describes the transformative power of being present in *The Spell of the Sensuous* and *Becoming Animal*. When I first read Abram I was struck by statements he makes about presence. At one point he writes, "When I allow the past and the future to dissolve, imaginatively, into the immediacy of the present moment, then the 'present' itself expands to become an enveloping field of *presence*. And this presence, vibrant and alive, spontaneously assumes the precise shape and contour of the enveloping sensory landscape. . . ."[272] In these moments, Abram continues, "every perceivable being . . . seems to vibrate with life and sensation."[273] Abram's comments here about "this presence" being "vibrant and alive" and things seeming to "vibrate with life" are similar to what I tried to describe earlier with my comment about things presencing themselves in their vibratory suchness.

We can tune in to these expressive presences when we allow ourselves to be more fully present with ourselves and our surroundings. On a hike, if I slow down and pay close attention rather than exerting myself to reach a summit or complete a loop, I can more fully sense what is happening around me and experience things in their presencing "just as they are," whether a chipmunk scurrying between nurse logs, a hawk soaring on updrafts above a ridge, or a deer with whom I have momentarily locked eyes. I am also intrigued by Abram's statement: "In this open present, I am unable to isolate space from time, or vice versa. I am immersed in the world."[274] Or, to use language I've used: when I am presencing in my *embodiedness*, I can realize my *embeddedness* in nature.

Abram goes beyond this similarity to Zen in stating that when we are fully present we are engaging in "direct sensory interactions with the land around us," and, in this way, getting in touch with the "direct sensuous reality"[275] in which we exist. These comments have helped me realize that Zen talk of spaciousness and the mind getting filled by the myriad things as they presence themselves may give the false impression that the observing mind is an aloof consciousness that is passively observing things. But as Abram is pointing out, we experience the presencing of things through the five senses as we *engage* the world and sensory data fills our minds. We see the waves, hear their crashing, smell them, taste the salt on our lips, and feel the water moving our body—and through these sensory experiences, we are "filled" with the surf. Or perhaps it is better not to talk of a mind as some*thing* that is separate from and filled by those sensations. Rather, what we have here is the immediate *givenness* of sense experience, without our minds commenting or reacting.[276] We might even say that in this immediacy there is no mind, but simply direct bodily/sensory experience. And, to use Abram's words, in that "untheorized, spontaneous lived experience," we are operating in a "preconceptual . . . world"[277]—that is, in a realm of direct experience prior to the overlay of conceptual thinking. Moreover, "Our spontaneous experience of the world, charged with subjective, emotional, and intuitive content, remains the vital and dark ground of all our subjectivity."[278] I assume that most Zen teachers would agree that this experience is fundamental, a "dark ground" existing prior to (or, we might say, deeper than) our normal thinking and worrying, and in that sense it is "preconceptual."

This spontaneous experience is a fully embodied experience insofar as it happens in and through our senses, Abram writes, "If this body is my very presence in the world, if it is the body that alone enables me to enter into relations with other presences, if without these eyes, this voice, or these hands I would be unable to see, to taste, and to touch things, or to be touched by them—if without this body, in other words, there would be no possibility of experience—then the body itself is the true subject of experience."[279] Abram also joins Buddhism in not seeing the body as an entity that we possess apart from the world, for as he puts it in relation to one of his own experiences, "my body was not, properly speaking, mine, but rather a piece of the sensuous world."[280]

Of course, many of us are out of touch with "direct sensuous reality." We're usually stuck in dualistic modes of experience, as a "me" in here separate from the "not me" out there. Walking in the woods, we may be thinking about what we're seeing, like when we are racking our brains and thumbing through a field guide to identify wildflowers. We may not even be thinking about the forest, for we may be obsessing about problems back home, as I often do. Either way, we rarely feel our embeddedness in and dependence upon nature. Abram writes,

We may acknowledge, intellectually, our body's reliance
upon those plants and animals that we consume as nour-
ishment, yet the civilized mind still feels itself somehow
separate, autonomous, independent of the body and of
bodily nature in general. Only as we begin to notice and
to experience, once again, our immersion in the invisible
air do we start to recall what it is to be fully a part of this
world.[281]

I think I once got a taste of being "fully a part of this world" during
a weeklong retreat forty years ago at the Mount Baldy Zen Center
in the San Gabriel Mountains northeast of Los Angeles. One evening, about five days into the retreat, I was standing in the shadows on the edge of a dirt road that ran alongside the meditation
hall. Though the retreat, like most Zen retreats, had been emotion-
ally and physically challenging, in that moment I was feeling calm
and present. As I stood there silently breathing, immersed in the
"invisible air," a coyote came sauntering along from my right. She
or he passed about four feet in front of me, seemingly oblivious to
my presence as I stood there in the shadows. I've always wondered
whether it would have picked up on my standing there if my mind
had been agitated or filled with desire and ill will, leaving me ener-
getically apart from that world rather than folded into it. Or maybe
the coyote was aware of me but didn't perceive me as a threat or
perhaps found me boring and not worthy of a passing glance.
Either way, in that tranquil state I felt like I was blended in with my
surroundings, with "sensuous reality," "fully a part of this world."

EXPRESSIVE INTELLIGENCES

In any case, Abram goes on to argue that when we realize that we
are part of a sensuous reality, we discern that other things aren't
simply presenting themselves but *expressing* themselves. As far as I
know, the Zen tradition does not teach this. As recognized in Indigenous cultures, however, ". . . everything is expressive, a thunder-

storm no less than a hummingbird. To the animistic, oral sensibility, a cedar tree's hushed and whispered phrasings may be as eloquent as a spider's fine-spun patternings, or the collective polyphony of a pack of wolves."[282] When I'm out in the woods, if I see or hear another animal I often stop to observe and listen so I can get at least some sense of what that fellow is expressing as they live their life in the moment. And as I walk along, I, too, am expressing myself, with my clothes, gait, grunts, and scent. In short, "Here in the forest, all is body language."[283] Though I prefer to hike in silence, perhaps I'm expressing my particular human voice most distinctly when I groan, hum a favorite tune, or talk with a companion.

Paying close attention, we may also see why many Indigenous peoples claim that everything is not only expressing itself but doing so in its own language. Abram writes that oral traditions affirm "that the other animals have their own languages, and that even the rustling of leaves in an oak tree or an aspen grove is itself a kind of voice."[284] I sometimes wonder what, exactly, the cardinals are communicating with their distinctive calls in the maple tree outside our kitchen window, or what the squirrels are saying with their chattering as they encounter each other on the retaining wall along the driveway. Last summer, when I was out back harvesting some cherry tomatoes, a catbird landed in the garden about ten feet from me and started making all sorts of utterances, not just the kind of repetitive "chirp chirp" we might expect from birds. I really felt that it was talking to me, saying all sorts of things in a language I didn't understand.

Of course, the languages of other beings are not necessarily systems of high-order conceptual verbalizations. "To the fully embodied animal, *any* movement might be a gesture, and *any* sound may be a voice, a meaningful utterance of the world. And hence to my own creaturely flesh, as well, everything speaks!"[285] So as they chatter, what are the squirrels also conveying with their twitching tails? What might the knotweed shoots be expressing with their two inches of growth on a spring day? What expressions am I missing as I walk across the backyard? How oblivious am I? Though

most of us don't pick up on—or don't know how to pick up on—the
expressiveness all around us, "[t]he sense of inhabiting an articu-
late landscape—of dwelling within a community of expressive presences that are also attentive, and listening, to the meanings that
move between them—is common to indigenous, oral peoples on
every continent."[286]

Abram and the Indigenous traditions that he draws upon see
that expressiveness as rooted in intelligence. Abram realized this
through his close attention to spiders: "It was from them [spiders]
that I first learned of the intelligence that lurks in nonhuman nature,
the ability that an alien form of sentience has to echo one's own, to
instill a reverberation in oneself that temporally shatters habitual
ways of seeing and feeling. . . ."[287] Gary Snyder echoes Abram when
he writes that "each creature is a spirit with an intelligence as bril-
liant as our own."[288] As Snyder implies with his viewing each animal as "a spirit," this intelligence goes beyond sentience as simply
the ability to feel physical pain and the instinctual urge to avoid it.
A few years back I was struck by the intelligent skill with which a
cardinal built a nest in the Japanese maple off our back deck and
reared several hatchlings in it. I'm always impressed by ants car-
rying bits of food along a scent trail back to their nest. Like many
others, I was moved by the actions of the octopus in *My Octopus
Teacher*. And just this week, while watching several segments of *Spy
in the Ocean*, Mishy and I were amazed at the intelligence of whales,
crabs, and cuttlefish. I've found that when I glimpse the intelligence
of animals, my concern for them is immediately enhanced.

Some people have even regarded plants as having a kind of intelligence. Thich Nhat Hanh writes, "When we look deeply at a blade
of grass or at a tree, we can see that it's not mere matter. It has its
own kind of intelligence. For example, a seed knows how to grow
into a plant with roots, leaves, flowers, and fruit. A pine tree is not
just matter; it possesses a sense of knowing."[289] With this "sense
of knowing," the trees around us do sophisticated things: they
order matter and energy, they respond to stimuli (droughts, pests,

warmer winters), and they send warnings about insect threats by releasing chemicals that are detected by nearby trees. Thanks to Suzanne Simard, Peter Wohlleben, and Paul Stamets, many of us have recently become aware of "the hidden life of trees"[290] as they coexist with fungi in a "wood wide web."[291] Reading their books and watching their YouTube videos, I've become especially intrigued by how trees share nutrients through mycorrhizal networks and, in this sharing, may give preference to their offspring. And I've often stood in awe of how old trees have been doing their thing with calm dignity and without ego since before any of us was born. On a recent outing with students in the woods on the Stonehill campus, I found myself commenting on how older white pines had "experienced" many seasons and stood before us as "elders." At other times when I have been in forests, especially old-growth forests, I have felt that I am in a community of special beings, sensing and perhaps communicating with each other in ways I can't begin to comprehend.

Some botanists have also seen this intelligence as extending beyond individual trees. Simard writes, "I discovered that they are in a web of interdependence, linked by a system of underground channels, where they perceive and connect and relate with an ancient intricacy and wisdom that can no longer be denied,"[292] which has led her to speak of "the intelligence of the forest."[293] Similarly, Wohlleben writes, "It appears that nutrient exchange and helping neighbors in times of need is the rule, and this leads to the conclusion that forests are superorganisms with interconnections much like ant colonies."[294]

I can see why botanists attribute a kind of "intelligence" to trees, though I find it hard to proceed from there to attribute sentience to them (not that Simard and Wohlleben are doing so). For this reason, when I think about other-than-human suffering caused by climate disruption, I'm inclined to keep my focus on animals. And rather than being content with broad, generic affirmations of the sentience of animals, which may not lead to compassion or action to protect them, I follow Abram's lead and try to attend to the *particularity* of the animals around me: how different species and individual members of those species express themselves, communicate, seek mates, protect their young, mourn losses, intelligently secure food and safety, innovate, celebrate a beautiful day, and perhaps even play. By paying close attention to animals living their lives in nearby parks or wilder places—and yes, in documentaries—we can realize that the place we inhabit is also home to thousands of *animal societies*, with individuals in those communities trying to stay alive and, presumably, reach their full potential (and reproduce!). I recently did a guided meditation with a class of students that prompted them to reflect on how Stonehill College's 375-acre campus usually appears in their minds as buildings, sidewalks, and lawns where students do their thing, but how it is also the site of countless anthills, bee hives, crow families, and squirrel communities.

When we discern the active embodiment, expressiveness, language, and intelligence of other animals, we can better appreciate them as fellow sentient beings. Many of us have experienced this with our pets, which may lead us to feel a kinship with them, and perhaps even to see them as relatives. In this limited way, perhaps we're getting a glimpse of why some Indigenous peoples may refer to other-than-human beings as "all my relations." Insofar as we act in ways that support these beings' flourishing in biodiverse ecosystems and receive gifts from them, we exist in reciprocity with them. Some may even see the boundaries between these beings and ourselves breaking down, whether through shapeshifting or rebirth.[295] Snyder writes,

> [Indigenous Australians] live in a world of ongoing recurrence—comradeship with the landscape and continual exchanges of being and form and position; every person, animals, forces, all are related via a web of reincarnation—or rather, they are "interborn." It may well be that rebirth (or interbirth, for we are all actually mutually creating each other and all things while living) is the

objective fact of existence which we have not yet brought into conscious knowledge and practice.[296]

Though I find it hard to imagine literal reincarnation, I can go along with Snyder in his formulation of "interbirth," for it seems to be another way of expressing the conditioned arising or interbeing in which we are affecting—"mutually creating"—each other moment to moment as we live our lives.

THE GREAT EARTH SANGHA

When we recognize these features of our interrelationship with other-than-human animals, we can see how we live together with them in what Snyder calls the "Great Earth Sangha." David Barnhill writes, "We can call this the 'mythological, shamanistic community,' in which plants, animals, and humans are seen as part of an interactive social community."[297] Though it might be trivial compared to what Snyder is describing, the other day I realized how we humans interact with the red-tailed hawks nesting up in the woods on Palfrey Hill at the end of our block. Sloppiness in our neighbors' handling of garbage has led to an upsurge in the rat and squirrel populations, and this has provided prey for the hawks. In turn, their predation has helped me avoid running into rats when I take out the garbage.

In the expanded community of the Great Earth Sangha we realize that we are, as Snyder puts it, just "another being in the Big Watershed," and we, other people, and other animals "can accept each other as barefoot equals sleeping on the same ground,"[298] or, as I sometimes put it, peeing together in the woods. Similar to Snyder, the pioneering environmentalist Aldo Leopold spoke of the need for each of us to see ourselves as a "plain member and citizen" of the land-community.[299] Though I rarely experience this here at home, I feel this when I am out on the trail in the homes of other animals, and possibly part of the food chain (and not at the apex). Thomas Berry spoke of how we live in a community of subjects, not in a world of objects. I feel this when I encounter bears on the trail or talk with that catbird in our vegetable garden. With the intimacy that we discover in this community with other-than-human animals, we may hear "an occasional voice for the nonhuman rising within the human realm,"[300] and Snyder himself offers that voice: "My political position is to be a spokesman for wild nature."[301]

At the very least, however, we can realize that, like us, other animals are affected by the climate crisis and an array of other environmental problems, and that we humans need to secure a safe habitat for ourselves and our other-than-human kin. We may also realize that intimacy can be a mixed blessing: as warming, habitat loss, and urban sprawl bring humans and other animals closer together, viruses and bacteria will hop more frequently between us. Humans will suffer more zoonotic diseases, and animals will be on the receiving end when viruses like the coronavirus hop back to them in a variant form. In this respect as well, all of us animals—human, domesticated, and wild—are in it together.

This more holistic way of looking at our place in, and as, nature propounded by oral cultures, Abram, and Snyder, can help us go beyond traditional Buddhist views of animals. In particular, these more holistic frameworks can help us see other-than-human animals as kindred beings who are participating in this world—presencing themselves—with their own specific sentience, intelligence, and expressiveness.[302] This, in turn, grants us a more substantial basis on which we can, in the lingo of environmental ethics, grant certain animals moral standing as "moral patients" with "considerability," in the sense of having interests that need to be considered when we make decisions. This approach may even lead us to see them as "subjects of a life" [303] with purposes, a certain dignity and, by extension, certain rights or simply certain claims on us relative to how we treat them. This may even prompt us to see them as kin, similar to how they are seen by many Indigenous peoples and by Buddhists who regard animals as possible relatives from past lifetimes. It can also help us broaden our compassion beyond humans to all of the other-than-human animals who have been suffering in droughts, wildfires, and floods.

Engaging Abram's ideas can also help expand the Buddhist notion of conditioned arising. When Abram writes, "... each entity— earthworm, musk ox, thundercloud, cactus flower—is held within an interdependent lattice of relationships, a matrix of exchanges and reciprocities. . . ,"[304] he is not thinking simply of event-things interacting with each other but a "breathing landscape,"[305] an "inter- twined web of experience."[306] In recognizing this breathing matrix, Buddhists can expand their concept of conditioned arising beyond a network of event-things constituting or affecting each other—like all of the non-flower things that constitute a flower, to use Thich Nhat Hanh's example—to a network of experiences, of sentiences, of expressive intelligences.

A deeper engagement with the natural world and its inhabitants can also help expand Buddhist conceptions of how one cultivates and discerns the truth of interconnection, of interbeing. Buddhism has typically seen such insight as happening internally through meditation. Abram, however, looks to sensory experience as a source of that insight, saying,

> As we return to our senses, we gradually discover our sen- sory perceptions to be simply our part of a vast, interpen- etrating webwork of perceptions and sensations borne by countless other bodies—supported, that is, not just by ourselves, but by icy streams tumbling down granitic slopes, by owl wings and lichens, by the unseen, imper- turbable wind.[307]

As I wrote before on a parallel track, we can realize our embed- dedness in nature through our embodiedness, through the imme- diate sense experience our bodies give us. For starters, checking in with our five senses when we step outside can help us get out of our heads and into more direct contact with the world around us. Abram echoes this focus on embodiedness and embeddedness when he describes how, as we "return to our senses," we can also realize that we exist in "a world all alive, awake, and aware,"[308] which is "nothing other than the biosphere—the matrix of earthly life in which we are embedded."[309] The biosphere that Abrams describes is not some inert object of scientific study but, rather, "the biosphere as it is experienced and *lived from within* by the intelligent body—by the attentive human animal who is entirely a part of the world that he, or she, experiences."[310] When we live within the biosphere in this way, we can grasp the wisdom of conditioned arising in a more vivid and profound way than if we were to approach it only through formal meditation.

Recognition of this intertwining and reciprocity can help us attend more deeply to the biosphere around us, recognize what we humans are doing to it, and discern that our actions affect *all* animals, ourselves and our other-than-human relatives included. This recognition can enhance our care about, and care for, our world here in the midst of climate disruption. That is to say, this recognition, which can augment traditional Buddhist forms of insight and wisdom, can stimulate our compassion for other-than-human animals and prompt us to take greater action—such as working to mitigate climate change—to alleviate their suffering.

BUILDING HUMAN COMMUNITY

Appreciating and preserving the natural systems that support the web of life on this planet is not something to be done alone. At this critical point in history, we can't underestimate the importance of community. As studies have shown, and as we all know in our hearts, happiness derives largely from feeling connected to other people and being loved, valued, and respected by them. John Cobb writes that in contrast to the desiring, self-interested individual presupposed by mainstream economic theories,

> Most of us today believe (I am even inclined to say 'know') that human beings do not exist in isolation. We

are largely constituted by our social relations. The health
of the community in which we participate is crucial to our
own well-being. We are persons-in-community rather
than isolated individuals unaffected by our relations to
others.[311]

Similarly, the Buddhist doctrine of conditioned arising emphasizes
selfhood as relational and describes how we are constituted in and
through our relationships with others. As I stressed above, conditioned arising does not posit that we are born into the world as a
separate entity that secondarily enters into relationships with other
people and things but, rather, that we emerge through interrelationship as one facet of a nature-culture nexus. This view of human
selfhood realizes that none of us is a "self-made" person and that
we all depend on ecological and social supports, such as a clean
and safe environment, healthy food, adequate healthcare, nurturing families, good friends, personal safety, strong schools, and
other public services.

Maybe there are spiritual seekers who can find fulfillment living
an eremitic life in a cabin on a mountain, but for most of us, being
a hermit is a recipe for loneliness and, in some cases, insanity. Even
Kamo no Chōmei, a paragon of the Buddhist poet-hermit tradition,
wrote about his loneliness, and the renowned Zen recluse Ryōkan
regularly played hacky-sack with village children and enjoyed saké
with those who sought him out in the woods. And despite such her-
mits being sprinkled across Buddhist history, the dominant model
of Buddhist religious practice has been the sangha, whether a community of practitioners living together in a monastery or, more
recently, a group of people, often under the guidance of a teacher,
practicing together in a meditation center or home.

When I think about when I have felt most happy in my life, I
recall times when I was hanging out with friends—sitting with my
high school pals on a bench up on the green in Litchfield, Connecti-
cut, lingering around the dinner table at Tyler House when I was an
undergraduate at Williams College, going on outings with students

in Japan, relaxing with friends around fire pits back here in the United States. As I tell my students, in the last years of my life I'd rather be poor with loved ones around me than rich and all alone.

If we're going to rethink "rich," try to live in a fulfilling green way, and engage the climate crisis, we must recognize the importance of community, whether our family, circle of friends, neighborhood, religious congregation, or local environmental group. Feeling camaraderie strikes me as essential to sustaining our efforts to mitigate the crisis. If we get serious about changing our lifestyle, about simplifying our activities and staying off of airplanes, it will be hard to do this alone. We will need friends who are committed to rethinking wealth with us, especially if certain people step back from us when we don't want to fly off to the Caribbean together for a week on the beach, when we're told that our kids will be deprived if we don't take them to Orlando, or when naysayers portray simple living as deprived living, akin to being in a gulag, with exhausted, somber faces all around. Granted, in certain moments simple living can be austere, but when pursued as a spiritual path, it's the austerity of monastics, who talk of fulfillment far beyond any materialistic and frenetic way of living. And when we restrain ourselves from dealing with our angst by buying something online, heading to the mall, or booking a flight to Las Vegas, the feeling of deprivation can be handled by getting together with friends and sharing a meal, heading out on a walk, sitting by a fire, or making music together. This may be something done spontaneously. Show up at a neighbor-friend's door someday and say, "What are you doing? Do you want to come out and play? Let's go somewhere." This spontaneity may even bring surprises and joy. You don't have to bowl alone.

For me, the building of community starts with primary relationships. We commit to our relatives and other loved ones. We cultivate friendship with, as Buddhism puts it, "friends on the path,"[312] whether fellow Buddhists or close acquaintances. Whoever they are, the key is to build a community of loving, kindred spirits. It may just be a group of friends, or several overlapping groups. Either way, a great blessing is having an intimate community with whom we can share meals, milestones, traditions, seasons, good news, and yes, bad news.

The next circle of community may be our apartment building or neighborhood. The initial step here is getting to know people. From Snyder's perspective, people having strong bonds at this level "means that they know each other personally on a first-name basis; it means that they know a *considerable* amount of the personal history of the individuals concerned. . . ."[313] I find that knowing the names and stories of our neighbors here on Oliver Street gives me some comfort as I gaze into our uncertain future.

To foster connection with neighbors, we can talk with them on their stoops, go for walks together, hold block parties. We can share food, plants, tools, cars.[314] We can share information, whether out on the street or through social media.[315] Snyder writes, "The community: Sharing and creating. The inherent aptness of communal life—where large tools are owned jointly and used efficiently. The power of renunciation: If enough Americans refused to buy a new car for one given year, it would permanently alter the American economy. Recycling clothes and equipment. Support handicrafts, gardening, home skills, midwifery, herbs—all the things that can make us independent, beautiful and whole."[316] This community is, according to David Barnhill, "physical and mundane rather than industrial or technologically sophisticated."[317] Or as Snyder puts it, with its connection to a local place in all its specificity, this is "a *natural* community," and, "A natural community is a *culture*."[318]

By doing what Snyder advocates, we can invest in our neighborhood or town and secure a return on that investment: "Referred to as 'social capital,' the web of supportive relationships within a neighborhood is a form of wealth that improves the quality of our lives."[319] This notion of wealth accords with Sulak Sivaraksa's claim that an optimal society is attainable "to the degree that the people . . . [are] honest, moral, generous, tolerant, and confident . . . energetic, industrious, and skillful; live in a good environment; associate with good people; have a balanced livelihood; and direct themselves."[320] And in the challenging times ahead, we will need social capital and local self-direction in order to adapt to changing conditions.

The community I'm describing here is not just an arena for daily living or a springboard for taking action; it can also function as a support for our spirituality. Snyder writes, ". . . by being in a place, we get the largest sense of community. We learn that community is of spiritual benefit and health for everyone, that ongoing working relationships and shared concerns, music, poetry, and stories all evolve into the shared practice of a set of values, visions, and quests. That's what the spiritual path really is."[321] This view is a valuable counterweight to prevailing views of spirituality as an individual, inner experience divorced from society.

Of course, not all local communities are nurturing. Hence the importance of building new types of local communities. And even if some of us don't want to put time and energy into doing this, as we increasingly suffer the effects of climate change and transition beyond peak oil, we will be compelled to do so. As Bill McKibben puts it, "The project we're now undertaking—maintenance, graceful decline, hunkering down, holding on against the storm—requires a different scale. Instead of continents and vast nations, we need to think about states, about towns, about neighborhoods, about blocks."[322] Strong community at this local level will become increasingly valuable as we try to maintain connection and hope.

Bringing community into discussions of Buddhist environmental ethics can serve those of us green Buddhists who live comfortably with all of our needs and most of our wants met and slip into privileging wilderness over groups who have relied on wild places for food and other resources.[323] We must take their interests into account, and in this way ensure that we integrate environmental justice into our reflection and praxis.

To fully (re)inhabit our places and engage the climate crisis, we need to do more than foster community. We need to be stewards. In this regard, Snyder comments,

> Stewardship means, for most of us, find your place on the
> planet, dig in, and take responsibility from there—the tire-
> some but tangible work of school boards, county super-
> visors, local foresters—local politics. Even while holding
> in mind the largest scale of potential change. Get a sense
> of workable territory, learn about it, and start acting point
> by point.[324]

In taking this stance, Snyder is urging us to move beyond just getting our personal act together to getting involved; to shift from a
focus on individual lifestyle change to collective structural change;
from a limited focus on actions that make our way of living greener
to activism that makes our society greener and, ultimately, mitigates the climate crisis.

Before we consider this shift, we need to reflect on the relationship between Buddhism and activism and how Buddhist teachings
might be able to inform and enrich our efforts to confront and mitigate the climate crisis.

10. Buddhism and Activism

Whatever travails or transitions you are facing
in this moment, please remember: we were
made for these times.
—Kaira Jewel Lingo[325]

A strong community and the collaboration it affords can help us expand our focus beyond lifestyle change to structural change. In making this shift, we might wonder what Buddhism has to offer us in support of our efforts to confront economic and political conditions in our society. In this chapter we will look at how the Buddhist tradition might be able to inform and enrich climate activism. We will see that Buddhist teachings contain an implicit call to activism and that elements of Buddhism can support activists and activism. But before we consider how Buddhism can support and encourage efforts to challenge the status quo, we need to acknowledge the ways in which the Buddhist tradition has *avoided* challenging established power structures throughout its history.

The Conservative Nature of the Buddhist Tradition

Many of us who first encountered Buddhism in the 1960s embraced an image of the tradition as politically detached or even somewhat subversive. At the very least, most of us saw it as a religion of peace and nonviolence that would never collaborate with militarists or oppressive rulers. Hippies even imagined Zen Buddhists to be hermit tricksters who tweaked their noses at those in power. Self-immolations by Vietnamese monks gave the impression that Buddhism is radically activist. Historically, however, very few Buddhists have engaged in activism that challenges the social, political, and economic status quo of Asian societies. We can identify a variety of reasons for this.

To begin with, in early Buddhism and certain forms of the tradition today, nirvana has been construed to be a permanent state that transcends this world of impermanence and suffering. Accordingly, the ultimate goal lies above and beyond the natural world and the social, political, and economic arenas in which activists do their thing. This focus militates against trying to effect change in those arenas.

Moreover, for most of its history, Buddhism has focused on the suffering of individuals, not collectives, and the individual suffering on which it has focused is the existential or "religious" suffering caused by our entanglement in unhealthy mental states and entrapment in dualistic modes of experiencing rather than such "mundane" forms of suffering as poverty, discrimination, and violence. Granted, mundane or physical suffering is one of the three main types of suffering identified in Buddhist texts, but it gets overshadowed by concern about existential suffering. This concern has even led some Buddhists to argue that a focus on the transformation of society rather than on the purification of individual minds is misplaced.

Another factor that has worked against Buddhist activism is the idea that suffering is ubiquitous and afflicts people regardless of their socio-economic situation. "Historically," as Gary Snyder once wrote, "Buddhist philosophers have failed to analyze out the degree to which ignorance and suffering are caused or encouraged by social factors, considering fear-and-desire to be given facts of the human condition."[326] This failure has often been coupled with the stance that people can awaken in any and all circumstances. We see this in traditional Zen discourse that implies that one does not have to have all of one's needs met or live in a safe and just community or in a healthy ecosystem to wake up. Perhaps this is true, at least in principle, but in actuality I, as a privileged white male, do not face the obstacles that many others face as they try to secure the resources—access to the Dharma, good teachers, time to practice, retreats—supportive of following the Buddhist path.

A further hindrance to Buddhist activism is the deterministic view of karma. Zen ethicist Ichikawa Hakugen writes, "Differing social positions, abilities, and circumstances," from the perspective of most traditional Buddhists, "are the retributive fruits of good and bad actions in previous existences."[327] That is to say, Buddhist thinkers have explained, accepted, and even justified societal differences as the result of karma from past lifetimes,[328] and for this reason they have been less inclined to take action to change societal conditions. Granted, Buddhists have engaged in a range of charitable activities, but one is hard pressed to find historical instances in Buddhist societies of social concern expanding beyond charity to include efforts to bring about structural change that would eliminate the causes of the problems from which the recipients of charity suffer. Although B. R. Ambedkar's direct criticism of caste and Bhikkhu Buddhadasa's "Dhammic socialism" stand out as important exceptions to this pattern, Buddhist leaders have usually advocated acceptance of one's karmic lot and the performance of good deeds (such as giving alms to monks) as the way to better one's prospects in the future, usually a future lifetime.

Such acceptance gets exacerbated when Zen figures see the resolution of suffering as a kind of peace of mind secured by "according with circumstances" (J. nin-un). This view results in what Ichikawa refers to as "accommodationism" (junnō-shugi): accepting the status quo, with all of its socio-economic problems, rather than working to change it and create a society that embodies core Buddhist values. In the case of the climate crisis, Buddhism runs the risk of promoting a peace of mind in which we simply go with the flow and adjust to our changing climate. Those of us who are privileged and not as affected by the crisis need to be vigilant around this, especially if we tend to lie low in our comfort zones and focus on things other than the crisis, like work, family, sports, entertainment, and

consumption. I see this operating in myself—at least at a subconscious level—when I slip into passivity at times and simply muddle
through my days.

Such passive accommodation can find support in the Buddhist
celebration of humility, which encourages letting go of concern
about oneself and, by extension, not asserting one's self-interest or
personal rights. This value of humility has been accentuated by the
collectivist cultures in which Buddhism has flourished. In a related
vein, Buddhism also tends to pathologize anger, leaving little space
for any notion of the value of righteous anger. In most cases, this
celebration of humility and rejection of anger have led to an avoid-
ance of conflict and a rejection of violence, except when done by
people seen as protecting the Dharma.

Another reason Buddhists have not engaged in much activism is
the fact that for the past 2,500 years in Asia, Buddhist institutions
have—with few exceptions—existed in a symbiotic relationship
with the most powerful political institutions and actors (rulers,
merchants, military leaders) in their societies. The result is that
Buddhists have tended to lack the critical distance that is necessary for fostering criticism of the status quo in the manner of, for
example, biblical prophets. In the case of Japan, we see this sym-
biosis between Buddhism and worldly power conveyed by such
expressions as the "unity of the ruler's law and Buddha's law [the
Dharma]" (ōbō-buppō ichinyo) and "Buddhism for the protection of
the realm" (gokoku Bukkyō).

This coziness with ruling powers has fostered Buddhist nationalism, in which Buddhist leaders have advocated protecting the
Dharma by supporting the ruler who protects the Dharma and
by joining with the state in police and military endeavors against
others who are seen as threatening the Dharma, whether outsid-
ers or non-Buddhist minorities. This historical pattern is evident in
Buddhist collaboration with Japanese imperialism during World
War II,[329] Buddhists' violence against the Hindu Tamil minority
in Sri Lanka, and Buddhists' oppression of the Muslim Rohingya
minority in Burma.

This accommodation of the status quo combined with deterministic readings of the doctrine of karma have meant that few Buddhists have made arguments about social justice or taken steps to
secure it, at least in terms of distributive justice—though they have
allowed for *retributive* justice through the workings of karma. Here,
when I say "distributive justice" I am referring to equitable ways
of distributing the "goods" and "bads" in society, such as ensuring
that public funds support public schools equitably, or making sure
that toxic waste dumps are not created disproportionately in poorer
communities. Even contemporary "engaged Buddhists," while making strong and convincing arguments for reducing consumption
and pollution, have usually not given much attention to such distributive justice questions, such as who suffers the effects of climate
change the most or who should shoulder most of the burdens in
any solution to the crisis.

When it comes to activism to bring about such forms of structural change as restricting corporate influence on elected officials
and reducing the power of the fossil fuel industry, we encounter
one other limitation of Buddhism. To effect such structural changes,
a great many people will need to get involved and take action. Bill
McKibben has written,

> We need . . . increased engagement. Some of the engage-
> ment will be local: building the kind of communities and
> economics that can withstand what's coming. And some
> of it must be global: we must step up the fight to keep cli-
> mate change from getting even more powerfully out of
> control, and to try to protect those people most at risk,
> who are almost always those who have done the least to
> cause the problem.[330]

To succeed, this engagement will need to generate a mass movement, and most religions can play a role here insofar as they can
mobilize their adherents.[331] But with its numerous denominations
and cultural locations, Buddhism in general has been decentralized

if not splintered, which poses challenges to mobilizing people across the many forms and locales of the tradition.

Finally, we must recognize, as Amod Lele has done in a recent article, that contrary to the contemporary celebration of "engaged Buddhism," numerous Buddhist thinkers over the centuries have argued for *disengaged* Buddhism. Lele writes that "many revered Buddhist thinkers have not merely refrained from social engagement, they have actively discouraged it," seeing it as "unfruitful and even harmful."[332] This, too, has militated against activism.

As a result of these various hindrances to activism, the Buddhist tradition has offered few models for prophetic critique, nonviolent protest, and the kind of activism needed for structural change.

EXAMPLES OF BUDDHIST ENVIRONMENTAL ACTIVISM

Nevertheless, Buddhists around the world have started to take action in response to the climate crisis and other environmental problems. Buddhist institutions have made efforts to lower their carbon footprints while planting trees and managing forests. Though not explicitly a response to the climate crisis, monks in Southeast Asia have "ordained" trees to protect local forests from logging. Drawing heavily from Buddhism, Joanna Macy has addressed the climate crisis in her Work that Reconnects Network, envisioned as part of a cultural "Great Turning" toward ecological thinking and living. One Earth Sangha takes as its mission "expressing a Buddhist response to climate change and other threats to our home," and it has offered "The Ecosattva Training," described as "a course to cultivate wisdom, connection, and an unwavering response."[333] The Rocky Mountain Ecodharma Retreat Center in Colorado and the Eco-Dharma Centre in the Pyrenees have offered retreats and workshops for people wanting to engage the ecological crises before us.

Buddhists have crafted declarations about the climate crisis. In 2009 eco-Buddhists John Stanley, David Loy, and Gyurme Dorje edited *A Buddhist Response to the Climate Emergency*, which led to the formulation of an organization, Ecological Buddhism, and a declaration, "The Time to Act is Now: A Buddhist Declaration on Climate Change"; this declaration was delivered in May 2015 to the Obama Administration by the first-ever Buddhist delegation to the White House. Another group of Buddhists, many of whom are connected to Spirit Rock Meditation Center, founded the Dharma Teachers International Collaborative on Climate Change in 2013 and issued a declaration of their own: "The Earth is My Witness." In the months leading up to the 2015 climate conference in Paris, the Dalai Lama, Thich Nhat Hanh, and other Buddhist leaders signed the "Buddhist Climate Change Statement to World Leaders." In April 2016 a group of Zen teachers issued "A Western Soto Zen Statement on the Climate Crisis."

In addition to the ecological precepts I discussed earlier, Buddhists have also crafted new practices, including the "earth relief ceremony" performed by the Zen Center of Rochester, a ritual memorializing plants and animals that have died in the gardens of Green Gulch Farm, and retreats led by Thich Nhat Hanh for environmentalists. Buddhists have created new chants, prayers, and verses. Thich Nhat Hanh has crafted "earth gathas,"[334] one of which reads,

> In this plate of food,
> I see the entire universe
> supporting my existence.[335]

Joanna Macy started the Nuclear Guardianship Project as a way to deal with toxic nuclear waste, and together with John Seed, she created the Council of All Beings, in which participants speak for animals, plants, and inorganic things affected by destructive human actions. Such Buddhist institutions as Zen Mountain Monastery in the Catskills, San Francisco Zen Center's Green Gulch Farm, Zen Mountain Center in southern California, Spirit Rock Meditation Center in northern California, and the Barre Center for Buddhist

Studies in Massachusetts have taken steps to make themselves into green communities.

One Earth Dharma, EcoBuddhism, and the Buddhist Peace Fellowship have made use of websites, blogs, and social media to promote discussion, education, and collaboration around environmental problems. These groups are pan-Buddhist and based more in cyberspace than in particular denominations, temples, or locations, and hence their praxis is trans-sectarian and trans-local.

A range of other Buddhist organizations and institutions have been offering additional responses to environmental issues, including the International Network of Engaged Buddhists (led by Sulak Sivaraksa), the Earth Holder Community (part of Thich Nhat Hanh's sangha), Ordinary Dharma, Green Sangha, the Zen Environmental Studies Institute at Zen Mountain Monastery in New York State, as well as the Ikeda Center for Peace, Learning, and Dialogue in Boston, Wonderwell Mountain Refuge in New Hampshire, the Sarvodaya Movement in Sri Lanka, the Tesi Environmental Awareness Movement in Tibet (also known as Eco-Tibet), and the headquarters of Sōtō Zen Buddhism in Japan. Complementing a range of writings on "Buddhist economics," the Bhutanese have adopted a novel economic indicator, Gross National Happiness, which takes into account the degree of just and sustainable development there.

Some Buddhists joined across sectarian divisions in 2015 to form the Buddhist Climate Action Network, though this online group has since disbanded, leaving a statement on their Facebook page:

> Now there are a number of vibrant, rapidly growing social movement organizations working valiantly to sustain our collective future and broadly embracing values of non-violence and mindful action. We've recently come to the conclusion that a larger contribution can be made by joining and supporting these dynamic groups rather than by putting our energy into independently organizing relatively small numbers of Buddhist practitioners.[336]

Along the lines of what the Network advocates, individual Buddhists have participated in environmental groups, protests, climate marches, decarbonization initiatives, and other responses to the climate crisis that were not initiated by Buddhists.

This may be the biggest impact Buddhism will have on the climate crisis: a large number of individual Buddhists getting engaged in activism through non-Buddhist organizations and actions that are making a difference. As I will sketch in the next chapter, this is what I have been doing. If the core focus of Buddhism is reducing suffering, getting involved in non-Buddhist organizations and making a difference constitutes a response to the climate crisis that is genuinely Buddhist. That is to say, Buddhist activists do not need to create an organization of their own, unless such an organization can prove more impactful—can reduce more suffering—than existing environmental groups.

A Buddhist Case for Climate Activism

So what do we make of this? If we are Buddhists, do we have an obligation to get involved in one or more of these ways? Can we make a Buddhist case for engaging in activism? Would activism distract us from the core Buddhist path, perhaps even dilute it? If Buddhists do engage in activism, should their focus and actions take a uniquely Buddhist form? And how might Buddhism support the efforts of activists—both Buddhist and non-Buddhist?

If we consider core Buddhist values and commitments, we can make a Buddhist case for getting involved in activism. First, as we saw before, the suffering that the Buddha attempted to alleviate is not limited to existential suffering but includes physical suffering, as experienced by those who are sick, hungry, and on the receiving end of violence. Alleviating physical suffering hence falls within the scope of normative Buddhist concern.

Even if we focus primarily on existential suffering, we need to recognize that the specific contours of that suffering are shaped by social and economic conditions. Though Buddhists have often discussed existential suffering as something universal (if not uniform), the mental anguish of a secure white male like me is different from that of people who are continually in a state of insecurity, whether worrying about their personal safety or struggling to find healthy food and pay bills. As a result, any skillful means of remedying suffering needs to take into account how the suffering of individual people *takes particular forms in particular sets of conditions* and then to respond to those conditions, not just to the individual in isolation.

Social conditions not only play a role in causing suffering but affect our ability to ameliorate it. Reginald Ray writes, ". . . as Buddhism throughout its history affirms, the health, safety, well-being, and sanity of one's life situation often determines one's ability to follow the path."[337] Having healthy food, medical care, personal safety, access to a sangha with good teachers—or simply to the Dharma through books and podcasts—and time to practice the Dharma is integral to reducing our suffering, and for a variety of social, political, and economic reasons some people don't have those requisites.[338] Needless to say, it is also hard to practice if one's community is constantly plagued with violence, wildfires, or flooding.

Because certain social conditions both play a role in causing "mundane" physical suffering and affect our ability to remedy it, our analyzing, criticizing, and offering alternatives to those social conditions falls squarely within the "proper" purview of Buddhism. Despite all of the historical factors militating against Buddhist social activism, stepping up and taking action to create these alternatives through structural change is what we would expect a buddha or a bodhisattva to do at this historical moment. I would even argue that working to construct an alternative society is a necessary but overlooked part of the perfected conduct of a bodhisattva. And not just bodhisattvas, for all Buddhists are called on to act with wisdom and compassion to reduce suffering.[339] The first line of the Fourfold Great Vow reads, "However innumerable suffering beings are, I vow to liberate them," and in this way we are all called to be bodhisattvas, or at least to do our best to reduce suffering. The climate crisis is causing immense suffering, and actively responding to it is one way to fulfill the Fourfold Great Vow.

Though most of us would resist seeing ourselves as bodhisatt-vas (it does come across as a bit grandiose), the way of living I'm sketching here can free us up to engage the climate crisis. Slowing down and paying attention can help us extricate ourselves from the freneticism and distraction that leads to ignor-ance, while declutter-ing our lives can open up time to respond to the crisis. The calming and presencing cultivated in meditation provide a remedy for the paralyzing effects of eco-anxiety and can provide a psychological and spiritual foundation that enables us to stay present with what is happening around us. Progressively realizing the truth of inter-connection—whether through meditative insight or absorption in Buddhist teachings—enhances our awareness of the causes of our predicament. This realization also leads to greater awareness of our impact on the world, and insofar as it has been cultivated together with compassion and non-harming, this realization can generate a greater sense of responsibility in both senses of the term (account-ability for our actions and the obligation to take care of someone or something).

These realizations of interconnection and responsibility gained through Buddhist practice can provide a basis on which we can take action. We should not, however, view this action as some sort of appendage tacked onto Buddhism. Again, if the goal of Buddhism is the alleviation of suffering in its various forms, including the suf-fering that is being caused by climate disruption, Buddhists have an implicit duty to act to reduce suffering. In this respect, Buddhist ethics are reminiscent of Immanuel Kant's deontological ethics. The Greek term *deon* means "duty," and Kant argued that the most ethical people feel a sense of duty to do the right thing, not because doing so will serve their interests or have other good consequences but simply because it is the right thing to do. At this point, one right thing to do is to take action to mitigate climate disruption and the suffering it's causing. When considering what that action might be, most of us will try to figure out which actions will have the largest positive impact, perhaps understood as the greatest mitigation of global warming and, by extension, the greatest net alleviation of climate suffering for the greatest number of sentient beings. This ethical approach resonates with utilitarianism and its cost-benefit analyses. As we saw before, Buddhists can also cultivate mental states that reduce their ecological impact and support their taking action, and these mental states include contentment, generosity, mindfulness, perseverance, and compassion. In this respect, Buddhism, like Aristotle, offers a helpful virtue ethic.

And just as Buddhist practice can support our activism, activism can help us cultivate the virtuous mental states that the Buddhist path prescribes. When we engage in activism, we are giving our time, energy, expertise, and talents—often over long periods of time—and in this respect, activism provides an opportunity to cultivate generosity. Activism is also a way to put compassion into action and thereby move beyond simply *feeling* concern to *actively caring* for others and the environment. Often rendered in English as "compassion," the Sanskrit term *karuṇā* does not refer simply to feeling the pain of others (com-passion) but also to taking action to mitigate it. This is why, as we saw earlier, some Buddhists prefer to translate *karuṇā* as "caring," which connotes both being concerned (caring *about* others) and taking action to help them (caring *for* others). If we engage in climate activism as a way to extend loving-kindness and compassion to humans, other animals, plants, and perhaps even ecosystems, that activism becomes a way to cultivate these mental states in ourselves and thereby reduce our ill will. In the process of caring for others through climate activism, we can realize another personal benefit: we can stop focusing only on our own personal problems and experience the gratification that comes from helping others. In these ways, serving others serves oneself, something Buddhism has recognized over the centuries.

Activism also parallels and supports another Buddhist practice: letting go of attachments. Engaging in activism is a way to free ourselves of self-preoccupation and our ego's desire to hold back and hunker down in a castle of apparent security. By stepping out of our comfort zone to take action, we also learn what scares us, whether it's conflict, getting arrested, losing our job, or getting criticized by our neighbors. In this way, activism holds up a mirror to us as we work on our attachments and fears.

In this hyper-individualized society, many of us feel isolated and powerless to make a difference. Taking action with others to lobby for a carbon fee or protest a pipeline can help us experience camaraderie in a community of kindred spirits and the empowerment that typically comes from being part of a movement. We can conspire and *con-spire*—"breathe together"—with our activist group, which can function as a kind of sangha within this dimension of our Buddhist practice. Moreover, the kind of local networks fostered by civic engagement and activism will be increasingly important going forward as the challenges get bigger and economic activity becomes increasingly decentralized.

Educating ourselves about our situation and engaging in activism also helps us realize the truth of conditioned arising—of interbeing—not just at the micro-level of our individual psyches and the food on our plate but at the macro level of collaboration aimed at mitigating the problem and economic systems causing the problem. Describing the benefits of such collaboration, Macy and Johnstone write, "When we share our cause with others, allies appear; synergy occurs. And when we act for causes larger than ourselves, the larger community for whom we do this will be acting through us."[340] This larger community includes, I might add, the more-than-human world. Moreover, as we take action on the basis of this deeper knowledge of interbeing at various levels, we can engage in our activism as a way to express gratitude to this world that has birthed and nurtured us.

Taking action also helps us avoid a downside of passivity. Not taking action in response to the climate crisis can leave us with doubts about ourselves, or at least with eroded self-esteem, which can contribute to thoughts such as "If even I, someone who knows about the problem, am not doing anything significant, we really are doomed." By getting involved and "walking the talk," we can overcome our inertia—in Buddhist terms, *thīna-middha*, sloth-and-torpor, one of the five hindrances. And by taking action we also discover a sense of integrity as someone who acted rather than retreated into self-indulgence and distraction. This sense of integrity can empower us over the long haul. By taking action, we can also avoid the guilt of not having done more as well as the shame in the future when our grandchildren ask us why we didn't do more.

Activism supports us on the path in one other way. I've noticed that changing my lifestyle and getting politically involved—even to a minor extent—is also a good antidote to depression and despair. When I cut back on meat, fly less, buy fewer unnecessary things, and work with environmental groups, I lessen the sense of gloom and doom I often feel in the night when I can't sleep. Katherine Hayhoe writes, "It's a true positive feedback cycle. When we feel empowered to act, individually and communally, that makes us not only more *likely* to act, but to support others who do. . . . It also inoculates us against despair: young people who are anxious about climate change, one survey found, aren't paralyzed by it if they are able to act."[341] Taking action not only diminishes "negative" feelings like despair but fosters an array of "positive" feelings. Marianne Krasny writes, "For some, the climate crisis is leading to depression, paralysis, and despair. Taking action, especially with others, may counteract paralysis by instilling feelings of agency, purpose, hope, and connection."[342] As Katharine Hayhoe realized after installing solar panels, "Yes, solar panels cut my carbon emissions, but they also make me feel empowered, as if what I do matters. They gave me a sense of *efficacy*."[343] I, too, find that becoming more engaged fosters these feelings of agency and efficacy. It also helps me feel hope.

At times, I've been skeptical of celebrations of hope in relation to the climate crisis and other large challenges, thinking that hope often devolves into a passive feeling that something good will happen because of actions by others or forces beyond our control. I am struck, however, by how Joanna Macy and Chris Johnstone have described "Active Hope":

> Active Hope is waking up to the beauty of life on whose
> behalf we can act. . . . With Active Hope we realize that
> there are adventures in store, strengths to discover, and
> comrades to link arms with. Active Hope is a readiness
> to engage. Active Hope is a readiness to discover the
> strengths in ourselves and in others, a readiness to dis-
> cover the reasons for hope and the occasions for love.[344]

Macy and Johnstone are careful to explain that this hope is not
something we *have* but something we *do*, and this doing consists of
three steps: "First we start from where we are by taking a clear view
of reality, acknowledging what we see and how we feel. Second, we
identify what we hope for in terms of the direction we'd like things
to move in or the values we'd like to see expressed. And third, we
take steps to move ourselves or our situation in that direction."[345]

When I act without attachment to outcome but with confidence
that my actions will reduce at least some suffering even if they
won't necessarily solve the larger problem, and when I do so with
an "I-don't-know mind" that recognizes that my actions may have
impacts I can't imagine, I feel hopeful. Along these lines, I appreciate
Thomas Homer-Dixon's distinction between "'hope that,' which is a
passive and timid locution, and 'hope to,' which is active and bold—a
difference that bears crucially on the issue of our agency as we try
to deal with humanity's problems."[346] He continues, "[w]e need to
turn our hope THAT the desired future will happen into a hope TO
make it happen."[347] And though the possibility of the needed structural changes may seem small when we consider the power of the
fossil fuel industry and our society's attachment to a carbon-dense
way of living, the chaos in which we find ourselves these days may
allow for dramatic changes. Madeline Ostrander writes that "a time
of unruliness is also a moment of rearrangement—there can be sudden shifts in who holds sway and what people value."[348]

More broadly, taking action contributes to a sense of satisfaction: "First, when we act in alignment with our deepest values,
we experience an inner sense of rightness behind what we do.

Second, when we apply ourselves to facing a challenge in a way that absorbs our attention, we are more likely to go into the flow states that psychologists like Mihaly Csikszentmihalyi have linked so strongly to life satisfaction."[349] Taking action can also give us a sense of purpose and meaning in our lives. Christiana Figueres and Tom Rivett-Carnac write, "When your mind tells you that this is all too depressing to deal with and that it is better to focus on the things you can directly affect, remind yourself that mobilizing for big generational challenges can be thrilling and can imbue your life with meaning and connection."[350]

In all of these respects, activism can be an extension of the Buddhist path, not a distraction from pursuing that path, as some Buddhist teachers have claimed with statements like "You can't liberate the world from suffering until you liberate yourself, so focus on your individual practice and deal with societal problems after you wake up." Our activism can reduce suffering and promote the common good. It also can give us a sense of living a life of meaning and purpose. And so, as I've been saying, living ecologically and engaging in activism is not a miserable endeavor in which we have to sacrifice our happiness but a way to find a deeper fulfillment.

Once a Buddhist becomes involved in activism, their tradition can support them. Stephanie Kaza has laid out five Buddhist teachings that activists can draw upon:

1. The tradition's "relational understanding of interdependence [conditioned arising] and no-self," through which, for example, we can assess "the relationships of the players in an environmental conflict from a context of historical and geographical causes and conditions" as well as the distribution of power across those relationships.
2. The teachings on non-harming and compassion, which can prompt activists to recognize not only the oppression of humans but the oppression of things in the more-than-human world.

3. The "non-dualistic view of reality," which can keep activists from slipping into an adversarial us-vs-them approach to perceived enemies and can help to "stabilize a volatile situation and establish new grounds for negotiation."

4. The Buddhist emphasis on intention and its effect on actions and their karmic consequences, which can help activists avoid launching their campaigns "out of spite, revenge, or rage."[351]

5. A focus on "detachment from the ego-centering self," which frees activists from attachment to their identity and opinions and from their attachment to the attainment of certain results.[352]

In addition to these five areas, I would add the ways in which Buddhism can help us cultivate presence as a foundation for facing the climate crisis. Practices such as seated meditation can equip us with the patience and perseverance needed for sustained activism and thereby help us avoid the burnout that plagues so many committed activists. And insofar as it cultivates loving-kindness and compassion, Buddhist practice can help us approach the crisis from a place of love that avoids demonizing others and deepens our care for suffering beings, human and other-than-human alike.

We can find yet another Buddhist support of activism in the teachings on bodhicitta, the "mind of awakening" that aspires to liberate all suffering beings. Joanna Macy and Chris Johnstone describe bodhicitta as "the deep desire to act for the welfare of all beings. When we feel this strongly in our hearts, it acts as our foundation stone, something we can count on, whatever else is happening."[353] Macy and Johnstone echo other key elements in the Buddhist path when they write, "By strengthening compassion, we give fuel to our courage and determination. By refreshing our sense of belonging to the world, we widen the web of relationships that nourishes us and protects us from burnout."[354] I am struck by their reference to courage. Buddhists typically do not talk much about courage, but we need it as we speak truth to power, face blowback from powerful interests, and possibly aggravate loved ones and neighbors. Another way to put it is to say that we need to cultivate non-fear. Kaira Jewel Lingo writes,

> Not-self means we are empty of a separate self, but full of everything else.... With the insight of not-self, we neither chase after pleasure or fame, nor fear pain or disrepute, because we know we are larger than these forces and they can't define us. This non-fear is what gives people courage to make big sacrifices and take incredible risks, knowing we are acting on behalf of the whole, and that our actions will still have an impact even if we, in our small selves, will not be there to see it.[355]

Recognizing how my own fear or dread can immobilize me, and how I succumb to doubting whether my efforts will have any significant impact, I find these words inspiring.

Of course, if and when these words or other factors inspire us to act, we have to address a question: What actions can we take to mitigate the climate crisis?

11. Taking Action

If we can begin to act with genuine compassion for
all, we still have a window of opportunity to protect
each other and our natural environment.
—DALAI LAMA XIV[356]

I see the great adventure of our time as not losing
heart or going crazy but regaining humanity in the
course of fighting for a planet where our children's
children can flourish.
—SUSAN MURPHY[357]

THE COMPLEXITY and magnitude of the climate crisis is daunting. At times, I feel like I'm living in a dystopian science fiction
movie. It's getting harder and harder to feel hope. I often doubt that
I can have any sort of impact on the problem: I'm just one person.
I'm not an elected official with the ability to effect policy change.
I'm not a wealthy lawyer who might have the contacts, expertise,
and means to move the needle. And even if I were, the power of the
fossil fuel industry is immense and entrenched.

However, probably like you, I feel called to act. But even with this
urge, figuring out what, exactly, to do is daunting. Myriad groups
are working to reduce emissions and sequester carbon. Which is
most effective: a famous environmental organization like Green-
peace or the Sierra Club, a group like Bill McKibben's 350.org with a
focus on all facets of the climate crisis, or a group like Citizens' Climate Lobby, with a narrower focus on lobbying Congress to pass

a revenue-neutral carbon-fee-and-dividend program? Should my focus be local, regional, national, or international? Where should I direct my efforts?

A Foundation for Taking Action

In my attempts to see the crisis clearly, hold the anxiety, and take action, I've found that cultivating a psychological foundation has been helpful. One cornerstone in that foundation is my practice of zazen. As I shared earlier, it centers on pouring myself into the simple act of breathing, settling down, opening sky mind, and being present. Meditative practices like this help us stay centered and maintain our focus rather than getting rattled and averting our gaze. They can also help us deal more calmly and effectively with what's happening around us—even if that's simply figuring out how to get a good heat pump installed.

Spaciousness is the second cornerstone. As much as possible, I try to slow down and keep space in my day so I'm not hurrying and feeling stressed out by the "not enough time" mindset. This way I can be more fully in my body, in my senses, in the moment, and able to care for other beings and savor the little things as I move through the day. With this spaciousness I am more able to be creative and try new approaches to greening my way of life or effecting structural change. And needless to say, when things feel spacious it's easier to add activism to my cluster of daily routines.

The third cornerstone is getting outside. Walking, hiking, bodyboarding, and open-water swimming help me de-stress, in large part, I assume, because of the vigorous movement of my body and the endorphins it triggers. Needless to say, these activities are good for my physical health, too, which will serve my efforts over time. As I plug into my sense experience during these activities, I can better realize my embeddedness in nature. By paying attention to what is around me, I can appreciate it and savor its beauty. I may feel awe and wonder. And perhaps even love. This love for our beautiful world—not fear and disturbing data—is what gets me out of depression and into action.

Connection to others is the fourth cornerstone. First and foremost is having a loving and supportive partner, family, and/or group of friends. Beyond cultivating these primary relationships, it is also important to move out into the next concentric ring of our social circle: getting to know other people, helping each other, exchanging information, and collaborating. In this way we can feel less isolation and more solidarity. Being part of an active community can also reduce our climate anxiety and give us the strength, joy, and hope that comes through camaraderie. This can sustain us in our efforts over the long haul to mitigate the crisis and transform the systems that cause it.

These four corners of my foundation—meditation, spaciousness, getting outside, and social connection—serve me on my Buddhist path as well, as they center on meditation and spaciousness, deepen my realization of how I am interconnected with nature and people around me, and grant me a supportive community—a sangha of sorts. And it is upon such a foundation that I take action, which, in turn, serves as an antidote to despair. Perhaps you have a foundation of your own, based on your faith, your centering practices, your way of feeling connected to something larger than yourself.

Changes We Can Make as Individuals

Regardless of the foundation on which we base ourselves, what actions can we take? A good place to start is our individual lives, for we have more control over actions and their consequences at that level. From there, we can move on to activism directed toward structural change.

As a first step, we can perform actions—or stop doing certain actions—to reduce our environmental impact. This will vary from person to person, depending on whether we own or rent a property (unless we are unhoused), whether it is a single-family dwelling or an apartment, and whether we have access to healthy food, clean energy, and public transportation. But here is a list of possible actions, many of which my students at Stonehill College have suggested in recent years.

- Reduce or (ideally) eliminate our consumption of meat. This not only reduces our carbon footprint but decreases animal suffering and improves our health.
- Try to be a locavore to reduce the farm-to-table carbon footprint of our food; this may take such forms as shopping at a farmers market or buying a share in an organic CSA (community supported agriculture) if we have access to one.
- If possible, grow some of our own food.
- Reduce food waste.
- Avoid plastic single-use items (plastic straws) and buy reusable items such as reusable straws and refillable water bottles.
- Buy durable products and avoid fast fashion—and fast food.
- Stay off of airplanes as much as possible.
- Use public transportation as much as possible.
- Consider ride sharing (carpools) and vehicle sharing.
- If having a personal vehicle is necessary, buy an electric or fuel-efficient vehicle (but first investigate how to keep our current vehicle from ending up in a junkyard).
- If still using gas, drive 20 percent slower on freeways for better fuel efficiency.
- Get an energy audit for our home.
- Install energy efficient windows and add insulation to outer walls if needed.
- Use only electricity generated without carbon, perhaps by wind farms or solar panels on our roof.
- Figure out how to heat our homes without using fossil fuels, perhaps by using a geothermal or air-source heat pump that runs on clean electricity.
- If our electricity and heating are not free from fossil fuels,

turn down the heat in the winter and wear warm layers, raise the set temperature if using air conditioning, use LED light bulbs, turn off lights when they're not needed, and turn off power strips when we go away.

- Dry at least some of our clothes on a clothesline.
- If we have to travel and stay in a hotel, stay in a green hotel.
- Practice right livelihood by not working for or investing in companies and institutions that play significant roles in causing or exacerbating the climate crisis.
- Try to practice the Five Rs: reduce, reuse, repair, rot, recycle.

This list is just for starters. I encourage you to take some time and think of what else you would add to this list.

The most important thing is to *do something*. Try to do at least one or two of these at first. Make them a practice. You may find that over time they'll become habitual and you'll no longer have to remind yourself or make a special effort to do them.

These actions also provide an immediate benefit to us in supporting our spiritual path. They call on us to slow down and pay attention, to keep certain guidelines in mind (mindfulness!), to restrain our desires, and to simplify. They are all based on the first precept—to avoid harming others—and our efforts to make this non-harming a core value and commitment. In this respect, we might even ground them in a vow: "I vow to do no unnecessary harm." Ideally, we will do these actions in collaboration with others who are making the same efforts, and thereby support each other and cultivate "friends on the path."

BECOMING MORE ENGAGED IN CLIMATE ACTIVISM

While greening our lifestyle in these ways, we can also get involved in activism. From the outset, it's good to realize that we don't all need to do something dramatic or groundbreaking. We don't all have to start organizations like Bill McKibben did or write incisive best-sellers like Naomi Klein does. We can simply take steps, regardless of their size. Along these lines, I've benefited from an article that I use in my teaching: "How to Stop Freaking Out and Tackle Climate Change." The author, Emma Marris, offers a five-part plan:

1. Ditch the shame.
2. Focus on systems, not yourself.
3. Join an effective group.
4. Define your role.
5. Know what you are fighting for, not just what you are fighting against.[358]

I appreciate this approach because it directs our attention to systems and the need for systemic (structural) change. I also value how it directs us to join a group and play a role that draws on our strengths, which reduces the burden of feeling like we have to start a new group or do everything on our own. Marris's exhortation to know what we are fighting for is compelling, too.

To figure out how to engage the climate crisis, we can start by following Marris's advice and get clear about what strengths we might bring to the struggle. I'm going to pose a series of questions. See what comes to mind in response, and consider taking notes on a pad or in a journal.

What are your passions?

What gives you joy?

What are you good at? What skills do you have?

Do you have any knowledge, connections, or resources that might prove helpful as you get engaged?

Next, we can turn to the facets of the climate crisis that interest us and toward which we can direct our talents. Read through the following list and note which topics catch your attention. As you'll see, most of them have to do with mitigation rather than adaptation.

- protecting habitats and biodiversity
- forests: protecting them as carbon sinks, planting trees, clearing invasive species
- nature-based solutions in general: not only protecting forests but soil conservation and regenerative agriculture
- opposing fracking
- acting in solidarity with Indigenous people around issues such as fracking, mining, oil drilling, pipelines, and destruction of ancestral burial grounds and ceremonial sites on their homelands
- retrofitting buildings: lobbying local officials to create and/or enforce building codes aimed at net zero emissions
- exploring alternative energy possibilities such as wind farms and solar energy (solar farms)
- installing heat pumps
- supporting a clean energy policy
- eliminating subsidies to the fossil fuel industry
- advocating for campaign finance reform
- supporting legislative initiatives like a carbon tax or a revenue-neutral fee-and-dividend program
- overturning the Citizens United ruling
- educating girls around the world
- prioritizing use and/or expansion of public transportation systems
- opposing private jet expansion (a current issue here in Massachusetts with a proposal to build more hangars for private jets at Hanscom Air Force Base)
- installing charging stations for electric vehicles (EV)
- "smart-growth" planning
- decreasing food waste
- adopting a plant-based diet
- organic gardening to grow food wherever there is soil
- participating in local agriculture (including CSAs, farmers markets)

- creating community gardens
- working with kids to grow food and green their schools
- envisioning an alternative economic paradigm
- creating a new indicator of well-being (like GNH in Bhutan)

The next question is how to engage the facet(s) of the climate crisis that caught our eye in the above list. Of course, we may feel over-extended with work, family, and other commitments. Belonging to yet another organization may feel like an overload. We may feel resistance to getting involved in local politics. Participating in rallies and marches may not be our thing. Perhaps we're afraid that our activism will get us in trouble with the powers that be or cause conflict with our neighbors. When I've considered getting more involved in environmental groups, I've found myself groaning at the thought of frequent meetings (and on Zoom), long discussions, drawn-out planning processes, and all the messiness of group decision-making. Scan the following list to see what actions draw your attention, and which turn you off:

- donating to environmental groups
- getting actively involved with an environmental group
- talking with friends and neighbors about what they can do in response to the crisis
- writing letters to politicians and newspapers about issues or pieces of legislation
- attending public hearings and providing oral or written comments
- lobbying elected officials
- soliciting signatures on petitions
- starting a study-action group
- educating others by giving talks or handing out information at fairs and festivals
- organizing film screenings
- working with local teachers and schools
- participating in protest marches and vigils

- picketing outside the headquarters of a complicit organization
- engaging in nonviolent civil disobedience with a willingness to get arrested
- playing a leadership role in an environmental group (helping run it, organizing initiatives and events)
- taking legal action
- working to create a movement by getting different organizations to collaborate
- using social media to support one or more of these actions

Ideally, each of us can find a focus that draws on our talents, experience, and resources. You may be a good writer, so crafting letters to editors or vision statements for environmental groups may be your thing. You may be an artist and want to create murals and billboards. You may be good at web design. You may have extensive skills and savvy around social media. Perhaps you are an extrovert and organizing demonstrations gives you joy.

The next question is the group with which you might want to affiliate. Do you know of any groups that focus on the facet of the crisis that draws your attention? Do you have any friends who are engaged in activism? Where have they plugged in? Getting involved with friends is an invaluable way to stay engaged and find greater joy in the work.

Let me share some of the things I've discovered in taking this approach to activism. I spent much of my youth in the woods—fishing, building forts, playing hide-and-seek. The son of a scoutmaster, I also spent a lot of time out on the trail, which spawned my lifelong love of hiking and backpacking. As I get older, and sit here recovering from knee-replacement surgery, my desire to climb mountains has been slowly shifting to a desire to walk in forests. Rather than feeling an urge to do "epic" hikes or scamper up "gnarly" peaks, I find myself simply wanting to be in the woods. In this shift from doing to *being*, my desire is to tap in, not top out. I've also found myself getting intrigued by trees, especially how they connect through mycorrhizal networks and communicate with one another. I stand in awe of them as fellow beings, living their lives in ways that are beyond my comprehension.

In light of this, the facet in the above list that most catches my attention is working to protect and expand forests as important carbon sinks and as crucial supports of healthy ecosystems, biodiversity, and clean water. I've been trying to educate myself about forests in Massachusetts, their ecology, the agencies controlling them, regulations about uses of public and private land, and forest bills before the legislature. Here in this state, a number of organizations have been working to preserve forests (proforestation) and plant trees in urban and rural locations (reforestation and afforestation) while also lobbying state officials and representatives around how forests are managed. Recently I've gotten involved with the Natural Solutions Working Group of an organization called Elders Climate Action of Massachusetts. I've also been plugging into or tracking several related groups, such as Save Massachusetts Forests, Trees as a Common Good, Speak for the Trees, and Trees for Watertown.

ACTING LOCALLY

Of course, our engagement can go beyond working on just one facet of the crisis. There are numerous issues that need to be addressed and actions we can take. Let me share some thoughts about this, starting at the local level.

A first step is to educate ourselves about the impact of the climate crisis on our local area. Have winters changed? Are there new insects and diseases? Has there been more rain, and flooding, than in the past? Has it been drier? Are there more frequent fires? What are the main forms of damage to my ecosystem? This education is based on seeing reality clearly and, in this respect, we need to value the role that science and rigorously debated and agreed-upon facts play in the public sphere. We need to appreciate the value of seeking and telling the truth, even when it brings tension into our relationships or threatens the interests of certain individuals, organizations, and institutions.

Insofar as I've tried to adopt (and adapt) reinhabitation as my approach to where I live, I've had to recognize that it goes beyond connecting with and studying the natural world. To fully inhabit a place, we need to take action, which from Snyder's perspective, as we saw before, "means, for most of us, find your place on the planet, dig in, and take responsibility from there—the tiresome but tangible work of school boards, county supervisors, local foresters—local politics."[359] To do this effectively, we need to get a handle on what can be done at the local level to help mitigate climate disruption. Here in Watertown, I'm aware of initiatives around increasing public transportation and using electric buses. People are lobbying the city for its workers to drive electric vehicles and to create more EV charging stations. With a high-tech boom happening here, there's a push for constructing new buildings—and retrofitting existing buildings—in a way that will make them net zero carbon emitters, and as part of this push, advocates have called on the city to ban new natural-gas hookups. Some people are agitating for the creation of micro-grids with geothermal energy and for an increase in the number of households able to participate in a composting service.

The situation is likely different where you live, so see if you can educate yourself about issues and initiatives in your town. Share what you learn with friends and neighbors, whether in conversations or in letters to the editors of the local newspaper (if you still have one). Of course, not everyone will be open to what we share, so we need to learn—from writers like George Marshall[360] and Katherine Hayhoe[361]—how to talk about the climate crisis with people who may dismiss it. You can also find out if there is a local climate group where you live. This way you don't have to do things on your own and you can reap the benefits of joining with others. As

Marianne Krasny reminds us, "Acting collectively with policy-savvy organizations enables us to effectively influence government and business policies."[362] In my town, the main climate activist group is Watertown Faces Climate Change, members of which have played key roles in the local initiatives I just mentioned.

BEYOND THE LOCAL

Of course, we can't mitigate the climate crisis just at the local level. There are steps we need to take that can only be done at broader levels. Larry Rasmussen writes, "Consider climate change. Hoisting solar panels to rooftops here and there, starting community gardens, and reforesting floodplains, one community at a time, will not do what only bioregional, national, and international legislation and law enforcement can."[363]

To follow Rasmussen's lead and move beyond the local to promote such legislation and other remedies, we can join groups that are acting at the state or provincial level. Watertown Faces Climate Change is a node of 350 Mass, otherwise known as the Better Future Project, whose home page includes the statement, "We are building a powerful statewide movement to end the destructive dominance of the fossil fuel industry and transition to a just, equitable, and clean energy economy."[364] As I mentioned earlier, I'm involved with the Massachusetts chapter of Elders Climate Action, which on its homepage declares, "We are committed to using our voices, our votes, and our collective power to push for policies and practices that will reduce greenhouse gases to a level consistent with life thriving on our planet."

In connecting with trans-local organizations such as these, we can lobby for or against certain bills in our state legislature. We can do research on struggles in our area, such as the resistance to the expansion of oil pipelines or other fossil fuel projects. We can support broader initiatives, like the Regional Greenhouse Gas Initiative with eleven states in the northeastern United States, which sets carbon dioxide allowances for electric power plants in each state and provides a mechanism for auctioning those allowances in a type of cap-and-trade approach to greenhouse gases.

We can also plug into groups and initiatives at the national level. One option in the US is Citizens' Climate Lobby, which has been lobbying Congress for a revenue-neutral, carbon-fee-and-dividend program that will internalize the costs of greenhouse gases and thereby incentivize reduced use of fossil fuels.[365] We can also join groups and protests in opposition to large-scale fossil fuel infrastructure projects, such as the Keystone XL pipeline extension and the Line 5 pipeline. We can also educate ourselves about how the climate crisis disproportionately affects marginalized and vulnerable communities and how, more broadly, it relates to poverty, racism, and other forms of structural oppression in our capitalist system.

Of course, not all elected officials are responsive to their constituents and environmental groups. For decades, the fossil fuel industry has been making massive campaign contributions to friendly politicians and influencing elections in other ways such as super PACs. This exertion of influence has been supported by the 2012 US Supreme Court ruling in *Citizens United v. Federal Election Commission*, which allows corporations to spend unlimited amounts of money on elections as a form of free speech that is purportedly their right because of corporate personhood. For this reason, we need campaign finance reform so we can elect more people who represent *us*, not the fossil fuel industry, and who can get mitigation legislation through Congress. Whether by limiting the size of contributions or by publicly funding political campaigns, we need to shift power in the US away from corporations and the wealthiest one percent to the people as a whole. If you are interested in this effort, check out such organizations as End Citizens United, Open-Secrets, and the Brennan Center for Justice at New York University's School of Law.

At the very least, as engaged citizens at the local, state, and national level, we should educate ourselves about relevant initiatives and lobby our elected officials to support them, even if those politicians receive large contributions from fossil fuel companies. While urging them to support a revenue-neutral carbon-fee-and-dividend program, we can call on them to support regulations that reduce emissions from large industrial factories and power plants, especially those using coal; cut subsidies to the fossil fuel industry, such as the industry's ability to write off the cost of oil exploration as a tax deduction; free up additional funding for the scaling up of renewable energy sources such as wind, solar, and geothermal; and transfer renewable energy technologies to developing countries. We can also advocate for higher fuel-efficiency standards for cars and trucks, and for subsidies and rebates, as needed, to increase the production and purchasing of electric vehicles and heat pumps. We can ask our representatives to allocate federal funds to develop accessible, convenient, and green public transportation systems and to cover at least some of the cost of retrofitting buildings to make them more energy efficient. In the name of eco-justice, we can call for programs to train and employ in these initiatives people who have heretofore lacked access to adequate education, opportunities, and, by extension, a living wage, and who have more often than not been bearing the brunt of profit-driven policies that have polluted if not destroyed the ecosystems on which they depend.

There is much we need to do at the international level as well. We need to lobby Congress to promote international agreements like the Paris Accord and international institutions like the United Nations and the World Criminal Court. We need to push them to reject or revise trade agreements that undermine labor laws and environmental regulations by viewing such laws and regulations as barriers to "free trade"—"free" in the sense of trans-national corporations being free to do whatever they want, regardless of the impact on labor or the environment. Like tens of thousands of other citizens, I was on the streets of Seattle in 1999 during the WTO Ministerial Conference, joining union members and environmental activists to raise alarms about the deleterious effects of "free trade" and contemporary configurations of economic globalization.

What Are We Fighting *For*?

Activism around mitigating climate change goes beyond specific actions. As Marris suggested, we need to know not only what we are fighting *against* but what we're fighting *for*. We need to envision the kind of society that will support us in our efforts and stand as an alternative to the destructive political economies in which we find ourselves. Beyond what I sketched above about local communities, what sort of community, or society, might that be? What might be a Buddhist vision of such a society?

A central aspect of such a society, to my thinking, is participatory democracy, which embodies the Buddhist doctrine of conditioned arising in an optimal form. As I have written elsewhere, "'To be' means to be in relationship, to participate in—contribute to and receive from—the whole of which one is part. The social 'good' is achieved to the extent people actualize optimal participation and mutually supportive interaction in society."[366] This sort of participation takes specific forms: "Optimal participation requires the ability to participate—to give and receive—in a fulfilling way, which includes such things as education, rewarding work, the right to vote, the ability to run a viable campaign for political office, and basic freedoms of speech and assembly."[367] It means the ability to *vote into office* representatives who can take the bold action needed to mitigate the climate crisis.

Participatory democracy is built on and reinforces a public life based on a realization of our interconnectedness, of our dependence on a vast array of factors for our well-being, and on a deep sense that "we're all in this together," rather than "It's dog eat dog" or "It's all about me." In actual practice, this calls for trust, generosity, cooperation, and both individual and collective responsibility. When coupled with Buddhist compassionate concern about the suffering of others, this version of public life would also feature a commitment to reducing harm in all of its forms.

In the Buddhist world, we have at least a partial template for this alternative type of society in the Sarvodaya Shramadana Movement, which was started by Dr. A.T. Ariyaratne in 1958 in Sri Lanka. With its largely Buddhist approach to development, Sarvodaya tries to preserve cultural values and a healthy natural environment. It works toward six types of goals: social, economic, political, moral, cultural, and spiritual.[368] The core social goals are equality, solidarity, education, and health. To remedy villages stagnated in poverty and conflict, Sarvodaya works to create villages that embody economic cooperation, sharing, equality, selflessness, and love. Politically, Sarvodaya strives to promote decentralized decision-making, nonviolence, and freedom from coercion. The central moral goal is full practice of the five precepts. Cultural goals include artistic expression and harmonious relationships, and the spiritual goal is to awaken as a group ("Sarvodaya" literally means "universal uplift," or "the awakening of all").[369]

This vision stands in tension with most political economies. The dominant global economic paradigm accepts a view of humans we noted earlier: as selfish individuals competing to maximize their pleasure. John Cobb has criticized this view: "What troubles me most about economic theory is that it abstracts from the social or communal character of human existence and fails to notice that it does so. Underlying its neglect of motives other than self-interest is a radically individualistic view of human beings."[370] Dominant economic approaches also foster a set of values contrary to Buddhist teachings. As we have seen, most economic systems foster desire through advertising and other means to increase consumption and, by extension, increase economic activity and profits. In the process, as Cobb has pointed out, religious values get replaced by corporate values, such as the value placed on continuous growth of the economy even though it may hurt the vulnerable or undermine communities (including ecosystems), on short-term profits for shareholders rather than long-term interests of stakeholders, and on individual material acquisition rather than communal well-being.

In contrast, Buddhist approaches to economic life direct us to focus on *need*, not greed, or, as Sulak Sivaraksa has put it, toward "more being," not "more having." Sivaraksa has also argued that "[c]ontrary to the rationale of consumerism, where *more* is considered *better* and where the amount of personal gain and possessions marks the goodness of one's life, one learns from the Buddha to constantly reduce one's attachments and to envision the good life as the successful overcoming of attachment to gain."[371] Sivaraksa has also contrasted modern ways of thinking about economic development with Buddhist approaches to inner development, saying, "From the usual standpoint, when desires are increased and satisfied, development can proceed. From the Buddhist standpoint, when there are fewer desires there can be greater development. It is the reduction of desires that constitutes development."[372]

Other Buddhist thinkers have been giving thought to the sorts of economic systems that would not only be compatible with Buddhist values but also generate lower levels of greenhouse gases. Some have called for a steady-state economy with greener energy policies. For example, Bhikkhu Bodhi writes, "Policy formation must be motivated not by narrow self-interest but by a magnanimous spirit of generosity, compassion, and wisdom" leading to a "steady-state economy governed by the principle of sufficiency, which gives priority to contentment, service to others, and inner fulfillment as the measure of the good life."[373] Similarly, David Loy calls for decarbonizing the economy and creating renewable energy sources, which, when tapped, would contribute to a "well-reasoned 'steady-state' economy that operates mindfully within the Earth's resource and energy budget."[374] Loy and Bhikkhu Bodhi also argue that "From a Buddhist perspective, a sane and sustainable economy would be governed by the principle of sufficiency: the key to happiness is contentment rather than an ever-increasing abundance of goods."[375] Such a society would work to guarantee "a satisfactory standard of living for everyone while allowing us to develop our full (including spiritual) potential in harmony with the biosphere, which sustains and nurtures all beings, including future generations."[376]

Distilling this material, from a Buddhist perspective what seems worth fighting *for* is, at the very least, a society that is participatory, grounded in trust, generosity, compassion, responsibility, and non-harming, a society with a decarbonized steady-state economy and a political and legal system that promotes justice for everyone. Internationally, we can fight for collaboration to find ways to sufficiently mitigate climate disruption and help people, especially those who are most vulnerable, adapt to it.

Clearly, we have an array of options to choose from as we consider how we might engage the climate crisis and work to bring about a new sort of society. To get started, we can find a focus that speaks to us, that concerns something that is dear to us, like forests. Once we get clear about our focus, we can then begin to give of ourselves as an act of generosity and compassion. This will not only help mitigate the climate crisis but will serve our spiritual path insofar as acting with generosity and compassion simultaneously serves to purify our minds of desire and ill-will. Though we may be reluctant to think of ourselves as bodhisattvas (or even as eco-sattvas), our efforts will also help relieve the suffering that human and other-than-human animals are experiencing here in the midst of the crisis. In this way, we can pursue activism not as a distraction from the path but as an extension of it, benefiting ourselves, other sentient beings, and the natural world of which we are part.

More broadly, the way of living I've been sketching here—a way of living that is spacious, compassionate, embedded in nature, connected to others, and engaged—provides us with what I referred to earlier as a win-win scenario insofar as it mitigates the climate crisis while also enriching our spiritual and social lives. Living in this way is not some dismal self-sacrifice but, again, a path to a higher fulfillment.

I hope that you, my reader, have garnered from this book at least a couple of nuggets that can serve you in your own life. Some of what I've presented here may not be your cup of tea, and you may have different strategies of your own. I hope you will let me know what you are pursuing and share your thoughts about the path that I've sketched here. We *are* all in this together, and we can each do our part, however small, toward transforming our world while transforming ourselves.

Notes

1. What I am setting forth here is an environmental ethic in a certain sense, but I have not crafted this book as a contribution to Environmental Ethics. Nevertheless, some of what I write here, and relegate to notes like this one, falls within the realm of that academic field. As I've written elsewhere, as an intellectual endeavor Environmental Ethics delves into such topics as human nature; the reality in which we find ourselves (metaphysics); how we should view reality (epistemology); the status of non-human parts of reality (other animals, plants, inanimate objects, larger wholes like species and ecosystems); the respective values (and types of value) of human and other-than-human parts of reality; the respective values of individuals and wholes (and reflections on possible tensions between valuing individuals and valuing wholes); ecological virtues; formal principles and guidelines for making decisions and engaging in actions (or activism); an ecologically optimal state of affairs (a telos, whether in a local community, ecosystem, bioregion, country, or broader area); and the way to attain that goal, or at least get things moving in that direction. See my article "Resources for Buddhist Environmental Ethics," *Journal of Buddhist Ethics* 20 (2013): 541–71.

2. I realize that "embeddedness" might imply that something separate has been inserted into nature, as when a journalist has been embedded into a combat unit. As I hope will become clear as we proceed, when I use the term I am thinking of how we emerge organically from within nature *as* nature, and in this sense we are embedded in it. To try to convey this meaning, at other points I will speak of how we are part of nature, or woven into nature.

3. For an example of corporations deploying the construct of individual carbon footprint to shift responsibility away from themselves and onto consumers, see Mark Kaufman's article "The Carbon Footprint Sham: A 'Successful, Deceptive' PR Campaign," https://mashable.com/feature/carbon-footprint-pr-campaign-sham/; accessed October 22, 2023; cited by LaUra Schmidt, *How to Live in a Chaotic Climate: Ten Steps to Reconnect with Ourselves, Our Communities, and Our Planet* (Boulder, CO: Shambhala Publications, 2023), 44.

4. Stephen Batchelor, "The Practice of Generosity," in *Mindfulness in the Marketplace: Compassionate Responses to Consumerism*, ed. Allan Hunt Badiner (Berkeley: Parallax Press, 2002), 65.

5. See, for example, two of the more widely read volumes on Buddhism and ecology: *Mindfulness in the Marketplace: Compassionate Responses to Consumerism*, ed. Allan Hunt Badiner (Berkeley: Parallax Press, 2002), and *Hooked! Buddhist Writings on Greed, Desire, and the Urge to Consume*, ed. Stephanie Kaza, (Boston: Shambhala Publications, 2005).

6. Sallie McFague, *Blessed Are the Consumers: Climate Change and the Practice of Restraint* (Minneapolis: Fortress Press, 2013), x.

7. Joe Jackson nailed this excess in his song "It's All Too Much."

8. And then there's the commercialization of holidays. Commercial interests—especially those of greeting card companies, chocolatiers, and florists—led to the invention of holidays like Valentine's Day and Mother's Day. The custom of giving Christmas gifts exploded after department stores appeared in the late nineteenth century. And Christmas ads start earlier each year, with their advent now creeping back from Thanksgiving to Halloween.

9. Another trend I've witnessed in my lifetime is commodification. Things that historically were free and available, whether for recreation or some other purpose, are getting privatized and commodified. We see this with water, land (and beach access!), seeds, and other things that were part of the birthright of all people, not just those with enough cash to control them by buying them or securing patents.

10. Tim Wu, "Mother Nature is Brought to You By...," *New York Times*, December 2, 2016; https://www.nytimes.com/2016/12/02/opinion/sunday/mother-nature-is-brought-to-you-by.html?searchResultPosition=1; accessed April 7, 2020.

11. Our idolizing of the rich often harbors an ideology of merit. Many of us assume that all wealthy people got to where they are through hard work and that poor people are impoverished because of some moral failure or character flaw like laziness. This assumption can obscure how affirmative action in one form has helped folks get into Harvard or Stanford: rather than the standard form, "All other things being equal, give preference to the minority person," affirmative action can take the form of "Regardless of how equal, give preference to the alum's kid or the offspring of the wealthy donor." The college admissions scandal of 2019 outed not only how SAT scores can get fudged and fake athletes gain admission to play sports they've never played (the back door) but also how large donations can get children accepted (the side door), something that has been alleged about Jared Kushner's getting accepted to Harvard right after his father pledged 2.5 million dollars to the place. Of course, this gets blurry when privileged people downplay class differences and the advantages into which they were born. As some critics said about the second Bush president, "W was born on third base but actually thinks he hit a triple to get there." Wealthy people can also deceive themselves by believing that, with but few exceptions, "We're all middle class."

12. William Ophuls, "Notes for a Buddhist Politics," in *Dharma Rain: Sources of Buddhist Environmentalism*, ed. Stephanie Kaza and Kenneth Kraft (Boston: Shambhala Publications, 2000), 370.

13. Simon P. James, *Zen Buddhism and Environmental Ethics* (Hampshire: Ashgate Publishing Company, 2004), 125.

14. As Peter Timmerman writes, "Buddhism is well placed to analyze, assess, and perhaps dismantle . . . the Romanticized individual self." "Western Buddhism and the Global Crisis," in Kaza and Kraft, eds., *Dharma Rain*, 367.

15. Buddhism is not alone in its criticism of desire. Jack Turner writes, "Any spiritual tradition worthy of its name teaches the diminishment of desire, and it is desire in all its forms—simple greed, avarice, hoarding, the will to power, the will to truth, the rush of population growth, the craving for control—that fuels the destruction of our once-fair planet." *The Abstract Wild* (Tucson: University of Arizona Press, 1996), xvi.

16. Glenn A. Albrecht criticizes the use of the term "environment" as dualistically representing nature as something apart from us, surrounding us, and advocates "symbioment" in its stead. *Earth Emotions: New Words for a New World* (Ithaca, NY: Cornell University Press, 2019), 101.

17. The Buddhist rejection of ill will, however, is not without problems. It's unreasonable to expect people not to feel anger when they encounter injustice and environmental destruction, and a blanket condemnation of anger can stifle the outrage that often stirs people to action. As my wife said the other day, one problem in the United States is that privileged citizens do not feel sufficient anger at what's going on. And we all know how racism can lead to denunciations of "angry Blacks" or "angry Black women." Buddhists need to recognize the positive role of righteous anger. Perhaps what they need to do is to discern that anger can enhance our attention to problems and prompt us to act in response to those problems. Insofar as we mindfully monitor our anger, we are more apt to act in ways that do not indulge it, cause harm, and make situations worse. With mindfulness, we can tap the energy of anger to fuel our actions and stamina.

18. These are two of the four *brahma vihāras* or "divine abodes": loving-kindness, compassion, sympathetic joy, and equanimity.

19. Sulak Sivaraksa, "Alternatives to Consumerism," in Badiner, *Mindfulness in the Marketplace*, 135.

20. This perspective finds expression in the metaphor of the ocean as an underlying body of water that takes the temporary form of this or that wave.

21. Thich Nhat Hanh, *Love Letter to the Earth* (Berkeley: Parallax Press, 2013), 8.

22. As meditation teacher Joseph Goldstein puts it, "Greed is fed by one particularly strong aspect of delusion, namely, the delusion of a separate, independently existing self." "Desire, Delusion, and DVDs," in Kaza, *Hooked!*, 19.

23. Just as Catholicism has categorized various types of sins, Buddhism offers various lists of unwholesome mental states.

24. Batchelor, "The Practice of Generosity," 65.

25. Kaza, "Introduction," 8.

26. David Korten, "Ecological Civilization and the New Enlightenment," *Tikkun* (Fall 2017), 18.

27. Ruben L. F. Habito, "The Inner Pursuit of Happiness," in Kaza, *Hooked!*, 34–35.

28. Sulak Sivaraksa, "Alternatives to Consumerism," in Badiner, *Mindfulness in the Marketplace*, 136.

29. Kaza, "Introduction," 3.

30. David Loy and Linda Goodhew, "Consuming Time," in Kaza, *Hooked!*, 176.

31. Loy and Goodhew, "Consuming Time," 176.

32. David R. Loy, *The Great Awakening: A Buddhist Social Theory* (Somerville, MA: Wisdom Publications, 1997), 27. Loy also writes, ". . . Buddhism shifts our focus from the terror of death (our primal repression, according to [Carl] Becker) to the anguish of a groundlessness experienced here and now. The problem is not so much that we will die, but that we do not feel real now." *The Great Awakening* , 22.

33. Habito, "The Inner Pursuit of Happiness," 37.

34. Alan Greenspan, *The Age of Turbulence: Adventures in a New World* (New York: Penguin Press, 2007), 463.

35. David Domke, *God Willing?: Political Fundamentalism in the White House, the "War on Terror," and the Echoing Press* (London: Pluto Press, 2004), 18.

36. Kaza, "Introduction," 8.

37. Ken Jones, *Beyond Optimism: A Buddhist Political Economy* (Oxford: Jon Carpenter Publishing, 1993), 22.

38. With support systems like Social Security and Medicaid teetering, this fear and the sense that we need to look out for ourselves—that we have to continually add to our material (financial) foundation—gets enhanced.

39. Bo Lazoff, "How Not to Feast from the Poison Cake," in Badiner, *Mindfulness in the Marketplace*, 106.

40. John B. Cobb, Jr., *Sustaining the Common Good: A Christian Perspective on the Global Economy* (Cleveland: Pilgrim Press, 1994), 28.

41. Cobb, *Sustaining the Common Good*, 37. Cobb's analysis echoes that of Karl Polanyi in *The Great Transformation*, who wrote, "instead of [the] economy being embedded in social relations, social relations are embedded in the economic system." Polanyi, *The Great Transformation: The Political and Economic Origins of Our Time* (Boston: Beacon Press, 1957), 57; quoted by Loy, *The Great Awakening*, 67.

42. Cobb, *Sustaining the Common Good*, 114.

43. By "sustainability" I am not thinking of preserving parts of nature ("resources") so that we can use them for human ends down the line. And I recognize that the task before us in many cases is not sustaining systems but regenerating systems.

44. Joanna Macy and Chris Johnstone, *Active Hope: How to Face the Mess We're in with Unexpected Resilience & Creative Power* (Novato, CA: New World Library, 2022), 23.

45. Vajragupta, *Wild Awake*, 16.

46. Lazoff, "How Not to Feast from the Poison Cake," 105.

47. Yifa, *Authenticity: Clearing the Junk: A Buddhist Perspective* (New York: Lantern Books, 2007), xi.

48. Thich Nhat Hanh, *Love Letter to the Earth*, 28–29.

49. Robert D. Putnam, *Bowling Alone: The Collapse and Revival of American Community* (New York: Simon & Schuster, 2020), 367.

50. Carl Honoré, *In Praise of Slowness: Challenging the Cult of Speed* (New York: HarperCollins, 2004), 3.

51. Joanna Macy and Molly Brown, *Coming Back to Life* (Gabriola Island, BC: New Society Publishers, 2022), 169.

52. Honoré, *In Praise of Slowness*, 11.

53. David Loy, *Money, Sex, War, Karma: Notes for a Buddhist Revolution* (Somerville, MA: Wisdom Publications, 2008), 96–98.

54. Loy, *Money, Sex, War, Karma*, 96.

55. Loy, *Money, Sex, War, Karma*, 99–100.

56. Lazoff, "How Not to Feast from the Poison Cake," 105.

57. On a parallel track, Joanna Macy and Chris Johnstone lift up seven common types of resistance:
    1. I don't believe it's that dangerous.
    2. It isn't my role to sort this out.
    3. I don't want to stand out from the crowd.
    4. This information threatens my commercial or political interest.
    5. It is so upsetting that I prefer not to think about it.
    6. I feel paralyzed. I'm aware of the danger, but I don't know what to do.
    7. There's no point doing anything, since it won't make any difference.
    Macy and Johnstone, *Active Hope*, 58–62.

58. Per Espen Stoknes lays out five barriers (the Five D's) to thinking deeply about and responding to the climate crisis: Distance, our mind not thinking about the crisis because it sees the problem as far away in time and space; 2. a feeling of Doom; 3. Dissonance between what we know and what we do, which leads us to place less weight on what we know; 4. Denial; and 5. iDentity getting in the way of listening to others, acknowledging facts, and being willing to change. *What We Think About When We Try Not to Think About Global Warming: Toward a New Psychology of Climate Action* (White River Junction, VT: Chelsea Green Publishing, 2015), 82.

59. Kari Marie Norgaard has analyzed emotional dimensions of denial in Norway, the United States, and other countries in *Living in Denial: Climate Change, Emotions, and Everyday Life* (Cambridge, MA: MIT Press, 2011).

60. Michael E. Mann, *The New Climate War: The Fight to Take Back Our Planet* (New York: PublicAffairs, 2021), 61.

61. We see an important break from this sort of ideological justification in the case of Katharine Hayhoe and Richard Cizik, who have diverged from most other evangelicals and are taking climate change seriously, as have many younger evangelicals. See Hayhoe's *Climate for Change: Global Warming Facts for Faith-Based Decisions* (New York: FaithWords, 2009) and Cizik's Good Steward Campaign.

62. Tyrone Cashman, "Where Does It Come From? Where Does It Go?," in Badiner, *Mindfulness in the Marketplace*, 226.

63. Helena Norberg-Hodge, "Buddhism in the Global Economy," in Badiner, *Mindfulness in the Marketplace*, 16.

64. Richard Louv, *Last Child in the Woods: Saving Our Children from Nature-Deficit Disorder* (Chapel Hill, NC: Algonquin Books, 2008).

65. The Buddhist tradition also lays out more proximate elements of flourishing. The Sarvodaya Movement in Sri Lanka, for example, has identified ten

basic needs: water; food; housing; clothing; health care; communication; fuel; education; a clean, safe, beautiful environment; and a spiritual and cultural life. Joanna Macy, *Dharma and Development: Religion as Resource in the Sarvodaya Self-Help Movement*, rev. ed. (West Hartford, CT: Kumarian Press, 1985), 27.

66. Clair Brown, *Buddhist Economics: An Enlightened Approach to the Dismal Science* (New York: Bloomsbury Press, 2017), 22.

67. Quoted by Leslie E. Sponsel and Poranee Natadecha-Sponsel, "A Theoretical Analysis of the Potential Contribution of the Monastic Community in Promoting a Green Society in Thailand," in *Buddhism and Ecology: The Interconnection of Dharma and Deeds*, ed. Mary Evelyn Tucker and Duncan Ryūken Williams (Cambridge, MA: Harvard University Press, 1997), 50. Renowned Buddhists Buddhadāsa Bhikkhu and Phra Prayudh Payutto have set forth outlines of an ecologically sustainable way of life. See Donald K. Swearer, "The Hermeneutics of Buddhist Ecology in Contemporary Thailand: Buddhadāsa and Dhammapiṭaka," in Tucker and Williams, *Buddhism and Ecology*.

68. Needless to say, this value is not relevant to those whose basic needs are not being met.

69. Kaza, "Introduction," 3.

70. Kōshō Uchiyama, *Opening the Hand of Thought: Foundations of Zen Buddhist Practice* (New York: Penguin Arkana, 1993).

71. Jan Chozen Bays, *How to Train a Wild Elephant: And Other Adventures in Mindfulness* (Boston: Shambhala Publications, 2011), 78.

72. Bays, *How to Train a Wild Elephant*, 2.

73. Andrew Olendzki, *Unlimiting Mind: The Radically Experiential Psychology of Buddhism* (Somerville, MA: Wisdom Publications, 2010), 71.

74. Similar to what I am describing is the RAIN technique (recognize, accept, investigate, not-identify), through which, according to Teah Strozer, we "shift from the content of the mind to the observer," and when this happens "we can see that the content is not who we are." "RAIN: Getting started on a spiritual path takes guts," *Tricycle* (Spring 2015), 31.

75. Georg Wilhelm Friedrich Hegel, *The Philosophy of History*, trans. J. Sibree (New York: Dover Publications, 1956), 167. Marx's dialectical materialism derives in part from the dialectic of history that Hegel set forth in *The Philosophy of History*.

76. Bhikkhu Bodhi, trans., *The Connected Discourses of the Buddha: A Translation of the Saṃyutta Nikāya* (Somerville, MA: Wisdom Publications, 2000), 1143.

77. These precepts direct us to abstain from (1) harming living beings, (2) taking what which has not been given, (3) sexual misconduct, (4) false speech, (5) using intoxicants.

78. Sharon Salzberg, "Calm in the Midst of Chaos," *Lion's Roar* (November 2020), 50.

79. John Ross Carter and Mahinda Palihawadana, trans., *The Dhammapada* (New York: Oxford University Press, 1987), 34.

80. Other sets of cousins include "tri," the number three in Sanskrit, and "tri" as in tricycle, as well as "Agni," the Vedic god of fire, and "ignite."

81. Kittisaro, "Tangled in Thought: How to Beat Your Mind at Its Own Game," *Tricycle* (Winter 2014), 83.

82. Shodo Harada Roshi, *Morning Dewdrops of the Mind: Teachings of a Contemporary Zen Master*, trans. Daichi-Priscilla Storandt (Berkeley: Frog Books, 1993), 66.

83. Quoted by Yongey Mingyur Rinpoche, "Rest in Your Buddhanature," *Lion's Roar*, March 15, 2022. *https://www.lionsroar.com/rest-in-your-buddhanature/*, accessed September 14, 2023.

84. Joseph Goldstein, *The Experience of Insight: A Simple and Direct Guide to Buddhist Meditation* (Boston: Shambhala Publications, 1983), 59. Pico Iyer tells us, "Clouds and blue sky . . . are how Buddhists explain the nature of our mind: there may be clouds passing across it, but that doesn't mean a blue sky isn't always there behind the observations. All you need is the patience to sit still until the blue shows up again." Pico Iyer, *The Art of Stillness: Adventures in Going Nowhere* (New York: Simon & Schuster, 2014), 26.

85. Skt. *ārava*, J. *rō* (漏).

86. Uchiyama, *Opening the Hand of Thought*, 86.

87. The characters for this are 修証, *shushō*, with the first character connoting practice in the sense of self-cultivation and the second connoting realize, prove, and confirm.

88. Shunryū Suzuki, *Zen Mind, Beginner's Mind: Informal Talks on Zen Meditation and Practice* (New York: Weatherhill, 1970), 128.

89. Bays, *How to Train a Wild Elephant*, 79.

90. Bays, *How to Train a Wild Elephant*, 2.

91. J. *genjō suru*.

92. Shōhaku Okumura, *Realizing Genjōkōan: A Key to Dōgen's* Shōbōgenzō (Somerville, MA: Wisdom Publications, 2010), 14–15.

93. Okumura, *Realizing Genjōkōan*, 21.

94. Brett W. Davis, "The Presencing of Truth: Dōgen's *Genjōkōan*," in *Buddhist Philosophy: Essential Readings*, ed. William Edelglass and Jay Garfield (New York: Oxford University Press, 2009), 253.

95. Sharon Salzberg, "Calm in the Midst of Chaos," *Lion's Roar* (November 2020), 51.

96. Thomas Kasulis, *Zen Action, Zen Person* (Honolulu: University of Hawai'i Press, 1981), 57.

97. Bret W. Davis, "The Philosophy of Zen Master Dōgen: Egoless Perspectivism," in *Oxford Handbook of Japanese Philosophy*, ed. Bret W. Davis (New York: Oxford University Press, 2020), 211.

98. Or as some are wont to phrase it, we "expand" consciousness and "open" the doors of perception.

99. Thich Nhat Hanh writes, "The most precious gift we can offer others is our presence." *Living Buddha, Living Christ* (New York: Penguin, 2007), 20.

100. Thich Nhat Hanh, *Love Letter to the Earth*, 104.

101. Bays, *How to Train a Wild Elephant*, 63.

102. Thich Nhat Hanh, *You Are Here: Discovering the Magic of the Present Moment* (Boston: Shambhala Publications, 2010), 16.

103. Kaira Jewel Lingo, *We Were Made for These Times: Ten Lessons on Moving through Change, Loss, and Disruption* (Berkeley: Parallax Press, 2021), 34.

104. However innumerable suffering beings are, I vow to liberate them; however inexhaustible mental defilements are, I vow eliminate them; however

immeasurable Buddhist teachings are, I vow to learn them; however unsurpassable the Buddhist Way is, I vow to attain it.

105. J. *bosatsu-gyō*.

106. Stephanie Kaza, *Green Buddhism: Practice and Compassionate Action in Uncertain Times* (Boulder, CO: Shambhala, 2019), xii.

107. Some translators have rendered the Pali term for this fourth type of wrong speech as "gossip."

108. Rebecca Z. Shafir, *The Zen of Listening: Mindful Communication in the Age of Distraction* (Wheaton, IL: Quest Books, 2003), 1–2.

109. Bays, *How to Train a Wild Elephant*, 158.

110. Allan Lokos, "Skillful Speech," *Tricycle* (Winter 2008), 85.

111. Patience has found its way into both the Theravāda and Mahāyāna lists of the Ten Perfections.

112. Though I'm not sure I agree with her, Chozen Bays teaches that "Impatience is a form of anger, and underneath anger/aversion is always fear." *How to Train an Elephant*, 184

113. "Life Without Principle," *Atlantic Monthly* (October 1863), 484. https://www.theatlantic.com/magazine/archive/1863/10/life-without-principle/542217/

114. Thich Nhat Hanh, *Keeping the Peace: Mindfulness and Public Service* (Berkeley: Parallax Press, 2005), 85.

115. Bays, *How to Train a Wild Elephant*, 160.

116. Shafir, *The Zen of Listening*, 12.

117. Katharine Hayhoe, *Saving Us: A Climate Scientist's Case for Hope and Healing in a Divided World* (New York: One Signal Publishers/Atria Books, 2021), 69.

118. Hayhoe, *Saving Us*, xii.

119. Hayhoe, *Saving Us*, 19.

120. Edward Espe Brown, "Leavening Spirit," *Tricycle* (Fall 2002), 90.

121. Henry David Thoreau, *Walden and Civil Disobedience* (New York: Penguin Books, 1984), 135.

122. Sometimes when I teach about mindfulness as in part the act of remembering, I flag for my students the term "recollection" and how we talk about "collecting" ourselves and being "calm and collected."

123 Thoreau, *Walden*, 135.

124. Stephen Altschuler, *Sacred Paths and Muddy Places: Rediscovering Spirit in Nature* (Lincoln, NE: iUniverse, 2007), 4.

125. Gary Thorp, *Sweeping Changes: Discovering the Joy of Zen in Everyday Tasks* (London: Walter Books, 2000), 48.

126. This is an expansion of a list by Lorilee Lippincott, *The Simple Living Handbook: Discover the Joy of a De-Cluttered Life* (New York, Skyhorse Publishing, 2013), 4.

127. Thoreau, *Walden*, 126.

128. Though this varies a bit from hiker to hiker, mine consists of water, extra food, rain gear, extra layer(s) for warmth, sun gear (sunblock, hat, sunglasses), fire-starting materials, navigation (in my low-tech way, a map and compass), headlamp, first-aid kit, and some sort of shelter, like a tarp or bivy sack.

129. Bays, *How to Train a Wild Elephant*, 24.

130. Ou Baholyodhin, *Living with Zen* (Boston: Tuttle Publishing, 2000), 11.

131. Duane Elgin, *Voluntary Simplicity: Toward a Way of Life That Is Outwardly Simple, Inwardly Rich*, rev. ed. (New York: Harper, 1993), 148.

132. For more tips, and from people who have much more expertise in this area than I do, check out Marie Kondo's *The Life-Changing Magic of Tidying Up: The Japanese Art of Decluttering and Organizing* (Berkeley: Ten Speed Press, 2014); Stephanie Bennett-Vogt's *Your Spacious Self: Clear the Clutter and Discover Who You Are* (San Antonio: Hierophant Publishing, 2012); or Bennett-Vogt's *A Year to Clear: A Daily Guide to Creating Spaciousness in Your Home and Heart* (San Antonio: Hierophant Publishing, 2015).

133. Quoted by Walter Sullivan, "The Einstein Papers: A Man of Many Parts," *The New York Times*, (March 29, 1972), 20.

134. Padmasiri de Silva, "Buddhist Environmental Ethics," in *Dharma Gaia: A Harvest of Essays in Buddhism and Ecology*, ed. Alan Hunt Badiner (Berkeley: Parallax Press, 1990), 15.

135. Again, this is one function of precepts and the morality components of the eightfold path.

136. See Christopher Ives, "True Person, Formless Self: Lay Zen Master Hisamatsu Shin'ichi," in *Zen Masters*, ed. Steven Heine and Dale S. Wright (New York: Oxford University Press, 2010).

137. Initiated in 1994 by Maurice Strong, Secretary General of the Rio Earth Summit, and Mikhail Gorbachev, and written over the following decade by thousands of collaborators, the Earth Charter consists of sixteen principles deemed necessary for sustainable life in community on this planet.

138. Boston Research Center for the 21st Century, *Buddhist Perspectives on the Earth Charter* (Cambridge, MA: Boston Research Center for the 21st Century, 1997), 73.

139. Rupert Gethin, *The Foundations of Buddhism* (New York: Oxford University Press, 1998), 88.

140. Morinaga Sōkō, "My Struggle to Become a Zen Monk," in *Zen: Tradition & Transition*, ed. Kenneth Kraft (New York: Grove Press, 1988), 23.

141. Thich Nhat Hanh, *Interbeing: Fourteen Guidelines for Engaged Buddhism*, 3rd ed. (Berkeley: Parallax Press, 1998), 33.

142. Christopher Ives, *Zen Awakening and Society* (London: Macmillan, 1992), 129.

143. D. T. Suzuki, *An Introduction to Zen Buddhism* (New York: Grove Press, 1964), 131.

144. Helena Norberg-Hodge, *Ancient Futures: Learning from Ladakh* (San Francisco: Sierra Club Books, 1991), 25-26.

145. See Elgin, *Voluntary Simplicity*; David E. Shi, *The Simple Life: Plain Living and High Thinking in American Culture* (Athens: University of Georgia Press, 2007); Cecile Andrews, *The Circle of Simplicity: Return to the Good Life* (New York: HarperCollins, 1997); Michael Schut, ed., *Simpler Living, Compassionate Life: A Christian Perspective* (Denver: Living the Good News, 2007).

146. Elgin, *Voluntary Simplicity*, 24–25.

147. Elgin, *Voluntary Simplicity*, 25.

148. Elgin, *Voluntary Simplicity*, 150.

149. Carter and Palihawadana, trans., *The Dhammapada*, 208.

150. Bhikkhu Bodhi, trans., *The Connected Discourses of the Buddha*, 662.

151. Lambert Schmithausen, *Buddhism and Nature* (Tokyo: International Institute for Buddhist Studies, 1991), 18.

152. Pibob Udomittipong, "Thailand's Ecology Monks," in Kaza and Kraft, *Dharma Rain*, 191.

153. Robin Wall Kimmerer, *Braiding Sweetgrass: Indigenous Wisdom, Scientific Knowledge, and the Teachings of Plants* (Minneapolis: Milkweed Editions, 2013), 111. ·

154. For example, Galatians 6:7 says, "Do not be deceived: God cannot be mocked. A man reaps what he sows."

155. See my brief discussion of Sarvodaya in chapter 11 below. Also see Joanna Macy, *Dharma and Development*, and George D. Bond, *Buddhism at Work: Community Development, Social Empowerment, and the Sarvodaya Movement* (Bloomfield, CT: Kumarian Press, 2004).

156. Dale S. Wright, *The Six Perfections: Buddhism & the Cultivation of Character* (New York: Oxford University Press, 2009), 24–25.

157. Taigen Dan Leighton, *The Faces of Compassion: Classic Bodhisattva Archetypes and Their Modern Expression* (Somerville, MA: Wisdom Publications, 2003), 64.

158. Bays, *How to Train a Wild Elephant*, 24.

159. Macy and Brown, *Coming Back to Life*, 92.

160. Macy and Brown, *Coming Back to Life*, 92.

161. Norman Fischer, "Wash Your Bowls," in Kaza, *Hooked!*, 217.

162. Thorp, *Sweeping Changes*, 26.

163. Thich Nhat Hanh, *Zen and the Art of Saving the Planet* (New York: HarperOne, 2021), 102.

164. Richard P. Hayes, "Towards a Buddhist View of Nature," *ARC* XVIII (Spring 1990), 23. Lewis Lancaster has written, "Is it not the case that practices such as birth control, using less, saving, recycling, changing our diet, forgoing convenience in favor of conservation are all forms of a modern asceticism?" "Buddhism and Ecology: Collective Cultural Perceptions," in Tucker and Williams, *Buddhism and Ecology*, 15.

165. Rita M. Gross, "Personal Transformation and the Earth Charter," in Boston Research Center, *Buddhist Perspectives on the Earth Charter*, 57

166. Lily De Silva, "Early Buddhist Attitudes toward Nature," in Kaza and Kraft, *Dharma Rain*, 96.

167. This fear appears to be flagged by the claim in the *Laṅkāvatāra Sūtra* that eating meat causes terror in animals. Matthieu Ricard, *A Plea for the Animals: The Moral, Philosophical, and Evolutionary Imperative to Treat All Beings with Compassion* (Boulder, CO: Shambhala Publications, 2014), 29.

168. Kosho Yamamoto, trans. *The Mahayana Mahaparinirvana Sutra, revised and edited by Tony Page (web-published pdf, 2007)*, 52. http://www.shabkar.org/download/pdf/Mahaparinirvana_Sutra_Yamamoto_Page_2007.pdf

169. Christian climate scientist Katherine Hayhoe writes, "Love is key to acting on climate change: caring for the poor and the needy, those most affected by the impacts of a changing climate, as well as creation itself. It's not only our responsibility, *it's who Christians believe God made us to be.*" *Saving Us*, 142.

170. Thich Nhat Hanh, *Interbeing*, 21.

171. Hayhoe, *Saving Us*, 83.

172. Marc Bekoff, *Rewilding Our Hearts: Building Pathways of Compassion and Coexistence* (Novato, CA: New World Library, 2014), 43.

173. Shantigarbha, *The Burning House: A Buddhist Response to the Climate and Ecological Emergency* (Cambridge: Windhorse Publications, 2021), 55.

174. Damien Keown, "Buddhism and Ecology: A Virtue Ethics Approach," *Contemporary Buddhism* 8, no. 2 (November 2007), 110.

175. Simon James, *Zen Buddhism and Environmental Ethics*. (Burlington, VT: Ashgate Publishing Company, 2004), 128. With regard to the virtue of "insight into the nature of things," James asserts that "as one internalizes the teachings of emptiness, etc., and so develops the virtue of insight, one also learns to feel and act in ways appropriate to that vision of the world. Hence insight comes as part of a 'package deal,' bound up with virtues such as compassion, non-violence, selflessness and mindfulness" (128). He continues, ". . . to be compassionate is to feel compassion for all sentient beings, human and non-human, and to act so as to alleviate their suffering. To be non-violent is to treat all beings with respect and not as merely instrumentally valuable. To be selfless is not to be self-abnegating, but to be non-attached to oneself, and to therefore be free of the desire to greedily consume as many natural resources as possible" (128). And with regard to mindfulness, he writes, "To be mindful is to have made one's actions one's own, not to be carried through life by the inertia of habit, and to be aware of the consequences of one's actions, environmental or otherwise" (128).

176. Gary Snyder, *The Practice of the Wild: Essays by Gary Snyder* (San Francisco: North Point Press, 1990), 23–24.

177. Bill McKibben, *Eaarth: Making a Life on a Tough New Planet* (New York: Times Books, 2010), 103.

178. Madeline Ostrander, *At Home on an Unruly Planet: Finding Refuge in a Changed Earth* (New York: Henry Holt and Company, 2022), 278.

179. Christopher Reed has formulated five eco-precepts: (1) I vow to recycle everything I can; (2) I vow to be energy efficient; (3) I vow to be an active and informed voter; (4) I vow to be car conscious; and (5) I vow to exercise my purchasing power for the benefit of all sentient beings. Christopher Reed, "Down to Earth," in Badiner, *Dharma Gaia*, 235. Joanna Macy and Chris Johnstone have come up with another set of five vows:

> To commit myself daily to the healing of the world and the welfare of all beings.
>
> To live on Earth more lightly and less violently in the food, products, and energy I consume.
>
> To draw strength and guidance from the living Earth, the ancestors, the future generations, and my brothers and sisters of all species.
>
> To support others in our work for the world and to ask for help when I need it.
>
> To pursue a daily practice that clarifies my mind, strengthens my heart, and supports me in observing these vows.

Macy and Johnstone, *Active Hope*, 202–3.

180. Snyder, *The Practice of the Wild*, 148; quoted by David Landis Barnhill, "Great Earth *Saṅgha*: Gary Snyder's View of Nature as Community," in Tucker and Williams, *Buddhism and Ecology*, 205.

181. Snyder, *The Practice of the Wild*, 148; quoted by Barnhill, "Great Earth *Saṅgha*," 205.

182. Snyder, *The Practice of the Wild*, 149.

183. As the tradition would have it (though not most scholars), this advocacy of *samu* and, by extension, monastic self-sufficiency, was systematized by Baizhang (J. Hyakujō 720–814), purported author of the early monastic code *Chan-yuan ching-kuei*, which set Zen apart from other forms of Buddhism that relied more on lay patronage.

184. Michael Carroll, *Awake at Work: Facing the Challenges of Life on the Job* (Boston: Shambhala Publications, 2004), 55.

185. Bays, *How to Train a Wild Elephant*, 24.

186. The seven "leave no trace" principles are: (1) plan ahead and prepare, (2) travel and camp on durable surfaces, (3) dispose of waste properly, (4) leave what you find, (5) minimize campfire impacts, (6) respect wildlife, and (7) be considerate of other visitors.

187. Suzuki, *Zen Mind, Beginner's Mind*, 62.

188. As the Japanese engineers for whom I once interpreted were wont to say, *dandori hachibu*, "preparation is eighty percent."

189. Thich Nhat Hanh, *Love Letter to the Earth*, 93.

190. For further description of this ritualized meal, see my *Zen on the Trail*, 68.

191. Buddhism imagines six paths or levels of rebirth (J. *rokudō*): denizens of hell, hungry ghosts (*gaki*), animal beasts, humans, warrior titans, and heavenly beings. The *gaki*, living one level above the denizens of hell, are beings who because of greed in a previous lifetime have been born with tiny throats, leaving them constantly hungry. It's interesting that *preta*, the Sanskrit term that is translated in Japanese as *gaki*, derives from a term for ancestors.

192. Sutta Nipāta 1.8. Bhikkhu Bodhi, trans. *The Suttanipāta: An Ancient Collection of the Buddha's Discourses Together with Its Commentaries* (Somerville, MA: Wisdom Publications, 2017), 179.

193. See my *Meditations on the Trail* for more detailed instructions.

194. Thich Nhat Hanh, *Love Letter to the Earth*, 51.

195. See note 104.

196. That being said, it is important to note that some Zen Buddhists have cautioned against art appreciation, lest the things being appreciated and the aesthetic experiences themselves become objects of attachment.

197. Quoted by Richard Louv, *The Nature Principle: Human Restoration and the End of Nature-Deficit Disorder* (Chapel Hill, NC: Algonquin Books, 2011), 72.

198. James, *Zen Buddhism and Environmental Ethics*, 73.

199. Padmasiri de Silva, "Buddhist Environmental Ethics," in Badiner, *Dharma Gaia*, 15.

200. Barnhill, "Great Earth *Saṅgha*," 92.

201. Joan Halifax, *The Fruitful Darkness: Reconnecting with the Body of the Earth* (New York: HarperCollins, 2013), 84.

202. Claire Dunn, *Rewilding the Urban Soul: Searching for the Wild in the City* (London: Scribe Publications, 2021) 7.

203. Daniel R. Wildcat, *Red Alert!: Saving the Planet with Indigenous Knowledge* (Golden, CO: Fulcrum Publishing, 2009), 29–30.

204. This was one of my reasons for writing *Zen on the Trail* and *Meditations on the Trail*.

205. Ostrander, *At Home on an Unruly Planet*, 278.

206. For an example of this, see D. T. Suzuki's chapter on Zen and the Japanese love of nature in his *Zen and Japanese Culture*.

207. As I have written elsewhere, in Japanese arts it is usually a minimalist, miniature, stylized nature that is loved.

208. Han-Shan, "Cold Mountain Poems," trans. Burton Watson, in Kaza and Kraft, *Dharma Rain*, 54.

209. Patrick McMahon describes one of these backpacking retreats in "Meditating with Mountains and Rivers" (in Kaza and Kraft, *Dharma Rain*).

210. See my *Zen on the Trail* and *Meditations on the Trail*.

211. Macy and Brown, *Coming Back to Life*, 21.

212. This seems to be what Dōgen was getting at when he wrote, "for the myriad things to advance and realize-in-practice the self is awakening."

213. Kōshō Uchiyama and Shōhaku Okumura, *The Zen Teachings of Homeless Kodo* (Somerville, MA: Wisdom Publications, 2014), 48.

214. This is the stance of Immanuel Kant and other philosophers influenced by his epistemology.

215. Dōgen Zenji, "*Sokushin ze butsu*" fascicle of *Shōbō-genzō*, ed. Ōkubo Dōshū (Tokyo: Chikuma Shobō, 1971), 44; quoted by Ruben Habito, "Mountains and Rivers and the Great Earth," in Tucker and Williams, *Buddhism and Ecology*, 168. Contemporary Zen teacher Ruben Habito echoes Yangshan when he writes, "Mountains, rivers, and the great earth are experienced as manifestations of one's own true self; they are no longer seen as 'out there,' entities separate from oneself." Habito, "Mountains and Rivers and the Great Earth," 170.

216. Thich Nhat Hanh. *Being Peace*, 68–69. As I have written elsewhere, we need to be careful when we lift up "becoming one" with things. See my "In Search of Green Dharma: Philosophical Issues in Buddhist Environmental Ethics," in *Destroying Mara Forever: Buddhist Ethics Essays in Honor of Damien Keown*, ed. Charles Prebish and John Powers (Ithaca, NY: Snow Lion Publications, 2009).

217. Vajragupta, *Wild Awake: Alone, Offline & Aware in Nature* (Cambridge: Windhorse Publications, 2018), 143.

218. Chatsumarn Kabilsingh. "Early Buddhist Views on Nature," in Badiner, *Dharma Gaia*, 8–9.

219. Arne Naess, "Self-Realization: An Ecological Approach to Being in the World," in *Thinking Like a Mountain: Toward a Council of All Beings*, ed. John Seed, Joanna Macy, Pat Fleming, and Arne Naess (Gabriola Island, BC: New Catalyst Books, 2007), 29.

220. Of course, a question for all of us is how, in the face of a crisis calling for

immediate and momentous action, we are to cultivate this awareness quickly in a large enough number of people to make a difference.

221. Joanna Macy, "The Greening of the Self," in Badiner, *Dharma Gaia*, 53.

222. I set forth these practices in *Meditations on the Trail: A Guide to Self-Discovery* (Somerville, MA: Wisdom Publications, 2021).

223. Thich Nhat Hanh, *Zen and the Art of Saving the Planet*, 124.

224. Macy and Johnstone, *Active Hope*, 71.

225. Scott Russel Sanders, *Staying Put: Making a Home in a Restless World* (Boston: Beacon Press, 1993), 28.

226. In this vein, Joanna Macy and Chris Johnstone celebrate our "connected self," about which they write, "We can deepen our sense of belonging in the world. Like trees extending their root system, we can grow in connection, thus allowing ourselves to draw from a deeper pool of strength, accessing the courage and intelligence we so greatly need right now." *Active Hope*, 31–32. They see this connected self as the source from which "much of what people most value emerges, including love, friendship, loyalty, trust, relationship, belonging, purpose, gratitude, spirituality, mutual aid, and meaning." *Active Hope*, 89.

227. Bekoff, *Rewilding Our Hearts*, 40-41.

228. Christiana Figueres and Tom Rivett-Carnac write, "Our current crisis requires a total shift in our thinking. To survive and thrive, we must understand ourselves to be inextricably connected to all of nature." *The Future We Choose: The Stubborn Optimist's Guide to the Climate Crisis* (New York: Vintage Books, 2020), 39.

229. Philip Clayton and Wm. Andrew Schwartz, *What is Ecological Civilization?: Crisis, Hope, and Future of the Planet* (Anoka, MN: Process Century Press, 2019), 64.

230. Clayton and Schwartz, *What is Ecological Civilization?*, 64.

231. Wildcat, *Red Alert!*, 20.

232. Gary Snyder, "Reinhabitation," in *A Place in Space: Ethics, Aesthetics, and Watersheds* (Washington, DC: Counterpoint, 1995), 191.

233. Gary Snyder, *The Real Work: Interviews & Talks 1964–1979* (New York: New Directions, 1980), 117.

234. Wildcat, *Red Alert!*, 32.

235. Wildcat, *Red Alert!*, 38.

236. Snyder, *The Practice of the Wild*, 36.

237. Snyder, *The Practice of the Wild*, 94.

238. Gary Snyder, *Nobody Home: Writing, Buddhism, and Living in Places* (San Antonio: Trinity University Press, 2014), 71.

239. Snyder, "Reinhabitation," 190.

240. Julia Martin, "Coyote Mind: An Interview with Gary Snyder," *TriQuarterly* 79 (Fall 1990), 152; cited by Charles R. Strain, "The Pacific Buddha's Wild Practice: Gary Snyder's Environmental Ethic," in *American Buddhism: Methods and Findings in Recent Scholarship*, ed. Dunken Ryūken Williams and Christopher S. Queen (Richmond, UK: Curzon Press, 1999), 52.

241. Snyder, *The Practice of the Wild*, 44.

242. Snyder, *The Practice of the Wild*, 39.

243. Snyder, *The Real Work*, 16.

244. Charles R. Strain, "The Pacific Buddha's Wild Practice: Gary Snyder's Environmental Ethic," in Williams and Queen, *American Buddhism*, 152.

245. Sanders, *Staying Put*, 62.

246. Here in New England, we're indebted to John Hanson Mitchell, who has written *A Field Guide to Your Own Back Yard* and an array of other engaging books about this region.

247. It is important to note that in the United States many Indigenous peoples have never left the land that their ancestors inhabited. And other Indigenous peoples have been dispossessed of their homeland, which makes inhabitation and reinhabitation of that land challenging if not impossible for them. Most non-Indigenous people exist here as colonial settlers, as uninvited occupiers of the land they might (re)inhabit. And all non-Indigenous people have benefited from settler colonialism.

248. Snyder, *The Real Work*, 180–81.

249. Wildcat, *Red Alert!*, 62.

250. Snyder, *The Real Work*, 23.

251. Snyder, *The Real Work*, 172.

252. David W. Orr, *Earth in Mind: On Education, Environment, and the Human Prospect* (Washington, DC: Island Press, 2004), 147; quoted by Louv, *The Nature Principle*, 89.

253. Gary Snyder, *Turtle Island* (New York: New Directions, 1974), 99.

254. Snyder, *The Real Work*, 161.

255. Snyder, *The Real Work*, 64.

256. Aldo Leopold, *A Sand County Almanac And Sketches Here and There* (New York: Oxford University Press, 1969), 174.

257. Bekoff, *Rewilding Our Hearts*, 91–92.

258. Snyder, *A Place in Space*, 246–47.

259. Korten, "Ecological Civilization and the New Enlightenment," 23.

260. Gary Snyder, *Back on the Fire* (Washington, DC: Counterpoint, 2008), 98.

261. Snyder, *Back on the Fire*, 98. He also claims, "We speak of watershed consciousness, and the great water-cycle of the planet makes it all one watershed. We are all natives to this earth" (98).

262. Sanders, *Staying Put*, xiii.

263. As Snyder flags, in reinhabitation we may even feel identity with that larger something: "A people and a place become one." *A Place in Space*, 95.

264. U.S. Geological Survey, "Climate Change and Wildlife Health: Direct and Indirect Effects," https://pubs.usgs.gov/fs/2010/3017/pdf/fs2010-3017.pdf, accessed November 9, 2023.

265. Granted, Thich Nhat Hanh's discussion of interbeing highlights the larger system that provides the inputs constitutive of oneself and such things as a flower.

266. Such as the categorizing of animals in terms of different types of birth.

267. And only recently have Buddhists been extrapolating from the doctrine of conditioned arising to offer an ecological view of nature.

268. Gishin Tokiwa, trans. *The Laṅkāvatāra Sūtram: A Jewel Scripture of Mahāyāna Thought and Practice* (Osaka: Gishin Tokiwa, 2003) 453, *slightly adapted*.

269. That being said, Buddhism celebrates *nāga*, semi-divine serpents who, among other things, protected the Buddha.

270. Rafe Martin, "Thoughts on the Jatakas," in Kaza and Kraft, *Dharma Rain*, 106.

271. Christopher Gowans comments that these tales use the device of "depicting various living beings as proxies for human beings" and "are mainly morality tales about human beings." *Buddhist Moral Philosophy: An Introduction* (New York: Routledge, 2015), 282.

272. David Abram, *The Spell of the Sensuous* (New York: Vintage Books, 1996), 203–4.

273. Abram, *The Spell of the Sensuous*, 204.

274. Abram, *The Spell of the Sensuous*, 204.

275. Abram, *The Spell of the Sensuous*, x.

276. Granted, at a deeper level our minds may be organizing data à la Kant in a kind of perspectivism, but it is, as Brett Davis terms it, an "egoless perspectivism." See his "The Philosophy of Zen Master Dōgen: Egoless Perspectivism."

277. Abram, *The Spell of the Sensuous*, 33.

278. Abram, *The Spell of the Sensuous*, 34.

279. Abram, *The Spell of the Sensuous*, 45.

280. David Abram, *Becoming Animal: An Earthly Cosmology* (New York: Pantheon Books, 2010), 251.

281. Abram, *The Spell of the Sensuous*, 260.

282. Abram, *Becoming Animal*, 265.

283. Abram, *Becoming Animal*, 192.

284. Abram, *The Spell of the Sensuous*, 256.

285. Abram, *Becoming Animal*, 167.

286. Abram, *Becoming Animal*, 173.

287. Abram, *The Spell of the Sensuous*, 19.

288. Snyder, *Practice of the Wild*, 20; cited by Barnhill, "Great Earth *Saṅgha*," 198.

289. Thich Nhat Hanh, *Love Letter to the Earth*, 11.

290. This is the title of Wohlleben's 2015 bestseller.

291. Simard, quoted by Wohlleben, *The Hidden Life of Trees: What They Feel, How They Communicate, Discoveries from a Secret World* (Vancouver: Greystone Books, 2015), 11.

292. Suzanne Simard, *Finding the Mother Tree: Discovering the Wisdom of the Forest* (New York: Alfred A. Knopf, 2021), 4.

293. Simard, *Finding the Mother Tree*, 5.

294. Wohlleben, *The Hidden Life of Trees*, 3.

295. Stephanie Kaza writes, "Naess maintained that the most convincing environmental ethics rest on experiential insights of relationship with other life-forms that expand one's own sense of self." *Mindfully Green: A Personal and Spiritual Guide to Whole Earth Thinking* (Boston: Shambhala Publications, 2008), 88.

296. Gary Snyder, *Earth House Hold* (New York: New Directions, 1969), 129.

297. David Barnhill, "Great Earth *Saṅgha*," 194.

298. Snyder, *The Practice of the Wild*, 24.

299. Aldo Leopold, *A Sand County Almanac* (New York: Oxford University Press, 1949), 204.

300. Snyder, *The Real Work*, 159.
301. Snyder, *The Real Work*, 49.
302. This may also help Buddhists develop the doctrine of buddha-nature. His-
    torically, the ascription of buddha-nature to animals other than us was
    simply an affirmation of their potential to awaken, rather than an animistic
    stance that thought long and hard about their sentience, intelligence, and
    expressiveness in the sensuous field of our breathing universe.
303. An expression coined by animal rights thinker Tom Regan.
304. Abram, *Becoming Animal*, 300.
305. Abram, *The Spell of the Sensuous*, 53.
306. Abram, *The Spell of the Sensuous*, 65.
307. Abram, *The Spell of the Sensuous*, 65.
308. Abram, *The Spell of the Sensuous*, 19.
309. Abram, *The Spell of the Sensuous*, 65.
310. Abram, *The Spell of the Sensuous*, 65.
311. John B. Cobb, Jr., *Sustaining the Common Good*, 33.
312. Skt. *kalyāṇa-mitra*.
313. Snyder, *Nobody Home*, 31.
314. As John B. Cobb, Jr. tells us, "Prizing of individual autonomy could give way
    to [or be balanced with] prizing of communal sharing and mutual support."
    Sustainability: Economics, Ecology, and Justice (Eugene, OR: Wipf & Stock Pub-
    lishers, 2007), 33. He adds, "Food habits could change to achieve greater
    health and enjoyment at less expense to the world's resources" (33).
315. Bill McKibben has extolled the use of social media at the local level as a way
    to network and exchange information.
316. Snyder, *Turtle Island*, 98.
317. Barnhill, "Great Earth *Saṅgha*, 210.
318. Snyder, *Nobody Home*, 31–32. Snyder also writes, "To restore the land one
    must live and work in a place. To work in a place is to work with others. Peo-
    ple who work together in a place become a community, and a community,
    in time, grows a culture." *Place in Space*, 250.
319. Macy and Johnstone, *Active Hope*, 119.
320. Sulak Sivaraksa, *Seeds of Peace: A Buddhist Vision for Renewing Society* (Berke-
    ley: Parallax Press, 1992), 109.
321. Snyder, *The Real Work*, 141. In their attempts to envision and create an opti-
    mal society, Buddhists can also draw from Larry Rasmussen's notion of
    "anticipatory communities" of people who are already living in "Earth-hon-
    oring" ways. As Rasmussen puts it, "'Anticipatory communities' are home
    places where it is possible to reimagine worlds and reorder possibilities,
    places where new or renewed practices give focus to an ecological and
    postindustrial way of life. . . . Here eco-social virtues are consciously culti-
    vated and embodied in community practices. Here the fault lines of moder-
    nity are exposed." Larry L. Rasmussen, *Earth-Honoring Faith: Religious Ethics
    in a New Key* (New York: Oxford University Press, 2013), 227.
322. McKibben, *Eaarth*, 124; his emphasis.
323. Here, too, dialogue with Cobb can prove useful, especially for those of
    us who are drawn to deep ecology. He writes that "what is called 'deep

ecology' usually begins with the condition of the earth and moves from that to the well-being of the human species and its members. This is a rational approach to be fully respected. But it is not the Christian one. Christians typically begin with the 'neighbor' who is in need." Cobb, "Protestant Theology and Deep Ecology," in *Deep Ecology and World Religions: New Essays on Sacred Ground*, ed. David Landiss Barnhill and Roger S. Gottlieb (Albany: SUNY Press, 2001), 220.

324. Snyder, *Turtle Island*, 101.

325. Kaira Jewel Lingo, *We Were Made for These Times*, 114.

326. Snyder, *Earth House Hold*, 90.

327. Ichikawa Hakugen, "The Problem of Buddhist Socialism in Japan," *Japanese Religions* 6/3 (August 1970): 16D. T7. I partially adapted the translation on the basis of the original Japanese in *Bukkyōsha no sensō-sekinin*, vol. 4 of *Ichikawa Hakugen chosakushū* [The collected works of Ichikawa Hakugen] (Kyoto: Hōzōkan, 1993).

328. Wealth has been seen in many Buddhist societies as the result of meritorious actions in previous lifetimes.

329. See my *Imperial-Way Zen: Ichikawa Hakugen's Critique and Lingering Questions for Buddhist Ethics* (Honolulu: University of Hawai'i Press, 2009).

330. McKibben, *Eaarth*, xv.

331. Perhaps a shared desire for the kind of community sketched here is a promising candidate for common ground. In the United States, citizens across the political spectrum, in states "red" and "blue," grieve the loss of community, as they live, in many cases, in factory and farm communities with boarded up shops on main street, or in more affluent communities where people retreat into their hyper-individualistic worlds of gated communities, black screens, consumerism, and distraction.

332. Amod Lele, "Disengaged Buddhism," *Journal of Buddhist Ethics* 26 (2019), 241.

333. One Earth Sangha home page, oneearthsangha.org, accessed April 14, 2022.

334. Gathas are short verses that are recited.

335. Thich Nhat Hanh, "Earth Gathas," in Badiner, *Dharma Gaia*, 195.

336. https://www.facebook.com/buddhistclimateactionnetwork/; accessed on May 31, 2022.

337. Reginald A. Ray, "The Buddha's Politics," in *Mindful Politics: A Buddhist Guide to Making the World a Better Place*, ed. Melvin McLeod (Somerville, MA: Wisdom Publications, 2006), 66.

338. As Stephen Jenkins has pointed out, in some Buddhist texts the Buddha is said to have asked for his audience to be fed before he preached. See Jenkins's article, "Do Bodhisattvas Relieve Poverty? The Distinction between Economic and Spiritual Development and Their Interrelation in Indian Buddhist Texts," *Journal of Buddhist Ethics* 7 (2000).

339. Although at least some forms of Buddhism claim that vows and actions flow automatically from our awakening to emptiness, I do not see social and political activism as something that *necessarily* flows from Buddhist meditative praxis. As I just mentioned, resistance to the status quo and activism aimed at changing it have been exceedingly rare across the history of Buddhism, and this historical fact undermines claims about awakened Buddhists' *auto-*

matically taking action to alleviate suffering (at least forms of suffering other than the existential "religious" suffering of individual practitioners presenting themselves to Buddhist teachers for guidance).

340. Macy and Johnstone, *Active Hope*, 112.

341. Hayhoe, *Saving Us*, 202.

342. Marianne E. Krasny, *In This Together: Connecting with Your Community to Combat the Climate Crisis* (Ithaca, NY: Cornell University Press, 2023), 8.

343. Hayhoe, *Saving Us*, 199.

344. Macy and Johnstone, *Active Hope*, 35.

345. Macy and Johnstone, *Active Hope*, 4–5.

346. Thomas Homer-Dixon, *Commanding Hope: The Power We Have to Renew a World in Peril* (Toronto: Alfred A. Knopf Canada, 2020), 61.

347. Homer-Dixon, *Commanding Hope*, 81.

348. Ostrander, *At Home on an Unruly Planet*, 273.

349. Macy and Johnstone, *Active Help*, 219. Mihaly Csikszentmihalyi, *Flow: The Psychology of Optimal Experience* (New York: Harper and Row, 1990).

350. Figueres and Rivett-Carnac, *The Future We Choose*, 43.

351. Shantigarbha writes, "Given that actions have consequences depending on the motivations with which they are performed, it's not just what we do but *how* we respond that is crucial. How we respond now will provide a template for future responses. Acceptance, compassion, cooperation, and empathy will lead to different outcomes from aggression, competition, blame, and denial." *The Burning House: A Buddhist Response to the Climate and Ecological Emergency* (Cambridge: Windhorse Publications, 2021), 212.

352. Stephanie Kaza, "To Save All Beings: Buddhist Environmental Activism," in *Engaged Buddhism in the West*, ed. Christopher S. Queen (Somerville, MA: Wisdom Publications, 2000), 175–76.

353. Macy and Johnstone, *Active Hope*, 232. Macy and Johnstone also write, "Whenever we act from bodhicitta, the desire that all life be well, we are being an activist." *Active Hope*, 216.

354. Macy and Johnstone, *Active Hope*, 33.

355. Kaira Jewel Lingo, *We Were Made for These Times*, 78.

356. Dalai Lama XIV, "Universal Responsibility and the Climate Emergency," in *A Buddhist Response to the Climate Emergency*, ed. John Stanley, David R. Loy, and Gyurme Dorje (Boston: Wisdom Publications, 2009), 21.

357. Susan Murphy, *Minding the Earth, Mending the World: Zen and the Art of Planetary Crisis* (Berkeley: Counterpoint, 2014), 9.

358. Emma Harris, "How to Stop Freaking Out and Tackle Climate Change," https://www.nytimes.com/2020/01/10/opinion/sunday/how-to-help-climate-change.html, accessed April 15, 2022.

359. Snyder, *Turtle Island*, 101.

360. Author of *Don't Even Think of It: How Our Brains Are Wired to Ignore Climate Change* (New York: Bloomsbury, 2014).

361. See *Saving Us*.

362. Krasny, *In This Together*, 15.

363. Rasmussen, *Earth-Honoring Faith*, 120–21.

364. https://350mass.betterfutureproject.org/; accessed August 2, 2022.

365. Currently before the House of Representatives is a piece of legislation directed to this goal: the Energy Innovation and Carbon Dividend Act of 2023 (H.R. 5744).

366. Christopher Ives, *Zen Awakening and Society* (Honolulu: University of Hawai'i Press, 1992), 123–24.

367. Christopher Ives, "Liberation from Economic Dukkha: A Buddhist Critique of the Gospels of Growth and Globalization in Dialogue with John Cobb," in *The World Market and Interreligious Dialogue*, ed. Catherine Cornille and Glenn Willis. (Eugene, OR: Cascade Books, 2011), 122.

368. Macy, *Dharma and Development*, 35.

369. Macy, *Dharma and Development*, 34.

370. Cobb, *Sustaining the Common Good*, 33.

371. Sulak Sivaraksa, *Conflict, Culture, Change: Engaged Buddhism in a Globalizing World* (Somerville, MA: Wisdom Publications, 2005), 37.

372. Sulak Sivaraksa, *Seeds of Peace*, 44.

373. Bhikkhu Bodhi, "Climate Change is a Moral Issue: A Buddhist response to Pope Francis's climate change encyclical" *Tricycle*, June 18, 2015, http://tricycle.org/trikedaily/climate-change-moral-issue.

374. John Stanley and David Loy, "Buddhism and the End of Economic Growth," *Huffington Post*, September 19, 2011, http://www.huffingtonpost.com/john-stanley/buddhism-and-economic-growth_b_954457.html; accessed October 22, 2023.

375. David Loy and Bhikkhu Bodhi, "The Time to Act is Now: A Buddhist Declaration on Climate Change," in David Loy, *Ecodharma: Buddhist Teachings for the Ecological Crisis* (Somerville, MA: Wisdom Publications, 2019), 184.

376. Loy and Bhikkhu Bodhi, "The Time to Act is Now," 184.

Bibliography

Abram, David. *Becoming Animal: An Earthly Cosmology.* New York: Pantheon Books, 2010.

———. *The Spell of the Sensuous.* New York: Vintage Books, 1996.

Albrecht, Glenn A. *Earth Emotions: New Words for a New World.* Ithaca, NY: Cornell University Press, 2019.

Altschuler, Stephen. *Sacred Paths and Muddy Places: Rediscovering Spirit in Nature.* Lincoln, NE: iUniverse, 2007.

Andrews, Cecile. *The Circle of Simplicity: Return to the Good Life.* New York: Harper-Collins, 1997.

Barnhill, David Landis. "Great Earth *Saṅgha*: Gary Snyder's View of Nature as Community." In *Buddhism and Ecology: The Interconnection of Dharma and Deeds,* edited by Mary Evelyn Tucker and Dunken Ryūken Williams. Cambridge, MA: Harvard University Press, 1997.

Batchelor, Stephen. "The Practice of Generosity." In *Mindfulness in the Marketplace: Compassionate Responses to Consumerism,* edited by Allan Hunt Badiner. Berkeley: Parallax Press, 2002.

Bays, Jan Chozen. *How to Train a Wild Elephant: And Other Adventures in Mindfulness.* Boston: Shambhala Publications, 2011.

Bekoff, Marc. *Rewilding Our Hearts: Building Pathways of Compassion and Coexistence.* Novato, CA: New World Library, 2014.

Bennett-Vogt, Stephanie. *A Year to Clear: A Daily Guide to Creating Spaciousness in Your Home and Heart.* San Antonio: Hierophant Publishing, 2015.

———. *Your Spacious Self: Clear the Clutter and Discover Who You Are.* San Antonio: Hierophant Publishing, 2012.

Bhikkhu Bodhi, "Climate Change Is a Moral Issue: A Buddhist response to Pope Francis's climate change encyclical." *Tricycle,* June 18, 2015. http://tricycle.org/trikedaily/climate-change-moral-issue; accessed July 7, 2021.

———, trans. *The Connected Discourses of the Buddha: A Translation of the Saṃyutta Nikāya.* Somerville, MA: Wisdom Publications, 2000.

———, trans. *The Suttanipāta: An Ancient Collection of the Buddha's Discourses Together with Its Commentaries.* Somerville, MA: Wisdom Publications, 2017.

Bond, George D. *Buddhism at Work: Community Development, Social Empowerment, and the Sarvodaya Movement.* Bloomfield, CT: Kumarian Press, 2004.

Boston Research Center for the 21st Century. *Buddhist Perspectives on the Earth Charter.* Cambridge, MA: Boston Research Center for the 21st Century, 1997.

Brown, Clair. *Buddhist Economics: An Enlightened Approach to the Dismal Science*. New York: Bloomsbury Press, 2017.

Brown, Edward Espe. "Leavening Spirit." *Tricycle*, Fall 2002.

Carroll, Michael. *Awake at Work: Facing the Challenges of Life on the Job*. Boston: Shambhala Publications, 2004.

Carter, John Ross and Mahinda Palihawadana, trans. *The Dhammapada*. New York: Oxford University Press, 1987.

Cashman, Tyrone. "Where Does It Come From? Where Does It Go?" In *Mindfulness in the Marketplace: Compassionate Responses to Consumerism*, edited by Alan Hunt Badiner. Berkeley: Parallax Press, 2002.

Clayton, Philip and Wm. Andrew Schwartz. *What is Ecological Civilization?: Crisis, Hope, and Future of the Planet*. Anoka, MN: Process Century Press, 2019.

Cobb, John B. Jr. "Protestant Theology and Deep Ecology." In *Deep Ecology and World Religions: New Essays on Sacred Ground*, edited by David Landiss Barnhill and Roger S. Gottlieb. Albany: SUNY Press, 2001.

——. *Sustainability: Economics, Ecology, and Justice*. Eugene, OR: Wipf & Stock Publishers, 2007.

——. *Sustaining the Common Good: A Christian Perspective on the Global Economy*. Cleveland: Pilgrim Press, 1994.

Csikszentmihalyi, Mihaly. *Flow: The Psychology of Optimal Experience*. New York: Harper and Row, 1990.

Dalai Lama XIV. "Universal Responsibility and the Climate Emergency." In *A Buddhist Response to the Climate Emergency*, edited by John Stanley, David R. Loy, and Gyurme Dorje. Boston: Wisdom Publications, 2009.

Davis, Brett W. "The Philosophy of Zen Master Dōgen: Egoless Perspectivism." In *Oxford Handbook of Japanese Philosophy*, edited by Bret W. Davis. New York: Oxford University Press, 2020.

——. "The Presencing of Truth: Dōgen's *Genjōkōan*." In *Buddhist Philosophy: Essential Readings*, edited by William Edelglass and Jay Garfield. New York: Oxford University Press, 2009.

de Silva, Lily. "Early Buddhist Attitudes toward Nature." In *Dharma Rain: Sources of Buddhist Environmentalism*, edited by Stephanie Kaza and Kenneth Kraft. Boston: Shambhala Publications, 2000.

de Silva, Padmasiri. "Buddhist Environmental Ethics." In *Dharma Gaia: A Harvest of Essays in Buddhism and Ecology*, edited by Alan Hunt Badiner. Berkeley: Parallax Press, 1990.

Dōgen. "*Sokushin ze butsu*." In *Shōbō-genzō*, edited by Ōkubo Dōshū. Tokyo: Chikuma Shobō, 1971.

Domke, David. *God Willing?: Political Fundamentalism in the White House, the "War on Terror," and the Echoing Press*. London: Pluto Press, 2004.

Dunn, Claire. *Rewilding the Urban Soul: Searching for the Wild in the City*. London: Scribe Publications, 2021.

Elgin, Duane. *Voluntary Simplicity: Toward a Way of Life that is Outwardly Simple, Inwardly Rich*. Rev. ed. New York: Harper, 1993.

Figueres, Christiana and Tom Rivett-Carnac. *The Future We Choose: The Stubborn Optimist's Guide to the Climate Crisis*. New York: Vintage Books, 2020.

Fischer, Norman. "Wash Your Bowls." In *Hooked! Buddhist Writings on Greed, Desire, and the Urge to Consume*, edited by Stephanie Kaza. Boston: Shambhala Publications, 2005.

Gethin, Rupert. *The Foundations of Buddhism*. New York: Oxford University Press, 1998.

Goldstein, Joseph. "Desire, Delusion, and DVDs." In *Hooked! Buddhist Writings on Greed, Desire, and the Urge to Consume*, edited by Stephanie Kaza. Boston: Shambhala Publications, 2005.

——. *The Experience of Insight: A Simple and Direct Guide to Buddhist Meditation*. Boston: Shambhala Publications, 1983.

Gowans, Christopher. *Buddhist Moral Philosophy: An Introduction*. New York: Routledge, 2015.

Greenspan, Alan. *The Age of Turbulence: Adventures in a New World*. New York: Penguin Press, 2007.

Gross, Rita M. "Personal Transformation and the Earth Charter." In *Buddhist Perspectives on the Earth Charter*, edited by Boston Research Center for the 21st Century. Cambridge, MA: Boston Research Center for the 21st Century, 1997.

Habito, Ruben L. F. "The Inner Pursuit of Happiness." In *Hooked! Buddhist Writings on Greed, Desire, and the Urge to Consume*, edited by Stephanie Kaza. Boston: Shambhala Publications, 2005.

Halifax, Joan. *The Fruitful Darkness: Reconnecting with the Body of the Earth*. New York: HarperCollins, 2013.

Han-Shan. "Cold Mountain Poems." Translated by Burton Watson. In *Dharma Rain: Sources of Buddhist Environmentalism*, edited by Stephanie Kaza and Kenneth Kraft. Boston: Shambhala Publications, 2000.

Harada Shodo Roshi. *Morning Dewdrops of the Mind: Teachings of a Contemporary Zen Master*. Translated by Daichi-Priscilla Storandt. Berkeley: Frog Books, 1993.

Harris, Emma. "How to Stop Freaking Out and Tackle Climate Change." *The New York Times*, January 10, 2020. https://www.nytimes.com/2020/01/10/opinion/sunday/how-to-help-climate-change.html; accessed October 10, 2023.

Hayes, Richard P. "Towards a Buddhist View of Nature." *ARC* XVIII (Spring 1990).

Hayhoe, Katharine. *Saving Us: A Climate Scientist's Case for Hope and Healing in a Divided World*. New York: One Signal Publishers/Atria Books, 2021.

Hegel, Georg Wilhelm Friedrich. *The Philosophy of History*. Translated by J. Sibree. New York: Dover Publications, 1956.

Homer-Dixon, Thomas. *Commanding Hope: The Power We Have to Renew a World in Peril*. Toronto: Alfred A. Knopf Canada, 2020.

Honoré, Carl. *In Praise of Slowness: Challenging the Cult of Speed*. New York: HarperCollins, 2004.

Ichikawa Hakugen. "The Problem of Buddhist Socialism in Japan." *Japanese Religions* 6/3 (August 1970).

Ives, Christopher. *Imperial-Way Zen: Ichikawa Hakugen's Critique and Lingering Questions for Buddhist Ethics*. Honolulu: University of Hawai'i Press, 2009.

——. "In Search of Green Dharma: Philosophical Issues in Buddhist Environmental Ethics." In *Destroying Mara Forever: Buddhist Ethics Essays in Honor of Damien Keown*. Edited by Charles Prebish and John Powers. Ithaca, NY: Snow Lion Publications, 2009.

——. "Liberation from Economic Dukkha: A Buddhist Critique of the Gospels of Growth and Globalization in Dialogue with John Cobb." In *The World Market and Interreligious Dialogue*, edited by Catherine Cornille and Glenn Willis. Eugene OR: Cascade Books, 2011.

——. *Meditations on the Trail: A Guidebook for Self-Discovery*. Somerville, MA: Wisdom Publications, 2021.

——. "True Person, Formless Self: Lay Zen Master Hisamatsu Shin'ichi." In *Zen Masters*, edited by Steven Heine and Dale S. Wright (New York: Oxford University Press, 2010).

——. *Zen Awakening and Society*. Honolulu: University of Hawai'i Press, 1992.

——. *Zen on the Trail: Hiking as Pilgrimage*. Somerville, MA: Wisdom Publications, 2018.

James, Simon P. *Zen Buddhism and Environmental Ethics*. Hampshire: Ashgate Publishing Company, 2004.

Jenkins, Stephen. "Do Bodhisattvas Relieve Poverty? The Distinction between Economic and Spiritual Development and Their Interrelation in Indian Buddhist Texts." *Journal of Buddhist Ethics* 7 (2000).

Jones, Ken. *Beyond Optimism: A Buddhist Political Economy*. Oxford: Jon Carpenter Publishing, 1993.

Kabilsingh, Chatsumarn. "Early Buddhist Views on Nature." In *Dharma Gaia: A Harvest of Essays in Buddhism and Ecology*, edited by Alan Hunt Badiner. Berkeley: Parallax Press, 1990.

Kasulis, Thomas. *Zen Action, Zen Person*. Honolulu: University of Hawai'i Press, 1981.

Kaufman, Mark. "The Carbon Footprint Sham: A 'Successful, Deceptive' PR Campaign." https://mashable.com/feature/carbon-footprint-pr-campaign-sham/; accessed October 22, 2023.

Kaza, Stephanie. *Green Buddhism: Practice and Compassionate Action in Uncertain Times*. Boulder, CO: Shambhala, 2019.

——, ed. *Hooked! Buddhist Writings on Greed, Desire, and the Urge to Consume*. Boston: Shambhala Publications, 2005.

——, "Introduction." In *Hooked! Buddhist Writings on Greed, Desire, and the Urge to Consume*, edited by Stephanie Kaza. Boston: Shambhala Publications, 2005.

——. *Mindfully Green: A Personal and Spiritual Guide to Whole Earth Thinking*. Boston: Shambhala Publications, 2008.

——. "To Save All Beings: Buddhist Environmental Activism." In *Engaged Buddhism in the West*, edited by Christopher S. Queen. Somerville, MA: Wisdom Publications, 2000.

Keown, Damien. "Buddhism and Ecology: A Virtue Ethics Approach." *Contemporary Buddhism* 8, no. 2 (November 2007).

Kimmerer, Robin Wall. *Braiding Sweetgrass: Indigenous Wisdom, Scientific Knowledge, and the Teachings of Plants*. Minneapolis: Milkweed Editions, 2013.

Kittisaro. "Tangled in Thought: How to Beat Your Mind at Its Own Game." *Tricycle* (Winter 2014).

Kondo, Marie. *The Life-Changing Magic of Tidying Up: The Japanese Art of Decluttering and Organizing*. Berkeley: Ten Speed Press, 2014.

Korten, David. "Ecological Civilization and the New Enlightenment." *Tikkun* (Fall 2017).

Krasny, Marianne E. *In This Together: Connecting with Your Community to Combat the Climate Crisis*. Ithaca, NY: Cornell University Press, 2023.

Lancaster, Lewis. "Buddhism and Ecology: Collective Cultural Perceptions." In *Buddhism and Ecology: The Interconnection of Dharma and Deeds*, edited by Mary Evelyn Tucker and Dunken Ryūken Williams. Cambridge, MA: Harvard University Press, 1997.

Lazoff, Bo. "How Not to Feast from the Poison Cake." In *Mindfulness in the Marketplace: Compassionate Responses to Consumerism*, edited by Alan Hunt Badiner. Berkeley: Parallax Press, 2002.

Leighton, Taigen Dan. *The Faces of Compassion: Classic Bodhisattva Archetypes and Their Modern Expression*. Somerville, MA: Wisdom Publications, 2003.

Lele, Amod. "Disengaged Buddhism." *Journal of Buddhist Ethics* 26 (2019).

Leopold, Aldo. *A Sand County Almanac and Sketches Here and There*. New York: Oxford University Press, 1969.

Lingo, Kaira Jewel. *We Were Made for These Times: Ten Lessons on Moving through Change, Loss, and Disruption*. Berkeley: Parallax Press, 2021.

Lippincott, Lorilee. *The Simple Living Handbook: Discover the Joy of a De-Cluttered Life*. New York, Skyhorse Publishing, 2013.

Lokos, Allan. "Skillful Speech," *Tricycle* (Winter 2008).

Louv, Richard. *Last Child in the Woods: Saving Our Children from Nature-Deficit Disorder*. Chapel Hill, NC: Algonquin Books, 2008.

———. *The Nature Principle: Human Restoration and the End of Nature-Deficit Disorder*. Chapel Hill, NC: Algonquin Books, 2011.

Loy, David R. *The Great Awakening: A Buddhist Social Theory*. Somerville, MA: Wisdom Publications, 1997.

———. *Money, Sex, War, Karma: Notes for a Buddhist Revolution* (Somerville, MA: Wisdom Publications, 2008).

Loy, David R. and Bhikkhu Bodhi, "The Time to Act Is Now: A Buddhist Declaration on Climate Change." In David R. Loy, *Ecodharma: Buddhist Teachings for the Ecological Crisis*. Somerville, MA: Wisdom Publications, 2019.

Loy, David and Linda Goodhew. "Consuming Time." In *Hooked! Buddhist Writings on Greed, Desire, and the Urge to Consume*, edited by Stephanie Kaza. Boston: Shambhala Publications, 2005.

Macy, Joanna. *Dharma and Development: Religion as Resource in the Sarvodaya Self-Help Movement*. Rev. ed. West Hartford, CT: Kumarian Press, 1985.

———. "The Greening of the Self." In *Dharma Gaia: A Harvest of Essays in Buddhism and Ecology*, edited by Alan Hunt Badiner. Berkeley: Parallax Press, 1990.

Macy, Joanna and Molly Brown. *Coming Back to Life*. Gabriola Island, BC: New Society Publishers, 2022.

Macy, Joanna and Chris Johnstone. *Active Hope: How to Face the Mess We're in with Unexpected Resilience & Creative Power*. Novato, CA: New World Library, 2022.

Mann, Michael E. *The New Climate War: The Fight to Take Back Our Planet*. New York: PublicAffairs, 2021.

Martin, Julia. "Coyote Mind: An Interview with Gary Snyder." *TriQuarterly* 79 (Fall 1990); cited by Charles R. Strain, "The Pacific Buddha's Wild Practice: Gary Snyder's Environmental Ethic." In *American Buddhism: Methods and Findings in Recent Scholarship*, edited by Dunken Ryūken Williams and Christopher S. Queen. Richmond, UK: Curzon Press, 1999.

McFague, Sallie. *Blessed Are the Consumers: Climate Change and the Practice of Restraint*. Minneapolis: Fortress Press, 2013.

McKibben, Bill. *Eaarth: Making a Life on a Tough New Planet*. New York: Times Books, 2010.

McMahon, Patrick. "Meditating with Mountains and Rivers." In *Dharma Rain: Sources of Buddhist Environmentalism*, edited by Stephanie Kaza and Kenneth Kraft. Boston: Shambhala Publications, 2000.

Mingyur, Yongey. "Rest in Your Buddhanature." *Lion's Roar*, March 15, 2022. https://www.lionsroar.com/rest-in-your-buddhanature/; accessed September 14, 2023.

Morinaga Sōkō. "My Struggle to Become a Zen Monk." In *Zen: Tradition & Transition*, edited by Kenneth Kraft. New York: Grove Press, 1988.

Murphy, Susan. *Minding the Earth, Mending the World: Zen and the Art of Planetary Crisis*. Berkeley: Counterpoint, 2014.

Naess, Arne. "Self-Realization: An Ecological Approach to Being in the World." In *Thinking Like a Mountain: Toward a Council of All Beings*, edited by John Seed, Joanna Macy, Pat Fleming, and Arne Naess. Gabriola Island, BC: New Catalyst Books, 2007.

Nhat Hanh, Thich. *Being Peace*. Berkeley: Parallax Press, 1990.

———. "Earth Gathas." In *Dharma Gaia: A Harvest of Essays in Buddhism and Ecology*, edited by Alan Hunt Badiner. Berkeley: Parallax Press, 1990.

———. *Interbeing: Fourteen Guidelines for Engaged Buddhism*. 3rd ed. Berkeley: Parallax Press, 1998.

———. *Keeping the Peace: Mindfulness and Public Service*. Berkeley: Parallax Press, 2005.

———. *Love Letter to the Earth*. Berkeley: Parallax Press, 2013.

———. *You Are Here: Discovering the Magic of the Present Moment*. Boston: Shambhala Publications, 2010.

———. *Zen and the Art of Saving the Planet*. New York: HarperOne, 2021.

Norberg-Hodge, Helena. *Ancient Futures: Learning from Ladakh*. San Francisco: Sierra Club Books, 1991.

———. "Buddhism in the Global Economy." In *Mindfulness in the Marketplace: Compassionate Responses to Consumerism*, edited by Alan Hunt Badiner. Berkeley: Parallax Press, 2002.

Norgaard, Kari Marie. *Living in Denial: Climate Change, Emotions, and Everyday Life*. Cambridge, MA: MIT Press, 2011.

Okumura Shōhaku. *Realizing Genjōkōan: A Key to Dōgen's Shōbōgenzō*. Somerville, MA: Wisdom Publications, 2010.

Olendzki, Andrew. *Unlimiting Mind: The Radically Experiential Psychology of Buddhism*. Somerville, MA: Wisdom Publications, 2010.

Ophuls, William. "Notes for a Buddhist Politics." In *Dharma Rain: Sources of Buddhist Environmentalism*, edited by Stephanie Kaza and Kenneth Kraft. Boston: Shambhala Publications, 2000.

Orr, David W. *Earth in Mind: On Education, Environment, and the Human Prospect*. Washington, DC: Island Press, 2004.

Ostrander, Madeline. *At Home on an Unruly Planet: Finding Refuge in a Changed Earth*. New York: Henry Holt and Company, 2022.

Polanyi, Karl. *The Great Transformation: The Political and Economic Origins of Our Time*. Boston: Beacon Press, 1957.

Putnam, Robert D. *Bowling Alone: The Collapse and Revival of American Community*. New York: Simon & Schuster, 2020.

Rasmussen, Larry L. *Earth-Honoring Faith: Religious Ethics in a New Key*. New York: Oxford University Press, 2013.

Ray, Reginald A. "The Buddha's Politics." In *Mindful Politics: A Buddhist Guide to Making the World a Better Place*, edited by Melvin McLeod. Somerville, MA: Wisdom Publications, 2006.

Reed, Christopher. "Down to Earth." In *Dharma Gaia: A Harvest of Essays in Buddhism and Ecology*, edited by Alan Hunt Badiner. Berkeley: Parallax Press, 1990.

Ricard, Matthieu. *A Plea for the Animals: The Moral, Philosophical, and Evolutionary Imperative to Treat All Beings with Compassion*. Boulder, CO: Shambhala Publications, 2014.

Salzberg, Sharon. "Calm in the Midst of Chaos." *Lion's Roar* (November 2020).

Sanders, Scott Russel. *Staying Put: Making a Home in a Restless World*. Boston: Beacon Press, 1993.

Schmidt, LaUra. *How to Live in a Chaotic Climate: Ten Steps to Reconnect with Ourselves, Our Communities, and Our Planet*. Boulder, CO: Shambhala Publications, 2023.

Schmithausen, Lambert. *Buddhism and Nature*. Tokyo: International Institute for Buddhist Studies, 1991.

Schut, Michael, ed., *Simpler Living, Compassionate Life: A Christian Perspective*. Denver: Living the Good News, 2007.

Shafir, Rebecca Z. *The Zen of Listening: Mindful Communication in the Age of Distraction*. Wheaton, IL: Quest Books, 2003.

Shantigarbha. *The Burning House: A Buddhist Response to the Climate and Ecological Emergency*. Cambridge: Windhorse Publications, 2021.

Shi, David E. *The Simple Life: Plain Living and High Thinking in American Culture*. Athens, GA: University of Georgia Press, 2007.

Simard, Suzanne. *Finding the Mother Tree: Discovering the Wisdom of the Forest*. New York: Alfred A. Knopf, 2021.

Sivaraksa, Sulak. "Alternatives to Consumerism." In *Mindfulness in the Marketplace: Compassionate Responses to Consumerism*, edited by Alan Hunt Badiner. Berkeley: Parallax Press, 2002.

———. *Conflict, Culture, Change: Engaged Buddhism in a Globalizing World*. Somerville, MA: Wisdom Publications, 2005.

———. *Seeds of Peace: A Buddhist Vision for Renewing Society*. Berkeley: Parallax Press, 1992.

Snyder, Gary. *Back on the Fire*. Washington, DC: Counterpoint, 2008.

———. *Earth House Hold*. New York: New Directions, 1969.

———. *Nobody Home: Writing, Buddhism, and Living in Places*. San Antonio: Trinity University Press, 2014.

———. *A Place in Space: Ethics, Aesthetics, and Watersheds*. Washington, DC: Counterpoint, 1995.

———. *The Practice of the Wild: Essays by Gary Snyder*. San Francisco: North Point Press, 1990.

———. *The Real Work: Interviews & Talks 1964–1979*. New York: New Directions, 1980.

———. *Turtle Island*. New York: New Directions, 1974.

Sponsel, Leslie E. and Poranee Natadecha-Sponsel. "A Theoretical Analysis of the Potential Contribution of the Monastic Community in Promoting a Green Society in Thailand." In *Buddhism and Ecology: The Interconnection of Dharma and Deeds*, edited by Mary Evelyn Tucker and Dunken Ryūken Williams. Cambridge, MA: Harvard University Press, 1997.

Stanley, John and David Loy. "Buddhism and the End of Economic Growth." *Huffington Post*, September 19, 2011. http://www.huffingtonpost.com/john-stanley/buddhism-and-economic-growth_b_954457.html; accessed October 22, 2023.

Stoknes, Per Espen. *What We Think About When We Try Not to Think About Global Warming: Toward a New Psychology of Climate Action*. White River Junction, VT: Chelsea Green Publishing, 2015.

Stozer, Teah. "RAIN: Getting started on a spiritual path takes guts." *Tricycle*, Spring 2015.

Strain, Charles R. "The Pacific Buddha's Wild Practice: Gary Snyder's Environmental Ethic." In *American Buddhism: Methods and Findings in Recent Scholarship*, edited by Dunken Ryūken Williams and Christopher S. Queen. Richmond, UK: Curzon Press, 1999.

Sullivan, Walter. "The Einstein Papers: A Man of Many Parts." *New York Times*, March 29, 1972.

Suzuki, D. T. *An Introduction to Zen Buddhism*. New York: Grove Press, 1964.

Suzuki, Shunryū. *Zen Mind, Beginner's Mind: Informal Talks on Zen Meditation and Practice*. New York: Weatherhill, 1970.

Swearer, Donald K. "The Hermeneutics of Buddhist Ecology in Contemporary Thailand: Buddhadāsa and Dhammapiṭaka." In *Buddhism and Ecology: The Interconnection of Dharma and Deeds*, edited by Mary Evelyn Tucker and Dunken Ryūken Williams. Cambridge, MA: Harvard University Press, 1997.

Thoreau, Henry David. "Life Without Principle." *Atlantic Monthly*, October 1863. https://www.theatlantic.com/magazine/archive/1863/10/life-without-principle/542217/; accessed June 18, 2024.

———. *Walden and Civil Disobedience*. New York: Penguin Books, 1984.

Thorp, Gary. *Sweeping Changes: Discovering the Joy of Zen in Everyday Tasks*. London: Walter Books, 2000.

Timmerman, Peter. "Western Buddhism and the Global Crisis." In *Dharma Rain: Sources of Buddhist Environmentalism*, edited by Stephanie Kaza and Kenneth Kraft. Boston: Shambhala Publications, 2000.

Tokiwa, Gishin, trans. *The Laṅkāvatāra Sūtram: A Jewel Scripture of Mahāyāna Thought and Practice*. Osaka: Gishin Tokiwa, 2003.

Turner, Jack. *The Abstract Wild*. Tucson: University of Arizona Press, 1996.

Uchiyama, Kōshō. *Opening the Hand of Thought: Foundations of Zen Buddhist Practice*. New York: Penguin Arkana, 1993.

Uchiyama, Kōshō and Shōhaku Okumura. *The Zen Teachings of Homeless Kodo*. Somerville, MA: Wisdom Publications, 2014.

Udomittipong, Pibob. "Thailand's Ecology Monks." In *Dharma Rain: Sources of*

Buddhist Environmentalism, edited by Stephanie Kaza and Kenneth Kraft. Boston: Shambhala Publications, 2000.

U.S. Geological Survey. "Climate Change and Wildlife Health: Direct and Indirect Effects." https://pubs.usgs.gov/fs/2010/3017/pdf/fs2010-3017.pdf; accessed November 9, 2023.

Vajragupta. *Wild Awake: Alone, Offline & Aware in Nature*. Cambridge: Windhorse Publications, 2018.

Wildcat, Daniel R. *Red Alert!: Saving the Planet with Indigenous Knowledge*. Golden, CO: Fulcrum Publishing, 2009.

Wohlleben, Peter. *The Hidden Life of Trees: What They Feel, How They Communicate, Discoveries from a Secret World*. Vancouver: Greystone Books, 2015.

Wright, Dale S. *The Six Perfections: Buddhism & the Cultivation of Character*. New York: Oxford University Press, 2009.

Wu, Tim. "Mother Nature is Brought to You By . . . ." *New York Times*, December 2, 2016. https://www.nytimes.com/2016/12/02/opinion/sunday/mother-nature-is-brought-to-you-by.html?searchResultPosition=1; accessed April 7, 2020.

Yamamoto, Kosho, trans. *The Mahayana Mahaparinirvana Sutra*, revised and edited by Tony Page (web-published pdf, 2007). http://www.shabkar.org/download/pdf/Mahaparinirvana_Sutra_Yamamoto_Page_2007.pdf; accessed June 18, 2024.

Yifa. *Authenticity: Clearing the Junk: A Buddhist Perspective*. New York: Lantern Books, 2007.

Index

A

Abe, Masao, 106
Abram, David, 161–62, 163–64, 171
Active Hope (Macy and Johnstone),
    192–93, 195, 221, 227n179,
    230n226, 235n353
advertising, 11–12, 16–17, 212. *See also*
    commercialization
Altschuler, Stephen, 80–81
Ambedkar, B. R., 181
analogies
    for equanimity, 65
    for mind, 53–54
    "monkey mind," 29–30
    for non-duality, 58–60
    for right speech, 70
    for three poisons, 160
anger. *See* ill will
animals, 99, 105, 159–61, 165, 166,
    167–68, 170–71, 226n167, 231n266
anxiety, 2, 18–21, 65, 91, 115, 122, 189,
    198–99. *See also* fear
Aristotle, 88–89, 108
attachment, 13, 19, 23, 117, 190–91, 193,
    195, 213, 228n196. *See also* desire
attention spans, 33–34
Avalokiteśvara, 74, 106
awakening, 56, 60, 63, 106, 124,
    195, 212, 234–35n339. *See also*
    bodhicitta
awareness, 47, 48–49, 50, 53–54, 55,
    56–57, 60, 120, 123–24, 161
    bioregional, 146

See also consciousness; mind; mind-
    fulness; presencing

B

Baholyodhin, Ou, 83
Baizhang, 228n183
Barnhill, David, 131
Batchelor, Stephen, 9, 16
Bays, Jan Chozen, 48, 56–57, 117
    on listening, 72, 73
    on spatial clutter, 83
Bekoff, Marc, 107, 140, 151
Better Future Project, 208
Bhutan, 186, 204
bioregionalism, 146–47, 151–53, 208
Black Lives Matter, 29
Bodhi, Bhikku, 213
bodhicitta, 106, 195, 235n353
bodhisattvas, 66, 74, 99, 106, 107, 108,
    188–89
body, 39, 76, 81, 104, 133, 135, 137, 149,
    163, 171. *See also* forms
Bowling Alone (Putnam), 29
breathing, 47–48, 53, 63, 79, 90, 91,
    123, 140, 171
Brown, Edward Espe, 77
Buddha, 13, 14, 41, 49–50, 51, 63, 160,
    234n338. *See also* Jātaka Tales
buddha nature, 124, 159, 233n302
Buddhism
    conservative nature of, 179–84,
    234–35n339
    ecology of, 3, 4–5

environmental activism in, 184–96,
231n267
psychology of, 49
societal systems in, 186, 212–13,
233n321
See also Zen Buddhism
Buddhist Climate Action Network,
186–87
Buddhist Response to the Climate Emergency, 184–85

C

Carroll, Michael, 116
Cashman, Tyrone, 39
China, 74, 133
Christianity, 226n169, 233–34n323
Citizens' Climate Lobby, 209
climate activism, 183, 184–96, 211–15
individual, 199–201
international, 208–10
local, 206 (*see also* community)
organized, 201–6
climate crisis, 1, 35, 74, 112, 119, 153,
158, 176–77, 202–4, 221n58
adaptation, 38, 87, 153, 176, 207
mitigation, 66, 87, 119, 153, 172, 190,
203, 207, 209, 211, 214
Cobb, John, 212
Coming Back to Life (Macy and Brown),
31, 45, 101, 135
commercialization, 11, 40, 218n8–9.
See also advertising
community, 3, 20, 125, 157–61, 172–77,
199, 234n331
compassion (*karuṇā*), 14, 73, 105–7,
190, 194, 195, 197, 211. *See also*
non-harming
conditioned arising (*pratītya-
samutpāda*), 15, 55, 132–38, 171, 173,
189, 191, 194, 230n226, 231n265
consciousness, 54, 87, 139, 162,
231n261. *See also* awareness; mind
consumerism, 41, 97, 144
shortcomings of, 9–12, 24–25
and three poisons, 13–18
See also advertising; materialism

contentment, 3, 41, 97–98, 109, 213.
See also happiness
COVID-19 pandemic, 61–62, 89, 91

D

Dalai Lama, 74, 197
Davis, Brett, 57, 59
death, 19, 65, 74, 220n32
deep ecology, 137, 233–34n323
delusion, 9, 14, 49–50, 56, 67, 71, 87,
159, 219n22. *See also* ignorance
democracy, 20, 211
desire, 21, 49–50, 52, 56, 90, 95, 98,
112, 160, 205, 219n15
and consumerism, 13–14, 15–18, 164,
212–13
and suffering, 9–10, 180
See also attachment; consumerism;
greed; restraint; selfishness
Dhammapada, 51, 97
Dharma, 67, 181, 182, 188
distraction, 20, 28, 31–35, 36, 71, 89,
96, 234n331. *See also* freneticism
Dōgen, 47–48, 229n212
on presencing, 57
on self, 56
D.T. Suzuki, 95
dualism, 32, 141, 159, 163, 219n16

E

Earth Charter, 93, 225
economics, 37, 97, 172–73, 180, 183,
187, 191, 210, 220n41
Buddhist, 186, 204, 212–13
eightfold path, 50, 51–53, 67–68,
225n135
80 percent speed, 76, 78–79, 116, 124,
138
Einstein, Albert, 87
Elgin, Duane, 83, 96–97
embeddedness, 4, 15, 39, 133–140, 159,
162, 171, 217n2
embodiedness, 39, 162, 171
emptiness (*śūnyatā*), 19, 55–56, 59–60,
83, 97, 106, 227n175, 234n339
environmental organizations, 184–87,
197–98, 205, 206, 208–9

equanimity, 50, 57–58, 65, 219n18
ethics, 107
  Buddhist, 62, 67–68, 176
  environmental, 3, 170, 217n1,
    232n295
Experience of Insight, The (Goldstein),
  223n84

F

fear, 18–22, 40, 74, 180, 196, 220n38,
    224n112, 226n167
  of death, 220n32
  See also anxiety
Fischer, Norman, 101
food, 119–20, 130, 139, 148–49, 185,
    200, 203, 233n314. *See also* ōryōki;
    "Short Meal Gatha"; vegetarian-
    ism; Zen Buddhism: segaki ritual
forms, 59–60, 83, 91–92, 131. *See also*
    body
fossil fuel industry, 4, 35, 37, 200–201
four divine abodes, 109, 219n18
freedom. *See* liberation
freneticism, 27–32, 40–41, 89, 189. *See*
    also distraction
Future We Choose, The (Figures and
    Rivet-Carnac), 194

G

Garfield, Jay, 106
generosity (*dāna*), 3, 13, 61, 88,
    98–100, 103, 109, 120, 190, 214
Goldstein, Joseph, 54
gratitude, 62, 97, 100–102, 117,
    118–20, 137, 191
Great Earth Sangha, 169–72
greed, 13, 16, 71, 113, 119, 219n15,
    219n22, 227n175, 228n191. *See also*
    desire
Gross, Rita, 103

H

Habito, Ruben, 17, 229n215
Hakugen, Ichikawa, 181
Hanshan, 134
happiness, 9, 10, 16, 21, 40, 121, 153,
    172–74, 213. *See also* contentment

Harada, Shōdō, 54
Hayhoe, Katharine, 74, 75, 105–6, 192,
    226n169
Heart Sutra, 59–60, 64
Heschel, Abraham Joshua, 131
Hisamatsu Shin'ichi, 91
home, 3, 81–84, 111–12, 133, 200
  and bioregional awareness, 146–47
  rituals in, 113–23
Homer-Dixon, Thomas, 193–94
Honoré, Carl, 30, 31
hope, 71, 106, 192–93
humility, 133, 182
hungry ghosts (*gaki*), 120, 161,
    228n191

I

ignor-ance, 34–41
ignorance, 15, 34–41, 74, 160, 180
  and ill will, 14
  See also delusion
ill will, 13–14, 15, 49–50, 56, 90, 160,
    219n17, 224n112
  antidote to (*see* non-harming)
impermanence, 14–15, 19–20, 34, 180
India, 15, 52, 96, 103
Indigenous cultures, 141, 144,
    147, 150, 164–66, 168–69, 203,
    231n247
individualism, 11, 16, 19–20, 87–88,
    172–73, 191, 212
insight, 135, 136, 159, 171–72, 189, 196,
    227n175, 232n295
intelligence, 164–68, 171
interbeing. *See* conditioned arising
    (*pratītya-samutpāda*)
Intergovernmental Panel on Climate
    Change (IPCC), 36

J

James, Simon P., 109
Japanese tea houses, 84, 129–30
Jātaka Tales, 160
Jones, Ken, 21

K

Kabilsingh, Chatsumarn, 137

Kant, Immanuel, 90, 189
karma, 181, 183, 195
  bodily, 81
  negative, 51
  three arenas of, 29
Kasulis, Thomas, 58
Kaza, Stephanie, 67
  on activism, 194–95
  on advertising, 16
  on consumerism, 17, 20–21
  on Earth Charter, 93
  on environmental ethics, 232n295
Kimmerer, Robin Wall, 97
King, Martin Luther Jr., 157
Kittasaro, 53
Korten, David, 151–52
Kransy, Marianne, 192, 208

L
Lancaster, Lewis, 226n164
language. *See* speech
Laṅkāvatāra Sūtra, 159
lay Buddhists, 95, 98, 160, 228n183
Lazoff, Bo, 34
Leighton, Taigen, 100
Leopold, Aldo, 131, 169
liberation, 65, 89–90, 91, 108, 190–91
Lingo, Kaira Jewel, 63, 179, 196
listening, 46, 71–75, 166, 221n58. *See also* speech
Lokos, Allan, 72
loneliness, 9, 28, 30, 173
Louv, Richard, 39
love. *See* loving-kindness (*mettā*)
loving-kindness (*mettā*), 14, 41, 54, 98, 105–6, 107, 120–22, 193, 195, 197, 198–99, 226n169, 230n226
Loy, David, 18–19, 33–34, 213

M
Macy, Joanna, 137–38
Maezumi Rōshi, 60
Mahāparinirvāṇa Sūtra, 104
Mahāyāna Buddhism, 67, 70, 99, 108, 160
Mañjuśri, 83
mantras, 51, 63, 70, 72, 112, 124

Marris, Emma, 202
Martin, Rafe, 160
Marx, Karl, 49
materialism, 21–25, 32–33, 40, 87–88, 222n75. *See also* consumerism
McFague, Sallie, 9–10
McKibben, Bill, 109, 176, 183
meditation, 47–48, 60, 61, 63, 90, 118, 198
  and activism, 195
  activity as, 114–16
  goal of, 55
  and patience, 108
  and spaciousness, 51–52, 53
  zazen, 47, 138
  See also breathing; Zen temples
meditation hall (*zendō*), 47, 83, 84, 114
Meditations on the Trail (Ives), 4
merit, 98, 160, 218n11, 234n328
Mettā Sutta, 120–21
mind, 194, 232n276
  clutter, 45
  "monkey mind," 29–30
  spacious, 53, 54, 56–57, 64–65, 102, 110
  and thoughts, 46–50
  See also awareness; consciousness; thoughts
mindfulness, 41, 45, 48–49, 53, 56–57, 62, 63, 68, 77–78, 201, 224n122. *See also* presencing; spaciousness
misinformation, 35–36, 112
monasticism, 3, 83, 97, 98, 113–15, 160, 174
  "four requisites," 94–95
morality. *See* ethics
Morinaga Sōkō, 94–95
Morita, Shōma, 122
Murphy, Susan, 197

N
Naess, Arne, 137
nāga, 232n269
natural resources, 95–96
nature
  aesthetic appreciation of, 130–31
  disconnection from, 39–40

embeddedness in, 4, 35, 132–41, 162–63, 171–72, 198–99, 217n2, 229n215
nirvana, 49, 50, 180
non-duality, 58–60, 136, 144, 195
non-harming, 89, 102–5, 109, 111, 125, 137, 149, 194, 201. *See also* compassion (*karuṇā*)
Norberg-Hodge, Helena, 39
no-self, 19, 109, 194, 196, 212, 227n175

O
Olendzki, Andrew, 48
One Earth Sangha, 184
Orr, David, 148
ōryōki, 120
Ostrander, Madeline, 111, 193–94

P
patience, 66, 73, 107–10, 195, 223n84, 224n111
Pensées (Pascal), 20
Philosophy of History (Hegel), 49
plants, 119–20, 134, 139–40, 148, 149, 150, 166–67
politics, 14, 32, 35, 177, 204, 207, 209–10
precepts
   five eco-precepts, 227n179
   five precepts, 50, 67, 111–12, 222n77
   ten precepts, 67, 94
   See also vows
presencing, 45, 57–66, 101, 108, 117–18, 138, 159, 161–64, 195, 223n99. *See also* awareness; mindfulness

R
Rasmussen, Larry, 208
rebirth, 160, 168–69, 191, 231n266
   six paths of, 161, 228n191
Reed, Christopher, 227n179
regret, 30, 46, 50
reinhabitation, 141, 143–53, 207, 231n247, 231n263
religion, 15, 20–21, 38, 49, 64, 67, 74, 115, 118, 132, 160, 180, 183, 212
restraint, 72, 88–94, 103, 112, 125

rituals
   beyond home, 63, 123–25
   at home, 91, 113–23, 185
Ryōkan, 173

S
Salzberg, Sharon, 50, 57–58
Saṃyutta Nikāya, 49–50, 97
Sanders, Scott Russel, 140, 146, 153
Sarvodaya Shramadana Movement, 98–99, 212, 221–22n65
self, 14–15, 34, 48, 56, 57, 58, 91, 137–38, 159, 195, 219n14, 219n22
   emptiness of, 56
   nonattachment to, 227n175
   See also soul
selfishness, 12–13, 15, 24, 137, 212
sense experience, 84, 115, 116, 123, 135, 138–39, 162–63, 171–72
Shafir, Rebecca, 71, 73
Shantigarbha, 107, 235n351
Shepherd, Paul, 83
"Short Meal Gatha," 119
Shunryū Suzuki, 56, 77
Sigālovāda Sutta, 104
Silva, Padmasiri de, 88
Simard, Suzanne, 167
simplicity, 79, 83, 84, 88, 89, 94–97, 103, 109–10, 113
Sivaraksa, Sulak, 14, 17, 41, 175–76
skillful means, 106, 109, 188
sloth, 30, 49, 192
Snyder, Gary, 102, 103, 109, 113, 168–69
   on Buddhism, 180
   on community, 175, 176–77, 207
   on Great Earth Sangha, 169, 170
   on intelligence, 166
   on reinhabitation, 143, 144, 145, 148, 150, 152
social media, 1, 18, 29, 31, 32, 33, 80, 175, 186, 205, 233n315
society, 9–10, 29, 40, 102, 175–76, 191, 211–14
   Buddhist, 105, 180, 181, 188, 233n321
   disconnection from, 31–32
   and nature, 132, 177, 183

See also community; consumerism
soul, 15, 55
   See also self
spaciousness, 3, 45–46, 50–51, 54–55,
   60–61, 63, 64–65, 87, 93, 198
   temporal, 75–81
   verbal, 67–75
   See also mindfulness
spatial clutter, 46, 81–84
speech, 29, 165
   right, 50, 51, 67–68, 72, 74
   uncluttering, 45–46, 69–70, 92
   wrong, 30, 222n77, 224n107
   See also listening
Strain, Charles, 146
Strozer, Teah, 222n74
suchness, 74, 102, 131, 135, 162
suffering (*dukkha*), 13, 19, 20, 30, 41,
   187–88, 189, 234–35n339
   causes of, 49, 148
   and desire, 9

T
technology, 31, 79, 80, 207
ten detrimental actions, 29–30
ten perfections (*pāramitā*), 66, 99, 107,
   108, 224n111
Theravāda Buddhism, 94, 98, 224n111
Thich Nhat Hanh, 51, 129, 149
   "bell of mindfulness" practice, 64
   "earth gathas," 185
   Fourteen Mindfulness Trainings, 105
   on freneticism, 28
   on interconnection, 15
   on listening, 73
   on plants, 166
   on presencing, 61, 63
Thoreau, Henry David, 73, 79, 82. *See
   also Walden* (Thoreau)
Thorp, Gary, 81–82, 101–2
thoughts, 29–30, 45, 69, 83, 191
   and awareness, 46–49, 50, 53–55
   during meditation, 131
Three Jewels, 67
time, 46, 75–81, 90
travel, 11, 47, 93–94, 95, 123–24, 200,
   201, 228n186

True Dedication, Sister, 102, 139

U
Uchiyama Kōshō, 48, 55
Udomittipong, Pibob, 97
United States, 1, 14, 20, 27, 29, 32, 89,
   231n247
unwholesome mental states, 30, 119,
   192, 219n23
   five hindrances, 49–51
   three poisons, 98
US Supreme Court, 209

V
Vajragupta, 27, 136–37
vegetarianism, 104, 111, 160, 200
violence, 1, 105, 121, 180, 182, 186, 188
virtues, 3, 88–89, 95, 108–10,
   190, 227n175. *See also* ethics,
   environmental
Visalo, Phra Phaisan, 41
vows, 67–68
   Fourfold Great Vows, 188–89,
   223–24n104
   See also precepts

W
Walden (Thoreau), 77
wealth, 41, 174, 218n11, 234n328
What is Ecological Civilization? (Clayton and Schwartz), 141
Wildcat, Daniel, 143–44
wisdom (*prajñā*), 41, 50, 54, 55, 63,
   117–18, 153, 160, 172, 213
   and compassion, 106, 107, 119, 188
   and equanimity, 57–58
   and ignorance, 98
   See also Mañjuśri
Wohlleben, Peter, 167
Work That Reconnects Network, 184
Wright, Dale, 99

Y
Yangshan, 136
Yifa, 27–28
yoga, 11, 52, 114, 118

Z

Zen aesthetics, 113, 129–32, 228n196, 229n207. *See also* Japanese tea houses; meditation hall (*zendō*); Zen temples

Zen Buddhism, 2, 186
  misinterpretations of, 91–92
  segaki ritual, 120, 134

Zen Buddhism and Environmental Ethics (James), 227n175

Zen Center of Los Angeles, 60

Zen expressions, 112
  "accommodationism" (*junnō-shugi*), 181
  "according with circumstances" (*nin-un*), 181
  gūjin, 116
  "leave no trace" (*mu-seki*), 117
  mono no shō o tsukusu, 95
  "realize-in-practice," 56, 223n87
  shōyoku chisoku, 95
  "unity of the ruler's law and Buddha's law," 182
  See also mantras

Zen on the Trail (Ives), 4

Zen temples, 84, 125, 129, 130, 133–34. *See also* meditation hall (*zendō*)

About the Author

 CHRISTOPHER IVES is a professor of Religious Studies at Stonehill College in Easton, Massachusetts. In his teaching and writing, he focuses on ethics in Zen Buddhism and Buddhist approaches to nature and environmental issues. His publications include *Zen on the Trail: Hiking as Pilgrimage*; *Meditations on the Trail: A Guidebook for Self-Discovery*; *Imperial-Way Zen: Ichikawa Hakugen's Critique and Lingering Questions for Buddhist Ethics*; *Zen Awakening and Society*; a translation (with Masao Abe) of Nishida Kitarō's *An Inquiry into the Good*; and a translation (with Gishin Tokiwa) of Shin'ichi Hisamatsu's *Critical Sermons of the Zen Tradition*. He is on the editorial board of the *Journal of Buddhist Ethics* and on the board of the Barre Center for Buddhist Studies. He lives with his wife, Mishy, in Watertown, Massachusetts.

What to Read Next from Wisdom Publications

Meditations on the Trail
A Guidebook for Self-Discovery
Christopher Ives

"Practical, elegant, and personal, Christopher Ives's book is a treasure, transporting our hikes into the ordinary profundity of Zen practice. It will certainly be in my backpack!"—Judith Simmer-Brown, author of *Dakini's Warm Breath: The Feminine Principle in Tibetan Buddhism*

Zen on the Trail
Hiking as Pilgrimage
Christopher Ives

"Like John Muir, Chris Ives knows that going out into the natural world is really going inward. This book about pilgrimage is itself a pilgrimage: we accompany the author as he leaves civilization behind to enter the wilderness and encounter his true nature and original face."—David R. Loy, author of *Money, Sex, War, Karma: Notes for a Buddhist Revolution*

A Buddhist Response to the Climate Emergency
Edited by John Stanley, David R. Loy, and Gyurme Dorje

"If you read only one Dharma book, make it this one."—*The Mirror*

Ecodharma
Buddhist Teachings for the Ecological Crisis
David R. Loy

This landmark work is simultaneously a manifesto, a blueprint, a call to action, and a deep comfort for troubling times. David R. Loy masterfully lays out the principles and perspectives of Ecodharma— the Buddhist response to our ecological predicament, a new term for a new development of the Buddhist tradition.

Ecology, Ethics, and Interdependence
The Dalai Lama in Conversation with Leading Thinkers on Climate Change
Edited by John Dunne and Daniel Goleman

"We need this one. Here is a book that looks at the global ecological crisis from many, many angles, each one bringing the challenge— and what to do about it—more and more into focus. This is an important book."—Jeff Bridges, actor and environmental activis

Interconnected
Embracing Life in Our Global Society
The Karmapa, Ogyen Trinley Dorje

"We are now so interdependent that it is in our own interest to take the whole of humanity into account. Hope lies with the generation who belong to the twenty-first century. If they can learn from the past and shape a different future, later this century the world could be a happier, more peaceful, and more environmentally stable place. I am very happy to see in this book the Karmapa Rinpoche taking a lead and advising practical ways to reach this goal."—His Holiness the Dalai Lama

About Wisdom Publications

Wisdom Publications is the leading publisher of classic and contemporary Buddhist books and practical works on mindfulness. To learn more about us or to explore our other books, please visit our website at wisdom.org or contact us at the address below.

Wisdom Publications
132 Perry Street
New York, NY 10014 USA

We are a 501(c)(3) organization, and donations in support of our mission are tax deductible.

Wisdom Publications is affiliated with the Foundation for the Preservation of the Mahayana Tradition (FPMT).